DEFINING MOMENTS
THE
LEWIS AND CLARK
EXPEDITION

DEFINING MOMENTS
THE
LEWIS AND CLARK
EXPEDITION

Laurie Collier Hillstrom

155 W. Congress, Suite 200
Detroit, MI 48226

Omnigraphics, Inc.

Cherie D. Abbey, *Managing Editor*

Peter E. Ruffner, *Publisher*

Copyright © 2016 Omnigraphics, Inc.
ISBN 978-0-7808-1417-2

Library of Congress Cataloging-in-Publication Data

Hillstrom, Laurie Collier, 1965- author.
    The Lewis and Clark Expedition / by Laurie Collier Hillstrom.
      pages cm. -- (Defining moments)
    Includes bibliographical references and index.
    Summary: "A detailed summary of the epic journey through the western wilderness undertaken by Meriwether Lewis, William Clark, and their Corps of Discovery in 1804-1806. Discusses the effects of the expedition on Native American cultures and examines its legacy in American history and imagination. Includes biographies, primary sources, and more"-- Provided by publisher.
    Audience: Grade 9 to 12.
    ISBN 978-0-7808-1417-2 (hardcover : alk. paper) 1. Lewis and Clark Expedition (1804-1806)--Juvenile literature. 2. Lewis, Meriwether, 1774-1809--Juvenile literature. 3. Clark, William, 1770-1838--Juvenile literature. 4. West (U.S.)--Discovery and exploration--Juvenile literature. I. Title.
    F592.7.H56 2015
    917.804'2--dc23   2015033665

TABLE OF CONTENTS

NARRATIVE OVERVIEW

BIOGRAPHIES

PRIMARY SOURCES

PREFACE

Throughout the course of America's existence, its people, culture, and institutions have been periodically challenged—and in many cases transformed—by profound historical events. Some of these momentous events, such as women's suffrage, the civil rights movement, and U.S. involvement in World War II, invigorated the nation and strengthened American confidence and capabilities. Others, such as the McCarthy era, the Vietnam War, and Watergate, have prompted troubled assessments and heated debates about the country's core beliefs and character.

Some of these defining moments in American history were years or even decades in the making. The Harlem Renaissance and the New Deal, for example, unfurled over the span of several years, while the American labor movement and the Cold War evolved over the course of decades. Other defining moments, such as the Cuban Missile Crisis and the terrorist attacks of September 11, 2001, transpired over a matter of days or weeks.

But although significant differences exist among these events in terms of their duration and their place in the timeline of American history, all share the same basic characteristic: they transformed the United States' political, cultural, and social landscape for future generations of Americans.

Taking heed of this fundamental reality, American citizens, schools, and other institutions are increasingly emphasizing the importance of understanding our nation's history. Omnigraphics' *Defining Moments* series was created for the express purpose of meeting this growing appetite for authoritative, useful historical resources. This series will be of enduring value to anyone interested in learning more about America's past—and in understanding how those historical events continue to reverberate in the twenty-first century.

Each individual volume of *Defining Moments* provides a valuable resource for readers interested in learning about the most profound events in our nation's history. Each volume is organized into three distinct sections—Narrative Overview, Biographies, and Primary Sources.

- The **Narrative Overview** provides readers with a detailed, factual account of the origins and progression of the "defining moment" being examined. It also explores the event's lasting impact on America's political and cultural landscape.

- The **Biographies** section provides valuable biographical background on leading figures associated with the event in question. Each biography concludes with a list of sources for further information on the profiled individual.

- The **Primary Sources** section collects a wide variety of pertinent primary source materials from the era under discussion, including official documents, papers and resolutions, letters, oral histories, memoirs, editorials, and other important works.

Individually, each of these sections is a rich resource for users. Together, they comprise an authoritative, balanced, and absorbing examination of some of the most significant events in U.S. history.

Other notable features contained within each volume in the series include a glossary of important individuals, places, and terms; a detailed chronology featuring page references to relevant sections of the narrative; an annotated bibliography of sources for further study; an extensive general bibliography that reflects the wide range of historical sources consulted by the author; and a subject index.

New Feature—Research Topics for Student Reports

Each volume in the *Defining Moments* series now includes a list of potential research topics for students. Students working on historical research and writing assignments will find this feature especially useful in assessing their options.

Information on the highlighted research topics can be found throughout the different sections of the book—and especially in the narrative overview, biography, and primary source sections. This wide coverage gives readers the flexibility to study the topic through multiple entry points.

Special Note about *Defining Moments: The Lewis and Clark Expedition*

The journals kept by Meriwether Lewis, William Clark, and other members of the Corps of Discovery during their journey across North America are a tremendous historical resource. But they are also notable for their irregular and often creative spelling, punctuation, capitalization, and grammar. English language usage had not yet been standardized in the early 1800s, and many of the journal-keepers had little formal education. As a result, the journals include twenty-seven variations of the word "Sioux" and fifteen different spellings of the word "mosquito." In an effort to make the journals more accessible and meaningful for students, we have silently corrected these inconsistencies to bring quotations into alignment with modern English usage. Those who are interested in reading the original journals of the Lewis and Clark Expedition will find unedited versions widely available in print and online. Please refer to the Sources for Further Study section for more information.

Acknowledgements

This series was developed in consultation with a distinguished Advisory Board comprised of public librarians, school librarians, and educators. They evaluated the series as it developed, and their comments and suggestions were invaluable throughout the production process. Any errors in this and other volumes in the series are ours alone. Following is a list of board members who contributed to the *Defining Moments* series:

Gail Beaver, M.A., M.A.L.S.
Adjunct Lecturer, University of Michigan
Ann Arbor, MI

Melissa C. Bergin, L.M.S., NBCT
Library Media Specialist
Niskayuna High School
Niskayuna, NY

Rose Davenport, M.S.L.S., Ed.Specialist
Library Media Specialist
Pershing High School Library
Detroit, MI

Karen Imarisio, A.M.L.S.
Assistant Head of Adult Services
Bloomfield Twp. Public Library
Bloomfield Hills, MI

Nancy Larsen, M.L.S., M.S. Ed.
Library Media Specialist
Clarkston High School
Clarkston, MI

Marilyn Mast, M.I.L.S.
Kingswood Campus Librarian
Cranbrook Kingswood Upper School
Bloomfield Hills, MI

Rosemary Orlando, M.L.I.S.
Library Director
St. Clair Shores Public Library
St. Clair Shores, MI

Comments and Suggestions

We welcome your comments on *Defining Moments: The Lewis and Clark Expedition* and suggestions for other events in U.S. history that warrant treatment in the *Defining Moments* series. Correspondence should be addressed to:

Editor, *Defining Moments*
Omnigraphics, Inc.
155 West Congress, Suite 200
Detroit, MI 48231

HOW TO USE THIS BOOK

Defining Moments: The Lewis and Clark Expedition provides users with a detailed and authoritative overview of the first U.S.-sponsored exploration of the West, as well as background on the principal figures involved in this pivotal period in American history. The preparation and arrangement of this volume—and all other books in the Defining Moments series—reflect an emphasis on providing a thorough and objective account of events that shaped our nation, presented in an easy-to-use reference work.

Defining Moments: The Lewis and Clark Expedition is divided into three main sections. The first of these sections, the **Narrative Overview**, tells the story of the epic journey through the unknown western wilderness undertaken by Meriwether Lewis, William Clark, and their Corps of Discovery in 1804-1806. It begins by chronicling President Thomas Jefferson's efforts to wrest control of the vast Louisiana Territory from France and his determination to mount an expedition to map the region and catalog its flora, fauna, and Native American inhabitants. It then offers a detailed description of the explorers' struggles, triumphs, and discoveries as they make their way across the rugged continent and finally reach the Pacific Ocean. It then discusses how the successful expedition served as a milestone in opening the American West for settlement—at the expense of the Native American cultures encountered by Lewis and Clark. The volume concludes by examining the legacy of the Lewis and Clark Expedition in American history and imagination.

The second section, **Biographies**, provides valuable biographical background on key figures involved in the Lewis and Clark Expedition. Among the individuals profiled are Thomas Jefferson, the president whose lifelong fascination with the West led him to organize the expedition; Captains Meriwether Lewis and William Clark, the co-leaders whose complementary skills and temperaments made their extraordinary achievements possible; Sacagawea, the remarkable Shoshone Indian interpreter and guide who carried her infant son all the way to the Pacific; John Colter, a member of the Corps of Discovery who went on to become a legendary mountain man; and York, Clark's enslaved African-American servant who participated equally in the challenges and triumphs of the expedition. Each biography concludes with a list of sources for further information on the profiled individual.

The third section, **Primary Sources**, collects essential and illuminating documents related to the Lewis and Clark Expedition and its importance in American history. This diverse collection includes Jefferson's confidential 1803 message to Congress requesting funding for an expedition; the historic Louisiana Purchase Treaty, which launched the era of U.S. westward expansion; Jefferson's detailed instructions to Lewis outlining his ambitious goals for the expedition; Lewis's list of equipment and supplies to take along; excerpts from the men's journals describing beautiful waterfalls, treacherous mountain passes, and dangerous grizzly bear encounters; an 1806 speech by a delegation of Native American leaders expressing concerns about the future; and an assessment of the legacy of Lewis and Clark by historian James P. Ronda.

Other valuable features in *Defining Moments: The Lewis and Clark Expedition* include the following:

- A list of Research Topics that provides students with starting points for reports.
- Attribution and referencing of primary sources and other quoted material to help guide users to other valuable historical research resources.
- Glossary of Important People, Places, and Terms.
- Detailed Chronology of events with a *see reference* feature. Under this arrangement, events listed in the chronology include a reference to page numbers within the Narrative Overview wherein users can find additional information on the event in question.
- Photographs of the leading figures and major events associated with the Lewis and Clark Expedition and U.S. westward expansion.
- Sources for Further Study, an annotated list of noteworthy works about the Lewis and Clark Expedition and its impact.
- Extensive bibliography of works consulted in the creation of this book, including books, periodicals, and Internet sites.
- A Subject Index.

RESEARCH TOPICS FOR DEFINING MOMENTS: THE LEWIS AND CLARK EXPEDITION

When students receive an assignment to produce a research paper on a historical event or topic, the first step in that process—settling on a subject for the paper—can be one of the most vexing. In recognition of this reality, each book in the *Defining Moments* series now highlights research topics that receive extensive coverage within that particular volume.

Potential research topics/study questions for students using *Defining Moments: The Lewis and Clark Expedition* include the following:

- What value did President Thomas Jefferson see in acquiring the Louisiana Territory and organizing the Lewis and Clark Expedition? Did he pursue westward expansion and exploration for the sake of the country, or to satisfy his own intellectual curiosity?

- Read the instructions Jefferson sent to Captain Meriwether Lewis. Make a list of the major goals the president established for the Lewis and Clark Expedition. Discuss which ones the Corps of Discovery was most and least successful in accomplishing.

- Imagine that it is 1803 and Jefferson has invited you to lead an expedition into the unknown western wilderness. Make a list of the equipment and supplies you would consider most essential to bring along. Compare your list to the one Lewis compiled prior to launching the expedition.

- Pick a region that Lewis and Clark explored on their journey, such as the Great Plains, the Rocky Mountains, or the Pacific Coast. Make a list of the main geographical features, climate, plants, animals, and Native American cultures the expedition encountered there. What do you think the explorers found most and least surprising about that region?

- The Lewis and Clark Expedition faced many challenges on their journey, from homesickness, hunger, and exhaustion to extreme weather, wild animals, and difficult terrain. Which ones did they struggle with the most? If you had been a member of the Corps of Discovery, which would have been the toughest for you to endure?

• Discuss the ways in which Sacagawea contributed to the success of the Lewis and Clark Expedition. Make a list of the forms of assistance the Corps of Discovery received from other Native Americans they encountered. What would have happened to the explorers if they had been forced to survive on their own?

• Pick an American Indian nation that helped Lewis and Clark, such as the Mandan, Shoshone, or Nez Perce peoples. Write a report detailing what happened to them in the decades after they met the explorers, and provide information about their current status.

• Discuss the various "discoveries" made by the Lewis and Clark Expedition. Considering that Native Americans had lived in the West for generations before the explorers arrived—and the region's geography, plants, and animals were familiar to them—did the Corps of Discovery deserve its name?

• Explore Thomas Jefferson's attitude toward Native Americans, as shown in his confidential message to Congress, his instructions to Lewis, and his speech to the delegation of Indian leaders. To what extent did the U.S. government's treatment of Native Americans over the next few decades reflect Jefferson's attitudes? To what extent did it betray the promises Jefferson made?

• Define the term "manifest destiny" and discuss how the idea was made evident in the United States during the 1800s. Are the Louisiana Purchase and the Lewis and Clark Expedition examples of manifest destiny? Is the idea still relevant in the United States today?

• Imagine that you have been ordered to explore and catalog the area around your home. Create a journal describing some of the plants and animals that are native to the area, including their formal scientific names, appearance, behavior, and habitat. If you had to prepare a package containing representative samples for someone who was unfamiliar with the region, what would you include?

• Visit a location on the Lewis and Clark National Historic Trail. Write a description of how the landscape appears today and compare it to the descriptions in the explorers' journals. In what ways has it changed?

How do these changes reflect larger changes that have occurred in American society?

- Discuss the legacy of the Lewis and Clark Expedition and explore the relevance this episode in U.S. history holds for Americans today.

NARRATIVE OVERVIEW

PROLOGUE

In the twenty-first century, there are very few places left on Earth that have not been explored, mapped, and studied by humans. Geographic discoveries have become rare, while long-distance travel has become quick, easy, and commonplace. Global positioning system (GPS) technology allows anyone with a smartphone to instantly pinpoint their geographic location and access a detailed map or satellite image of their surroundings. Navigation is as simple as plugging a destination into an app and following the turn-by-turn directions it provides. As a result, most people have trouble imagining what it would be like to set off into an unknown wilderness, with no map or directions and only the most rudimentary navigational tools.

Two hundred years ago, however, large portions of the North American continent had yet to be explored. The majority of the U.S. population lived in a narrow strip of land along the East Coast, hemmed in between the Atlantic Ocean and the Appalachian Mountains. Although the western frontier of the young nation stretched to the Mississippi River, this area was sparsely populated by hardy farmers, hunters, and traders.

In 1803 President Thomas Jefferson made a deal to purchase the Louisiana Territory, doubling the size of the United States and extending its western border all the way to the Rocky Mountains. Very few Americans had ever ventured into the vast wilderness west of the Mississippi. The spotty information that was known about the West came from the reports of French fur traders, the journals of Spanish or British explorers, and the legends told by Native Americans.

Jefferson immediately decided to mount an official U.S. military expedition, jointly led by Captains Meriwether Lewis and William Clark, to explore and map the newly acquired land and search for an easy trade route to the Pacific Ocean. When Lewis and Clark and their hand-picked Corps of Discovery set forth from St. Louis, Missouri, in the spring of 1804, they stepped into the unknown—as well as into American history. Their epic two-and-a-half-year journey across the continent and back has been described as "the greatest camping trip of all time, a voyage of high adventure, an exercise in manifest destiny which carried the American flag overland to the Pacific," according to the National Park Service. "It was all of this and more."[1]

Lewis and Clark covered nearly 8,000 miles, traveling in canoes, on horseback, or on foot. Since no roads or railways existed in the West at that time, they followed river courses, ancient Indian routes, and game trails. They navigated by the sun and the stars, relied on advice and assistance from the Native Americans they encountered, and created maps as they went along. Most importantly—as far as securing their place in history—the captains kept journals relating their experiences, cataloguing the plants and animals they found, describing the geographic features they saw, and recording the Native American cultures they observed. Their detailed notes filled 5,000 journal pages and amounted to more than one million words—and much of this treasure trove of historical information has been preserved for future generations.

One of the major turning points for the Lewis and Clark Expedition came in the summer of 1805. After traveling up the Missouri River for 2,500 miles, they reached a spot known as Three Forks, where three smaller rivers converged to form the Missouri. At this point, the captains knew that their boats would soon become useless—they needed to switch to overland travel in order to cross the treacherous Rocky Mountains. The success of their mission, and perhaps their very survival, depended on acquiring horses to help carry their gear on the steep trails. They also needed guidance to help them find food and a safe route through the snow-covered peaks that seemed to stretch endlessly into the distance. The captains decided that their best hope was to locate and befriend the Shoshone Indians, who were believed to frequent that area. In the following excerpt from his journal dated July 27, 1805, Lewis tries to maintain a positive outlook as he describes the expedition's potentially dire situation:

> We begin to feel considerable anxiety with respect to the Snake [Shoshone] Indians. If we do not find them or some other nation who have horses I fear the successful issue of our voyage will be very doubtful or at all events much more difficult in its accomplishment. We are now several hundred miles within the bosom of this wild and mountainous country, where game may rationally be expected shortly to become scarce and subsistence precarious without any information with respect to the country,

not knowing how far these mountains continue, or where to direct our course to pass them to advantage or intercept a navigable branch of the Columbia [River, which flows westward to the Pacific], or even were we on such a one the probability is that we should not find any timber within these mountains large enough [to build dugout] canoes, if we judge from the portion of them through which we have passed. However I still hope for the best, and intend taking a tramp myself in a few days to find these yellow gentlemen if possible. My two principal consolations are that from our present position it is impossible that the [southwest] fork can head with the waters of any other river but the Columbia, and that if any Indians can subsist in the form of a nation in these mountains with the means they have of acquiring food, we can also subsist.[2]

Lewis and Clark overcame these and countless other challenges on their journey. Their success, and the information they brought back, helped launch an era of westward expansion that shaped American history. Their story also gives modern readers an opportunity to understand how it felt to set forth into unexplored territory, navigate through unknown hazards, and discover fascinating new places, people, and things.

Notes

[1] "Introduction." *Lewis and Clark Expedition: A National Register of Historic Places Travel Itinerary.* U.S. National Park Service, n.d. Retrieved from http://www.nps.gov/nr/travel/lewisandclark/intro.htm.

[2] Lewis, Meriwether. July 27, 1805, entry in *The Journals of the Lewis and Clark Expedition,* ed. Gary Moulton. Lincoln: University of Nebraska Press/Electronic Text Center, 2005. Retrieved from http://lewisandclarkjournals.unl.edu/journals.php?id=1805-07-27.

Chapter One

THE LOUISIANA PURCHASE

However our present interests may restrain us within our own
limits, it is impossible not to look forward to distant times, when
our rapid multiplication will expand itself beyond those limits
and over the whole ... continent, with a people speaking the
same language, governed in similar forms by similar laws.

—President Thomas Jefferson,
letter to James Monroe, November 24, 1801

At the time the United States gained its independence in 1783, most of
its population occupied a narrow strip of land along the Atlantic Ocean.
Thomas Jefferson, who took office as the third president of the United
States in 1801, wanted to expand the fledgling nation's territorial holdings westward across the continent of North America. Full of curiosity about the unexplored western frontier, Jefferson believed that laying claim to these lands would
increase national security, promote economic development, and establish the
United States as a world power. When Jefferson got an unexpected opportunity to purchase the vast Louisiana Territory from France in 1803, he immediately
launched a historic expedition to explore and map the region.

Jefferson Looks West

By the time Thomas Jefferson (see biography, p. 137) became president in
1801, the fifty-seven-year-old Virginian had already made his mark on American history as the main author of the Declaration of Independence. He had also
served as governor of Virginia and U.S. ambassador to France, secretary of state,
and vice president. Throughout his long political career, Jefferson had become

known for his boundless intellectual curiosity—especially about the unexplored territory west of the Mississippi River (see "Jefferson's Search for Knowledge," p. 9). Although he had never traveled there himself, Jefferson's fascination with the West was so deep that the library at his home, Monticello, contained more books about the region than any other library in the world.

Like other Founding Fathers, Jefferson was a product of the Enlightenment, or Age of Reason. Leading thinkers in this historical era emphasized questioning traditional authority, pursuing knowledge and individual improvement, and reforming government, society, and culture. These principles not only inspired the American Revolution, but also led to important scientific discoveries and created a strong desire for exploration. "His mind thirsted for facts, not just for curiosity's sake but for useful improvement, what the men of the Enlightenment called practical knowledge,"[1] wrote historian Stephen E. Ambrose.

President Thomas Jefferson's desire to explore the western frontier grew out of his boundless curiosity and thirst for knowledge.

When Jefferson took office, however, two-thirds of the 5.3 million citizens of the United States lived within fifty miles of the Atlantic Coast. They were cut off from the interior of the continent by the Appalachian Mountains, which formed a 1,500-mile-long barrier to east-west travel stretching from Maine to Georgia. In fact, in those days it was quicker and easier for residents of Boston, Massachusetts, to travel across the ocean to London, England, than to follow one of the four rugged, poor-quality roads that crossed the Appalachian range to points west. As a result, Americans living along the eastern seaboard maintained many economic and cultural ties to Europe at the turn of the nineteenth century.

Although the young nation's territory extended all the way to the Mississippi River, only half a million Americans—or 10 percent of the population—lived west of the Appalachians. The

Jefferson's Thirst for Knowledge

Thomas Jefferson began pursuing his dream of western exploration long before he became president. In 1783, for instance, Jefferson approached George Rogers Clark with a proposal for a scientific expedition of the lands west of the Mississippi River. Clark—who had become famous as the commander of frontier forces in Kentucky during the Revolutionary War—shared Jefferson's interest in science and often sent him seeds, shells, bones, and other specimens from his travels. Although Clark turned down the offer to lead an expedition, he provided advice on dealing with Native American tribes and also suggested that Jefferson consider his younger brother, William, for the job. (William Clark ended up becoming co-leader of the Lewis and Clark Expedition twenty years later.)

Jefferson's next effort to gain information about the western half of the continent came in 1786, when he was serving as U.S. ambassador to France. He and other investors commissioned John Ledyard, an American who had sailed throughout the Pacific with the famous British explorer Captain James Cook, to attempt to cross from Russia to North America over land. Starting from Northern Europe, Ledyard made it most of the way across Russia before Queen Catherine the Great learned of his unauthorized scheme and had him escorted out of the country.

In 1793 Jefferson and fellow members of the American Philosophical Society supported a scientific expedition by French botanist Andre Michaux. The plan was for Michaux to gather information about the flora, fauna, and geology of the West. As it turned out, though, the Frenchman was secretly involved in a French plot to stir up trouble between American and Spanish settlers on the western frontier. When the American backers learned about Michaux's divided loyalties, they pulled the plug on his expedition. Jefferson had to wait another decade before he was finally able to satisfy his thirst for knowledge about the West.

hardy farmers, hunters, and tradesmen of the western frontier had little connection with the East Coast. Instead, they sent their crops and trade goods down the Mississippi River to the port city of New Orleans, where these products were loaded onto ships to be transported around the world. Some frontier residents felt so cut off from the rest of the United States that they considered severing formal political ties and forming their own separate country.

Meanwhile, the United States was surrounded by the competing land claims of several powerful European nations. Spain owned Florida and the southwestern part of North America, from California to Texas. England controlled Canada and the Pacific Northwest, including what eventually became Washington and Oregon. Russia held present-day Alaska and had also established a military outpost in northern California. France owned the entire area between the Mississippi River and the Rocky Mountains, from the Gulf of Mexico in the south to present-day Montana in the north. This vast region on the western border of the United States was known as Louisiana.

The Struggle over New Orleans

France had lost most of its territory in North America in 1762, at the end of the French and Indian War. At that time, France had been forced to turn over control of Louisiana to Spain. Shortly after gaining its independence, the United States signed a treaty with Spain that gave American settlers the right to transport goods down the Mississippi River and use the port of New Orleans for shipping. U.S. leaders viewed Spain as a weak nation, and they believed that they could steadily increase the American presence in New Orleans and eventually gain control of the valuable port.

In 1799, however, Napoleon Bonaparte seized power in France and immediately began working to restore his country's standing as a world power. Part of Napoleon's plan involved reclaiming former French colonies in North America and the Caribbean. Rumors soon spread that Spain had secretly agreed to transfer control of the Louisiana Territory back to France. This news deeply alarmed U.S. leaders, who viewed France as a stronger and more dangerous adversary than Spain. They worried that Napoleon might cut off American shipping rights from New Orleans or use Louisiana as a staging ground for a military invasion of the U.S. western frontier. "Every eye in the U.S. is now fixed on this affair of Louisiana," Jefferson wrote to Robert Livingston, the U.S. ambassador to France. "Perhaps nothing since the revolutionary war has produced more uneasy sensations through the body of the nation."[2]

The rumors proved true in October 1802, when King Charles IV of Spain signed a decree transferring ownership of the Louisiana Territory back to France. Acting on Napoleon's orders, the Spanish agent in New Orleans immediately revoked American shipping rights. Jefferson knew that this development would have far-reaching consequences. "There is on the globe one single spot, the possessor of which is our natural and habitual enemy. It is New Orleans, through which the produce of three-eighths of our territory must pass to market,"[3] he wrote. "This little event, of France's possessing herself of Louisiana, is the embryo of a tornado which will burst on the countries on both sides of the Atlantic and involve in its effects their highest destinies."[4]

Jefferson's political rivals argued that the United States should declare war against France and take control of New Orleans by force. Meanwhile, concerned frontier residents claimed that the United States had failed to protect their interests and threatened to form their own government. Under pressure to take action from all sides, Jefferson nonetheless tried to resolve the issue with diplomacy. He authorized Livingston to offer France up to $10 million to purchase New Orleans. At the very least, Jefferson hoped the ambassador would be able to forge a new treaty that would restore American rights to use the port.

In January 1803 the president sent James Monroe to France as a special envoy to join in the negotiations. Although Monroe was a longtime friend and political ally of Jefferson, he was also a trusted figure among people on the western frontier. Jefferson hoped that Monroe's presence would help fend off the

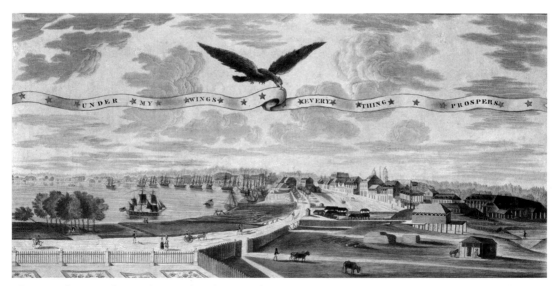

The city of New Orleans, depicted in this painting as it appeared in 1803, was considered vital to U.S. shipping interests and economic growth.

11

threat of disunion. "All eyes, all hopes, are now fixed on you," he told Monroe, "for on the event of this mission depends the future destinies of this republic."[5]

The Louisiana Purchase

When France initially regained Louisiana from Spain, Napoleon planned a military expedition to defend the territory and develop it as a French colony. On their way to New Orleans, however, the French troops stopped at the Caribbean island of Saint Domingue (present-day Haiti) to help French colonial officials put down a slave rebellion and independence movement. More than half of the 30,000 French soldiers contracted yellow fever and died, and the rest were badly defeated.

Following this turn of events, Napoleon began to rethink his plan to establish a foothold in North America. He felt that Louisiana was less valuable now that France had lost the sugar-producing colony of Saint Domingue. He also worried that without French troops to defend its borders, the vast territory would be vulnerable to takeover by the Americans or British. Finally, Napoleon knew that France was on the verge of going to war against England, and he

French finance minister François de Barbé-Marbois shows American negotiators Robert Livingston and James Monroe a map of the area covered by the Louisiana Purchase Treaty.

needed to concentrate his nation's resources on that conflict. When Napoleon's finance minister, François de Barbé-Marbois, advised him to sell Louisiana to the United States, the French leader decided to pursue the idea.

On April 11, 1803, French foreign minister Charles Maurice de Talleyrand told Livingston that France would be willing to sell all of Louisiana to the United States for $15 million. Livingston was shocked to receive this offer. After all, he had been trying fruitlessly for months to convince Napoleon to sell only New Orleans. The French negotiating position had changed so suddenly that he was uncertain how to proceed.

When Monroe arrived in France the following day, the two Americans discussed the situation. They realized that they would be taking a risk by accepting the French proposal. They would be exceeding their authority as well as the amount of money Jefferson had allotted for them to spend. It would take too long to send a letter across the ocean to get U.S. government approval, though, so they had to make a decision on their own. In the end, both men agreed that the deal was far too good to pass up. After signing the Louisiana Purchase Treaty on April 30, Livingston famously said, "We have lived long, but this is the noblest work of our whole lives.... From this day the United States take their place among the powers of the first rank."[6]

"We have lived long, but this is the noblest work of our whole lives," Robert Livingston said upon signing the Louisiana Purchase Treaty. "From this day the United States take their place among the powers of the first rank."

The United States Doubles in Size

When Jefferson received word of the agreement from his representatives in France, he was surprised but delighted at the opportunity to acquire the entire Louisiana Territory. When the president announced the impending purchase in the United States on July 4, many Americans responded with the largest Independence Day celebrations to date. But Jefferson's political rivals in the Federalist Party criticized the plan. An editorial in Boston's *Columbian Centinel* newspaper called Louisiana "a great waste, a wilderness unpeopled with any beings except wolves and wandering Indians," and warned that "we are to give money of which we have too little, for land of which we already have too much."[7]

On the French side, Napoleon was thrilled to get rid of territory that he had no way of defending in exchange for funds to pay off his country's debts and support his war aims. He also recognized that transferring Louisiana to the United States gave the young nation new standing among the world's powers. "Sixty million francs for an occupation that will not perhaps last a day!" Napoleon wrote. "The sale assures forever the power of the United States, and I have given England a rival who, sooner or later, will humble her pride."[8]

The Louisiana Purchase Treaty could not become official until it was approved by the U.S. Senate. At first Jefferson hesitated to present the treaty for a vote because he worried that it was unconstitutional. Jefferson had always been a leading proponent of following the U.S. Constitution exactly as it was written, rather than trying to interpret its underlying meaning or expand upon what it said. He knew that the Constitution did not include any provisions that allowed the president to purchase territory. To overcome this problem, Jefferson suggested amending or changing the Constitution to make the Louisiana Purchase legal. But the members of his cabinet insisted that Napoleon would

The United States made several major territorial acquisitions during the nineteenth century, including the 1803 Louisiana Purchase, which doubled the nation's land area.

not wait for the United States to ratify a constitutional amendment. They also convinced him that it was not strictly necessary, because the Constitution did allow the president to make treaties with other countries.

In the end, Jefferson decided that the Louisiana Territory held such great value for the United States that future generations of Americans would not quibble about the way he went about acquiring it. "It is the case of a guardian, investing the money of his ward in purchasing an important adjacent territory; and saying to him when of age, I did this for your good,"[9] he explained. The U.S. Senate agreed and voted to approve the treaty on October 20, 1803, by a margin of 24-7 (see "The Louisiana Purchase Treaty," p. 164).

Jefferson "wanted to create a country that was continent-wide, an empire of liberty stretching from sea to shining sea," wrote historian Stephen E. Ambrose. "The boldness and uniqueness of his vision were breathtaking."

Although the exact boundaries of the newly acquired territory had to be negotiated with England and Spain over the next few years, the Louisiana Purchase amounted to approximately 827,000 square miles, or 530 million acres. For the remarkably low price of $18 per square mile, or about 3 cents per acre, Jefferson doubled the size of the United States and shifted the nation's western border all the way from the Mississippi River to the Rocky Mountains. The region eventually comprised all or part of thirteen states: Arkansas, Colorado, Iowa, Kansas, Louisiana, Minnesota, Missouri, Montana, Nebraska, North Dakota, Oklahoma, South Dakota, and Wyoming.

Organizing an Expedition

When the United States came into possession of Louisiana, few Americans had ever visited the territory or knew anything about it. What little information Jefferson had about the West came from the reports of French fur traders, the journals of Spanish or British explorers, and the legends told by Native Americans. Now that the nation actually held title to lands west of the Mississippi River, he believed that he would finally be able to mount an official U.S. expedition. Jefferson not only sought to satisfy his own curiosity about the Louisiana Territory, he also wanted to reinforce U.S. ownership of the land by building forts and trading posts and encouraging settlement.

Although the Louisiana Purchase provided the impetus for the expedition, Jefferson had no intention of stopping at the western border of the new territory. Instead, he was determined to explore all the way to the edge of the continent at the Pacific Ocean. He eventually hoped to claim all of this land for the United States. "Jefferson had in mind the extension of the territory of the young Republic not only across the Mississippi River to the Rockies but also all the way to the Pacific Coast," Ambrose explained. "He wanted to create a country that was continent-wide, an empire of liberty stretching from sea to shining sea. The boldness and uniqueness of his vision were breathtaking."[10]

Even less was known about the vast area to the west of Louisiana. In fact, many people believed that mastodons and other prehistoric creatures still roamed through the western wilderness. Rumors also circulated that the landscape contained dangerous volcanoes, a giant mountain made of salt, and a tribe of blue-eyed Indians who spoke Welsh. More credible reports indicated that a great Rocky Mountain range ran from north to south through the middle of the continent. Jefferson and other American leaders had also collected bits of information about the Pacific Coast from people who had reached it by water. In 1792, for instance, an American sea captain named Robert Gray had sailed into the mouth of a large river that emptied into the Pacific. The reports of Gray's voyage up what he named the Columbia River raised hopes of finding a water route that would connect the Atlantic to the Pacific.

The successful overland journey across Canada completed by Scottish explorer Alexander Mackenzie made Jefferson even more determined to launch an American expedition.

Jefferson felt that time was of the essence, because he knew that the United States faced competition from other nations hoping to lay claim to the West. A Scottish explorer named Alexander Mackenzie had already become the first European to cross North America by land and reach the Pacific Ocean. Searching for new trade routes on behalf of the British-owned North West Company, Mackenzie traveled westward through the present-day Canadian provinces of Saskatchewan, Alberta, and British Columbia. He left the following inscription on a rock near Vancouver: "Alexander Mackenzie, from Canada, by land, the 22nd of July, 1793."

In 1801 Mackenzie published a book about his journey entitled *Voyages from Montreal, on the River St. Lawrence through the Continent of North America, to the Frozen and Pacific Oceans.* Jefferson read Mackenzie's book with great interest. Although he appreciated the new information it contained about the West, the book made the president uneasy. He worried that Mackenzie's accomplishment would bolster British claims to the land and its valuable furs and other trade goods. He viewed it as a direct challenge to U.S. authority and security as well as an affront to national honor. He vowed to respond by organizing an American expedition (see "Alexander Mackenzie Inspires American Exploration," p. 157).

On January 18, 1803, Jefferson delivered a confidential message to Congress. It presented his proposal for exploring the Louisiana Territory and the remainder of the continent, all the way to the "Western Ocean." The president requested an appropriation of $2,500 to finance the endeavor. As a strict follower of the Constitution, Jefferson worded his request carefully to make sure that Congress had the power to grant it. The Constitution did not allow Congress to appropriate funds for scientific exploration or for an invasion of foreign territory, so the president described the purpose of the expedition as promoting commerce (see "President Thomas Jefferson Asks Congress to Fund an Expedition," p. 160).

In addition to business and trade opportunities, however, Jefferson explained that the project offered many other benefits for the American people. For example, they could find out whether the geography and climate were suitable for farming, whether the land contained mineral deposits or other valuable natural resources, and what types of plants and animals could be found there. They could also learn about the distribution, population, languages, and cultures of the Native American tribes who inhabited the region. Finally, he emphasized the importance of claiming new territory for the United States before other countries beat them to it. "What Jefferson was proposing had neither precedent nor Constitutional authorization. The expedition would be an armed foray into foreign territory," Ambrose noted. "Never mind, Jefferson [thought]. Two-thirds of a continent was at stake. It had to be American. The race was on."[11]

Notes

[1] Ambrose, Stephen E. *Lewis and Clark: Voyage of Discovery.* Washington, DC: National Geographic Society, 1998, p. 26.

[2] Quoted in Lipscomb, Andrew A., and Albert E. Bergh, eds. *The Writings of Thomas Jefferson.* Washington, DC: Thomas Jefferson Memorial Association of the United States, 1903-04, Vol. 10, p. 315. Retrieved from http://www.monticello.org/site/jefferson/louisiana-purchase.

[3] Quoted in Ambrose, p. 28.

[4] Quoted in Lipscomb and Bergh, Vol. 10, p. 318.

[5] Quoted in Lipscomb and Bergh, Vol. 10, p. 344.

[6] Quoted in Muzzey, David Saville. *The United States through the Civil War.* Boston: Ginn, 1922, p. 216.

[7] Quoted in Duncan, Dayton, and Ken Burns. *Lewis and Clark: The Journey of the Corps of Discovery.* New York: Knopf, 1997, p. 15.

[8] Quoted in Ambrose, p. 40.

[9] Quoted in Lipscomb and Bergh, Vol. 10, p. 411.

[10] Ambrose, p. 30.

[11] Ambrose, p. 31.

Chapter Two

THE CORPS OF DISCOVERY

> We shall delineate with correctness the great arteries of this great country: those who come after us will fill up the canvas we begin.
>
> —Thomas Jefferson, May 1804

Once Congress approved President Thomas Jefferson's proposal to mount an expedition to explore the West, plans and preparations got underway immediately. Jefferson selected Meriwether Lewis, his personal secretary and protégé, as the leader of the historic expedition. Lewis spent the spring and summer of 1803 gaining the knowledge and skills the position would demand and gathering equipment and supplies for the challenging journey ahead. After William Clark signed on as co-leader, the two men recruited a group of tough, experienced outdoorsmen to join their team, which became known as the Corps of Discovery. Following a winter of training near the frontier town of St. Louis, Missouri, the Lewis and Clark Expedition finally set off into the unknown in the spring of 1804.

Choosing Leaders for the Expedition

After agreeing to spend millions of dollars to purchase Louisiana from France, members of the U.S. Congress barely blinked at Jefferson's modest request for $2,500 to fund an expedition to explore and map the newly acquired territory. They quickly approved the measure, with only a few murmurs of complaint from the president's Federalist rivals. As it turned out, Jefferson's request was merely a formality, because he had already begun making preparations for the historic undertaking.

Jefferson selected his personal secretary and protégé, Meriwether Lewis, to lead a U.S. military expedition into the unexplored territory of the West.

The president's first order of business was to select a man to lead the expedition. He chose Meriwether Lewis (see biography, p. 141), a young military officer who had grown up near Monticello in Virginia. Lewis was only five years old when his father, a wealthy planter and a friend of Jefferson, died during the Revolutionary War. Jefferson took the boy under his wing and spent hours tutoring him and lending him books from his extensive private library. As Lewis grew older, he came to share Jefferson's thirst for knowledge and his fascination with the West. He also learned many scientific skills, such as how to preserve plant and animal specimens and how to navigate by the stars.

After serving in the Virginia militia in 1794, Lewis joined the U.S. Army. He served on the western frontier in Ohio and Tennessee and eventually rose to the rank of captain. When Jefferson was elected president in 1801, he invited Lewis to return to the East and become his personal secretary. Lewis quickly accepted the position. Although Lewis's poor spelling and grammar and stiff manners made him a less-than-ideal secretary, he soon learned that Jefferson had a much larger role in mind for him. The president believed that Lewis possessed many of the qualities needed to lead an expedition into the unexplored territory of the West, including courage, wisdom, outdoor skills, frontier experience, and good health.

Even before the expedition received congressional approval, Jefferson helped Lewis brush up on various scientific subjects, such as botany, zoology, ethnology, and astronomy. The president also encouraged his protégé to read books written by explorers who had visited the West, like Robert Gray and Alexander Mackenzie, and to study their sketchy maps of the region. Once Congress agreed to fund the expedition, Jefferson officially appointed Lewis as its leader.

In the spring of 1803, Jefferson sent Lewis to Philadelphia to continue his studies with some of the leading scientists of the day. Jefferson sent a letter of introduction to these men—all members of the American Philosophical Society—describing Lewis's strengths and asking them to tutor him in their areas of specialization. "Capt. Lewis is brave, prudent, habituated to the woods, & familiar with Indian manners & character," the president wrote. "He is not regularly educated, but he possesses a great mass of accurate observation on all the subjects of nature which present themselves here."[1] Lewis studied medicine under physician Benjamin Rush, astronomy with mathematician Robert Patterson, botany under naturalist Benjamin Smith Barton, anatomy and fossils with physician Caspar Wistar, and mapmaking under surveyor Andrew Ellicott.

"If there is anything in this enterprise, which would induce you to participate with me in its fatigues, its dangers and its honors," Lewis wrote to Clark, "believe me there is no man on earth with whom I should feel equal pleasure in sharing them as with yourself."

While he completed his training, Lewis decided to add a co-leader to the expedition whose skills would complement his own. He chose William Clark (see biography, p. 121), a fellow Virginian who had moved to the frontier town of Louisville, Kentucky, at the age of fourteen. The two men had met in 1795, when Lewis served in a military unit of frontier riflemen with Clark as its commanding officer, and developed a high level of trust and respect for one another. The redheaded Clark possessed many skills that Lewis knew would be valuable to the expedition. He had an eye for details of the land, for instance, and was an accomplished surveyor and mapmaker. He also knew how to handle a boat on rivers and negotiate with Native Americans. Finally, he possessed engineering skills that would be useful in building forts and repairing equipment. Jefferson had learned of Clark's skills as a leader and outdoorsman from his older brother, Revolutionary War hero George Rogers Clark, and he approved of Lewis's choice.

On June 19, 1803, Lewis sent a letter to Clark asking him to be a partner in the expedition. Scholar Donald Jackson described it as "one of the most famous invitations to greatness the nation's archives can provide."[2] "From the long and uninterrupted friendship and confidence which has subsisted between us I feel no hesitation in making to you the following communication," Lewis wrote. "My plan is to descend the Ohio in a keeled boat thence up the Mississippi to the mouth of the Missouri, and up that river as far as its navigation is practicable with a keeled boat, there to prepare canoes of bark or raw-hides, and proceed to its source, and if practicable pass over to the waters of the Columbia or Oregon River and by descending it reach the Western Ocean.... If there is anything in this enterprise, which would induce you to participate with me in its fatigues, its dangers and its honors, believe me there is no man on earth with whom I should feel equal pleasure in sharing them as with yourself." Clark eagerly accepted the offer, replying, "My friend, I join you with hand & heart."[3]

Jefferson Provides Instructions

To ensure that the expedition accomplished everything he wanted, Jefferson provided Lewis with a long, detailed set of instructions. In a letter dated June 20, 1803, the president outlined his many scientific, political, and military goals and offered Lewis advice about how to achieve them (see "Jefferson Provides Meriwether Lewis with Detailed Instructions," p. 169). First and foremost, Jefferson emphasized that the primary mission of the government-sponsored expedition was scientific exploration and discovery—both for the sake of knowledge and for the purpose of evaluating the region's potential for future development.

In order to fulfill all of the president's expectations for the expedition, Lewis decided to add a co-leader, William Clark, whose skills would complement his own.

Jefferson listed all of the information he and his scientist friends hoped to gain about the plants, animals, soil, minerals, and climate of the West. He also instructed Lewis to record the latitude and longitude of all major landmarks and geographical features in order to create a detailed map of the region. Jefferson advised the expedition leader to make multiple copies of all of his records so they would not get damaged or lost.

The president also stressed that Lewis was undertaking a touchy diplomatic mission on behalf of the United States. He and his team would not only be exploring the newly acquired Louisiana Territory, but continuing beyond it to western territory that had been claimed by other European nations or remained in dispute. To avoid potential hassles, Jefferson informed the leaders of Great Britain, France, and Spain about the expedition and assured them that its goal was scientific discovery rather than military conquest.

In addition, Lewis and his team would be the first Americans to encounter many of the Native American nations of the West. Jefferson knew it would be tricky for them to avoid conflict and establish peaceful relations with these indigenous peoples. He wanted the Indians to be impressed by the wealth and strength of the United States, but he also sought to assure them of his desire for friendship and trade. "In all your intercourse with the natives, treat them in the most friendly & conciliatory manner which their own conduct will admit," Jefferson wrote to Lewis. "Allay all jealousies as to the object of your journey, satisfy them of its innocence, make them acquainted with the position, extent, character, peaceable & commercial dispositions of the U.S., of our wish to be neighborly, friendly, & useful to them, & of our dispositions to a commercial intercourse with them."[4]

Jefferson also instructed Lewis to gather as much information as possible about the Native Americans they encountered. He wished to know the names of the tribes; their populations, languages, religions, and customs; the extent of their territory; their relationships to each other; and the items they most desired to trade. The president also suggested that Lewis send representatives of various Indian nations back to Washington, D.C., for an official visit.

Assuming that Lewis and his team reached the Pacific Ocean, Jefferson authorized them to draw on the U.S. treasury to purchase whatever supplies they needed for their return journey. Finally, he urged Lewis to be careful and come back safely. "In the loss of yourselves, we should lose also the information you will have acquired. By returning safely with that, you may enable us to renew the essay [effort] with better calculated means," he wrote. "To your own discretion therefore must be left the degree of danger you risk, and the point at which you should decline, only saying we wish you to err on the side of your safety, and to bring back your party safe even if it be with less information."[5]

Gearing Up for the Journey

Even before the expedition became official, Jefferson asked Lewis put together a preliminary estimate of how much it would cost. Lewis tried to keep

The expedition carried a variety of gifts to exchange with Native Americans on the frontier, including silver peace medals engraved with a portrait of the president.

the expenses as low as possible so Congress would be more likely to approve the president's funding request. Once he received the $2,500 he asked for, Lewis began purchasing food and equipment in March 1803 (see "Lewis Buys Equipment and Supplies for the Expedition," p. 175).

The budget for the expedition included $696 for "Indian presents." Lewis knew that exchanging gifts was a traditional part of the interaction between white Americans and Native Americans on the frontier. Gifts served as a medium of exchange when bargaining for trade goods and supplies. They also demonstrated good intentions and helped establish friendly relations. The items Lewis purchased as Indian presents included colorful glass and metal beads, thimbles, small knives, scissors, mirrors, fish hooks, and other trinkets. The most impressive items were specially made silver peace medals. These medallions, which ranged from two to four inches in diameter, were engraved with a portrait of Jefferson on one side and an image of clasped hands on the other, along with the words "peace and friendship."

Lewis also visited the federal military arsenal at Harpers Ferry, Virginia, to obtain rifles, ammunition, and gunpowder. His gear also included a variety of scientific instruments for navigation and mapmaking, including a compass, sextant, and chronometer, along with sturdy paper and ink for recording observations. Lewis also purchased camping and cooking supplies for his expected crew of ten to twelve men, such as tents, pots and pans, eating utensils, fishing gear, and candles. Although he planned for the team to obtain most of its food by hunting and gathering, Lewis also bought some basic provisions, including salt, sugar, flour, corn, lard, 50 pounds of coffee, tobacco, 100 gallons of whiskey, and medicine. He also purchased 193 pounds of "portable soup," a concoction made by boiling down beef, eggs, and vegetables to create a thick paste. The paste was sealed in canisters for transport and then prepared later by adding water.

To be equipped for the variety of terrain he might face on the journey, Lewis also designed a collapsible, iron-framed boat. When covered with bark or animal skins, it could carry a load of up to 1,700 pounds and navigate through shallow rivers and swamps. If necessary, it could also be folded up into a bundle that weighed only 44 pounds and carried overland.

Lewis shipped the boat and all of the other gear and supplies he had collected to Pittsburgh, Pennsylvania. On July 5 he traveled from Washington to Pittsburgh, where he planned to load all of his equipment onto a keelboat. At 55 feet long and 8 feet wide, the keelboat could carry up to 12 tons of cargo. It had a 32-foot mast that allowed it to be sailed in favorable winds, or it also had oars and could be rowed by twenty men. Lewis intended to leave Pittsburgh immediately and follow the Ohio River west nearly 600 miles to Louisville, Kentucky, where he would meet up with Clark. They would continue sailing west on the Ohio another 400 miles until they reached the Mississippi River, then proceed north about 170 miles to St. Louis, Missouri. They planned to camp for the winter near St. Louis, which would be the launching point for the expedition the following spring.

To fill out the Corps of Discovery, Lewis told Clark to look for "good hunters, stout, healthy, unmarried men, accustomed to the woods, and capable of bearing bodily fatigue in a pretty considerable degree."

When Lewis reached Pittsburgh, however, he encountered the first problem of the expedition. He learned that the keelboat was still under construction and would not be ready for several weeks. While he waited impatiently for the shipbuilders to finish, Lewis bought a dog to lift his spirits. The large, black Newfoundland, which he named Seaman, would accompany the expedition from beginning to end as a watchdog, hunting dog, and companion.

Lewis finally departed from Pittsburgh on August 31, 1803. He marked the occasion by writing the first entry in his journal. Lewis was discouraged to find that the late-summer water level on the Ohio River was very low. He and his crew often had to get out of the boat and haul or lift it through shallow areas. "[We] proceeded to a ripple of McKee's rock where we were obliged to get out all hands and lift the boat over about thirty yards; the river is extremely low; said to be more so than it has been known for four years," Lewis wrote. "Halted for the night much fatigued after laboring with my men all day."[6]

Although their progress was slow, Lewis did get to enjoy some unusual sights along the way. On September 11, for instance, he mentioned seeing gray squirrels migrating across the river. "Observed a number of squirrels swimming the Ohio and universally passing from the West to the East shore," he wrote. "I made my dog take as many each day as I had occasion for, they were fat and I thought them when fried a pleasant food."[7]

Forming the Corps of Discovery

Lewis finally met up with his partner on October 14 in Clarksville, Indiana Territory—a settlement that had been founded by George Rogers Clark and was located across the Ohio River from Louisville, Kentucky. While waiting for Lewis to arrive, William Clark had begun selecting a team of men to accompany them on the expedition. The two leaders had initially agreed that their group should consist of about a dozen men. They felt that this number would provide some security but not alarm the Native Americans by appearing to be an invading army.

Among the most important characteristics Lewis and Clark wanted in members of the Corps of Discovery were strength, courage, and skills that would be useful in the wilderness. They needed tough, resourceful frontiersmen who could handle a wide variety of outdoor tasks, meet challenges, and endure hardships. In a letter to Clark, Lewis suggested that he avoid "gentlemen's sons" and instead look for "good hunters, stout, healthy, unmarried men, accustomed to the woods, and capable of bearing bodily fatigue in a pretty considerable degree."[8]

Clark interviewed many volunteers, and he had signed up several recruits by the time Lewis arrived. In order to take part in the exhibition, the men had to enlist in the U.S. military and receive a rank. Two of Clark's recruits—Charles Floyd and Nathaniel Pryor—became sergeants, ranking just below the two captains in the chain of command. Clark also signed up seven privates, which is the lowest army rank: William Bratton, John Colter, brothers Joseph and Reubin Field, George Gibson, George Shannon, and John Shields. This group of experienced hunters, trackers, boatmen, blacksmiths, and carpenters became known as the "nine young men from Kentucky." Shannon was the youngest member of the Corps at eighteen. Shields was the oldest at thirty-four, as well as the only married man. The expedition also included York (see biography, p. 150), an enslaved African-American man who was Clark's lifelong companion and servant. York, whose first name may have been Ben, was a valued team member for the duration of the journey.

After picking up Clark and his crew, the keelboat left Clarksville on October 26 and continued down the Ohio River toward the Mississippi. Lewis and Clark wrote ahead to the commanders of the U.S. Army posts along their intended route

Captain Clark bids farewell to his family as the other expedition members load the keelboat on the Ohio River and prepare to depart for St. Louis on October 26, 1803.

to notify them that they were recruiting men for the expedition. As a result, they picked up several more men from the forts they passed on the way to their winter camp near St. Louis. Lewis and Clark also recruited a few French settlers who were familiar with the waterways through Illinois and Missouri to serve as boatmen and guides. They were known as *engagés*, or hired men. Although most of the Frenchmen only traveled with the expedition temporarily, George Drouillard (see biography, p. 129)—who joined the group at Fort Massac, Illinois—became a permanent member. Of mixed French Canadian and Shawnee Indian ancestry, Drouillard not only contributed skills as a hunter, trapper, and woodsman, but was also fluent in several Indian languages and thus served as an interpreter.

On November 13 the group reached the junction of the Ohio and Mississippi Rivers and stopped to fix the latitude and longitude of the spot. Once the keelboat entered the Mississippi River and began moving upstream, Lewis and Clark found the heavy vessel difficult to maneuver in the swirling currents. They picked up another dozen volunteers from the army post at Kaskaskia, Illinois, about sixty miles south of St. Louis, to help out at the oars. Few details are available about the backgrounds of many of these men. "About the captains there is abundant information," editor Gary Moulton wrote in *The Journals of the Lewis and Clark Expedition.* "Most of the Corps of Discovery, however, lived obscure lives before and after their season of glory. For many there exists the scantiest record, or none at all, about their lives before 1803 and after 1806. The records of the expedition themselves provide, in most cases, only the barest hints about their personalities, virtues, and weaknesses."[9]

Making Camp for the Winter

The expedition finally reached St. Louis on December 10. They decided to make camp for the winter just upstream from the city at Wood River, Illinois, directly across from the confluence of the Mississippi and Missouri Rivers. They called their winter quarters Camp Dubois, after an early French explorer of the area. At this point, Lewis and Clark divided up the tasks that they needed to accomplish before embarking into the unexplored wilderness the following spring. Lewis spent much of his time in St. Louis on U.S. government business. He conferred with the Spanish authorities who were overseeing the details of the Louisiana Purchase, for instance, and attended a ceremony marking the official transfer of the territory to the United States on March 9, 1804.

Lewis also sent the first package of scientific specimens back to Jefferson. One of the objects included in this shipment was an Osage orange, a large, bumpy, green fruit that was previously unknown in the East. Historians claim that Jefferson planted some of the seeds near his home in Virginia, where the original trees continued to grow into the twenty-first century. Lewis also used his time in St. Louis to gather information about the Missouri River from fur traders, hunters, surveyors, merchants, and Native Americans who were familiar with the area. He also studied maps made by James Mackay and John Thomas Evans, who had ascended the Missouri from St. Louis to Three Forks, Montana, as part of a Spanish-sponsored expedition. Some historians believe that Lewis arranged a secret meeting with Mackay to go over details of the maps.

In the meantime, Clark remained at Wood River and oversaw the building and operation of the winter camp. He directed the Corps of Discovery to clear timber, cut logs, and construct cabins and a protective wall. Clark also made changes to the keelboat to be better prepared for the journey into Indian country. He installed a small cannon and some shotguns on the deck to deter

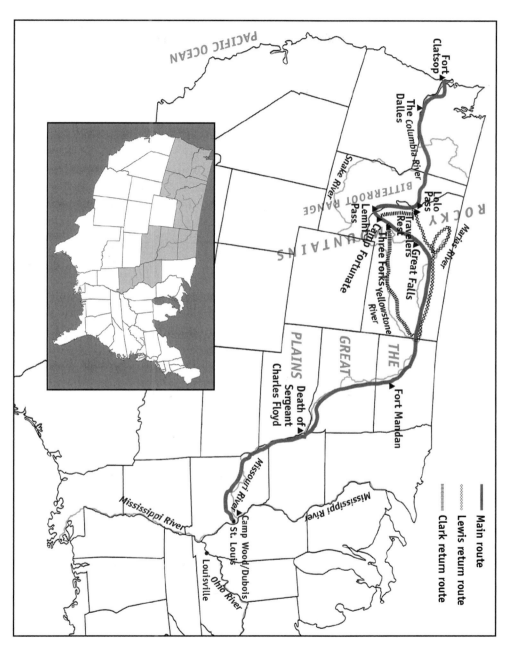

Route of the Lewis and Clark Expedition

Searching for Artifacts
from the Lewis and Clark Exhibition

One of the main goals of the Lewis and Clark Expedition was to gather scientific data about the West and bring back examples of plants, animals, minerals, and Native American culture for further study. The Corps of Discovery collected and catalogued hundreds of items over the course of their three-year journey. They sent back seeds and rocks, dried plants and animal skins, stuffed birds, and even a mastodon jawbone. They also shipped back a wide variety of Native American artifacts, from woven baskets and clay pots to beaded clothing and painted buffalo robes.

Sadly, most of the objects Lewis and Clark so carefully preserved for future generations to study have disappeared over time. In conjunction with the 200th anniversary of the expedition in 2004, historians attempted to solve the mystery of what happened to the artifacts and track down any that remained in existence. The surviving items were displayed in a traveling exhibition, and photographs were published in several commemorative volumes.

During the process of preparing the exhibition, researchers learned that Lewis and Clark sent many artifacts directly to President Thomas Jefferson. When Jefferson left office and shipped his belongings home to Virginia, some of the boxes sustained water damage during transit. He displayed the artifacts that survived, including a buffalo robe with a hand-painted map on it, at Monticello in a spectacular Indian Hall. Late in his life, Jefferson donat-

Indian attacks, for instance, and he added storage lockers along the sides with lids that could double as defensive shields. Recognizing that the expedition needed more room to transport men and supplies upriver, Clark purchased and refitted two pirogues—sturdy, flat-bottomed, dugout canoes that were 40 feet long, 12 feet wide, and had 3-foot-deep cargo holds. He painted one of the pirogues bright red and the other white.

Throughout the winter, Clark also worked to turn their ragtag collection of frontiersmen and soldiers into a highly trained and well-disciplined military unit. When the men were not busy with camp chores, he ordered them to perform drills, practice shooting, and sharpen the other skills they would need in

ed his collection of Indian artifacts to the University of Virginia. Over the years, though, the pieces were scattered to different campus buildings or simply thrown away. "They would have just become old artifacts," explained Elizabeth Chew, an associate curator at Monticello. "They were all organic, they would deteriorate, they would be eaten by bugs."

William Clark kept some artifacts himself. Upon his death, they were sent to the Western Academy of Science, where they were destroyed in a fire in 1869. Many of Clark's letters and documents were thrown out by a later owner of his house who did not realize their historical value. A number of artifacts from the expedition went to Charles Willson Peale, an artist who ran a private natural history museum in Philadelphia. The contents of the museum were sold following Peale's death, however, to circus showman P. T. Barnum and Boston politician and curiosity collector Moses Kimball. Although Barnum's collection was destroyed in a fire in 1865, Kimball's items eventually ended up at Harvard University's Peabody Museum, where they can be seen to this day.

Sources

Hunter, Frances. "The Lost Artifacts of Lewis and Clark." October 6, 2009. Retrieved from https://franceshunter.wordpress.com/2009/10/06/the-lost-artifacts-of-lewis-clark/.

Kelly, Matt. "Tracking Down Lewis and Clark Artifacts." *Inside UVA Online*, September 28–October 4, 2001. Retrieved from http://www.virginia.edu/insideuva/2001/30/artifacts.html.

the wilderness. As they got to know one another at the winter camp, Clark also evaluated the men's abilities and character.

He and Lewis had decided to expand the size of the group that would accompany them all the way to the Pacific—known as the permanent party—to around twenty-five men. They also planned to send a smaller group—known as the return party—back to St. Louis in the keelboat once they reached their next winter camp at the headwaters of the Missouri River (see "Searching for Artifacts from the Lewis and Clark Expedition," p. 30). "Such a party could carry back dispatches, maps, completed journals, and plant, animal, mineral, and anthropological specimens to President Jefferson, giving him a progress report and sparing the expedition the labor of carrying such objects for the entire journey," Moulton wrote. "The thought that something would be saved if they themselves failed to return must have been in their minds."[10]

Clark kept several lists of names as he continually reviewed the men's performance and behavior and separated them into two groups. Some of the men lost their spots in the expedition crew by drinking, fighting, and leaving camp without permission during the long winter months. On the other hand, a few new recruits signed up and earned spots in the Corps of Discovery. John Ordway joined the group at Wood River and was named a sergeant, while Patrick Gass (see biography, p. 133) was added as a private. Both men distinguished themselves by keeping their own journals of the expedition and publishing them after their return.

On April 1, 1804, Lewis and Clark filed a military detachment order indicating the final composition of the two parties. Around that time, Lewis received the official military paperwork from Washington regarding Clark's participation in the expedition. To the surprise and disappointment of both men, the War Department refused to honor Lewis's request to grant Clark the rank of captain. Claiming that there were no vacancies at that rank, the department offered Clark a commission as a lieutenant instead—meaning that he would rank below Lewis. But Lewis had promised his friend that they would lead the expedition as equals, even though it went against military protocol. "Divided command almost never works and is the bane of all military men, to whom the sanctity of the chain of command is basic," Ambrose explained. "But Lewis did it anyway. It felt right to him. It was based on what he knew about Clark, and what he felt for him."[11] As a result, Lewis decided to ignore the message. He never told any of the enlisted men about the situation and referred to Clark as "Captain" throughout the journey.

Getting Underway

After spending five months camped at Wood River, Clark set sail on May 14, 1804. Meanwhile, Lewis remained in St. Louis for an extra week to arrange transportation for an Osage Indian chief who had agreed to go to Washington to meet with Jefferson. He also picked up two local men who were half-French and half-Indian, Pierre Cruzatte and Francis Labiche, to serve as interpreters. Their addition brought the total number in the party to around forty-five.

As their epic journey got underway, the members of the Corps of Discovery had mixed feelings about the mysteries that lay ahead. Patrick Gass felt some trepidation, writing in his journal that he expected "to pass through a country possessed by numerous, powerful and warlike nations of savages, of gigantic stature, fierce, treacherous and cruel; and particularly hostile to white men."[12] Yet John Ordway expressed excitement in a letter to his parents. "I am so happy to be one of the party," he stated. "If we make great discoveries as we expect, the United States has promised to make us great rewards."[13]

Once Lewis rejoined the group at St. Charles on May 21, they prepared to leave the last American settlement on the Missouri River. Packed away in the keelboat and the two pirogues were all the equipment and supplies that the Corps of Discovery would take with them into the wilderness. "When they set off from St. Charles, they were on their own. They had no supply line. No orders from their Commander-in-Chief could reach them," historian Stephen E. Ambrose wrote. "The captains had an independence of command that matched the independence of Columbus, Magellan, and Cook. Like those great explorers, Lewis and Clark knew not what lay ahead, but whatever it turned out to be, they would have to deal with the challenges with what they had with them."[14]

Notes

[1] Quoted in Ambrose, Stephen E. *Lewis and Clark: Voyage of Discovery.* Washington, DC: National Geographic Society, 1998, p. 31.

[2] Quoted in Duncan, Dayton, and Ken Burns. *Lewis and Clark: The Journey of the Corps of Discovery.* New York: Knopf, 1997, p. 119.

[3] Quoted in Ambrose, p. 37.

[4] Jefferson, Thomas. Letter to Meriwether Lewis, June 20, 1803. Retrieved from http://memory .loc.gov/cgi-bin/query/r?ammem/mtj:@field%28DOCID+@lit%28je00048%29%29.

[5] Jefferson, letter to Meriwether Lewis, June 20, 1803.

[6] Lewis, Meriwether. August 30, 1803, entry in *The Journals of the Lewis and Clark Expedition,* ed. Gary Moulton. Lincoln: University of Nebraska Press / University of Nebraska-Lincoln Libraries-Electronic Text Center, 2005. Retrieved from http://lewisandclarkjournals.unl.edu/read/?_xmlsrc=1803-08-30.xml&_xslsrc=LCstyles.xsl.

[7] Lewis, September 11, 1803, entry in *The Journals of the Lewis and Clark Expedition.* Retrieved from http://lewisandclarkjournals.unl.edu/read/?_xmlsrc=1803-09-11.xml&_xslsrc=LCstyles.xsl.

[8] Quoted in Cavan, Seamus. *Lewis and Clark and the Route to the Pacific.* New York: Chelsea House, 1991, p. 33.

[9] Moulton, Gary, ed. *The Journals of the Lewis and Clark Expedition,* Volume 2, Appendix A: "Members of the Exhibition." Lincoln: University of Nebraska Press / University of Nebraska-Lincoln Libraries-Electronic Text Center, 2005. Retrieved from http://lewisandclarkjournals.unl.edu/read/?_xmls rc=v02.appendix.a.xml&_xslsrc=LCstyles.xsl.

[10] Moulton, *The Journals of the Lewis and Clark Expedition,* Volume 2, Appendix A: "Members of the Exhibition."

[11] Quoted in Duncan and Burns, p. 119.

[12] Quoted in Ambrose, p. 45.

[13] Quoted in Ambrose, p. 46.

[14] Ambrose, p. 47.

Chapter Three

UP THE MISSOURI RIVER, 1804

The plains of this country are covered with a leek green grass,... interspersed with copses of trees, spreading their lofty branches over pools, springs, or brooks of fine water. Groups of shrubs covered with the most delicious fruit [are] to be seen in every direction, and nature appears to have exerted herself to beautify the scenery by the variety of flowers.

—William Clark, northeastern Kansas, July 4, 1804

After setting out in May 1804, Captains Meriwether Lewis and William Clark spent the next six months traveling northwest up the Missouri River. By the time the onset of winter forced the Corps of Discovery to make camp among the Mandan Indians near present-day Bismarck, North Dakota, they had traveled over 1,600 miles. They had experienced a variety of terrain and climate conditions, encountered dozens of previously unknown species of plants and animals, and made contact with several Native American groups. Yet half a continent still lay between them and the Pacific Coast, and the most difficult parts of their journey were yet to come.

Life on the River

Once they left the last vestiges of civilization behind and began moving up the Missouri River, the men of the Corps of Discovery quickly settled into a routine. Each morning they woke up early, ate a quick breakfast consisting of cold leftovers from the previous night's dinner, and carefully packed their equipment into the keelboat and two pirogues. They always made sure to divide the gear among the boats so that they would not lose their entire stock of any one item if a particular boat capsized or sunk. Clark typically took charge of the keel-boat during the day. In addition to directing the men who rowed, sailed, or dragged the unwieldy craft upriver, Clark constantly charted the expedition's progress. He took compass readings, estimated distances between bends, and recorded the landmarks they passed.

Lewis, on the other hand, usually walked along the shore of the river and engaged in scientific pursuits. He spent his days collecting samples of soil and minerals, gathering specimens of plants and flowers, observing birds and wildlife, and noting promising locations for future American settlements, trading posts, or forts. George Drouillard, who was the most proficient hunter in the Corps of Discovery, often traveled overland as well. He and a few selected

The Lewis and Clark Expedition traveled 1,600 miles up the Missouri River during the summer and fall of 1804.

men rode on horseback and hunted for wild game to supplement the expedition's daily rations.

Whether they traveled on the river or by land, the members of the Corps of Discovery worked hard and faced many challenges. The men on the boats struggled against the current, which in some spots created treacherous rapids. On stretches where the river was too swift or too shallow to row the keelboat, the crew had to wrap a heavy towrope—known to the French boatmen as a *cordelle*—around its mast and drag it upriver. Cordelling, or pulling the boat, was a very strenuous job that required the men to tromp through thick brush on shore or wade through mud along the riverbank. One time the towrope broke midway through a rapid, and the keelboat bumped and spun its way downstream for two miles before the men on board managed to regain control.

The Missouri contained many other hazards in addition to rapids. Even when the river was wide and calm, its muddy waters hid rocks that could break oars, snags and sandbars that could cause a boat to run aground, and logs that could put a hole in its side. One day, when the keelboat unexpectedly hit a tree limb that was overhanging the river, its mast broke and it nearly overturned. Bad storms and high winds forced the Corps of Discovery to land their small boats on many occasions. At other times they had to deal with stifling heat. "Those men that do not work at all will wet a shirt in a few minutes," Clark wrote, "and those who work, the sweat will run off in streams."[1]

Conditions were not any easier for the men on shore. To protect themselves from ticks and mosquitoes, the men spread grease on their skin by day and slept under mosquito netting at night. Various members of the crew suffered injuries, such as cuts and bruises, puncture wounds from cactus thorns, snake bites, and dislocated shoulders. Others developed dysentery (an intestinal illness that causes diarrhea), sunburns, or skin boils from spending too much time in wet clothing.

Despite all of these issues, however, the Corps of Discovery generally remained in good spirits. Most days the expedition managed to travel between ten and twenty miles upriver. Whenever the captains decided to stop for the evening, the men made camp, distributed rations of corn, flour, lard, and salt pork, and cooked whatever wild plants and game the hunters had managed to procure. Before retiring for the night, Lewis and Clark updated their maps and recorded the day's events in their journals. Sometimes Pierre Cruzatte entertained the group by playing his fiddle.

Into the Great Plains

As the weeks passed by, Lewis and Clark noted many changes in the features of the landscape. On June 26 they reached the point where the Kansas River joins the Missouri River. This confluence, located nearly 400 miles upstream from St. Louis, is the site of present-day Kansas City, Missouri. Looking out from the top of a tall bluff, Clark described the surrounding countryside as "very fine." The Corps of Discovery spent four days there before resuming their journey. One night in camp, a couple of privates on night watch broke into a barrel of whiskey and got drunk on duty. Clark arranged a court-martial, and the men were found guilty and sentenced to be whipped.

On July 4 the Corps of Discovery held the first-ever Fourth of July celebration west of the Mississippi River. They camped on "one of the most beautiful plains I ever saw," according to Clark, "diversified with hills and valleys all presenting themselves to the river covered with grass and a handsome creek meandering through."[2] They named it Independence Creek, in honor of the holiday, and celebrated by firing their cannon and distributing draughts of whiskey to the men.

On July 21 Lewis and Clark passed the confluence of the Platte River in present-day Nebraska, nearly 650 miles upstream from Camp Wood. At this point they entered the Great Plains region, which was characterized by rolling grasslands and abundant wildlife. "The shortness and [freshness] of grass gave the plain the appearance ... of [a] beautiful bowling-green in fine order," Lewis wrote. "This scenery, already rich, pleasing and beautiful, was still further heightened by immense herds of buffalo, deer, elk."[3] Patrick Gass also expressed wonder at their surroundings. "A person by going on one of the hills may have a view as far as the eye can reach without any obstruction; and enjoy the most delightful prospects,"[4] he noted in his journal.

Not all members of the expedition found it enjoyable, however. In early August Private Moses B. Reed asked for permission to go downriver to retrieve a knife he had left behind. When he failed to return, Lewis and Clark discovered he had taken all his belongings with him—a clear indication that he had intentionally deserted his military unit. Recognizing that such a breach of discipline could jeopardize the safety of the group and the success of the expedition, the captains sent Drouillard to find him. In the meantime, the Corps of Discovery camped on a sandbar at the mouth of a creek. The men wove willow branches into a net and caught hundreds of fish to add to their provisions.

Members of the Lewis and Clark Expedition were amazed at the abundance and variety of wildlife on the Great Plains.

When Reed was finally captured, he was forced to run through a line of men who beat him with willow switches as he passed. He was also expelled from the permanent party, which meant that he would be sent back to St. Louis with the keelboat once the expedition reached the headwaters of the Missouri.

In mid-August Sergeant Charles Floyd became ill. He suffered from severe stomach pain, vomiting, and fever. Lewis and Clark tried a few common remedies, but his condition continued to worsen. On August 20 he died, probably from a ruptured appendix. Although this problem can be addressed with surgery today, the best medical care available at that time could not have saved Floyd. He became the first U.S. soldier to lose his life west of the Mississippi River. The men of the Corps of Discovery buried him on a bluff near Sioux City, Iowa, and

"He was buried with the honors of war, much lamented," Captain William Clark wrote of Sergeant Charles Floyd, the only member of the Corps of Discovery to lose his life during the expedition.

named a nearby river in his honor. "He was buried with the honors of war, much lamented," wrote Clark. "A cedar post with [his] name was fixed at the head of his grave. This man at all times gave us proofs of his firmness and determined resolution to do service to his country and honor to himself."[5] The group elected Gass to fill the vacant sergeant's post.

In early September Lewis and Clark grew concerned about another expedition member. George Shannon, the youngest member of the Corps, accidentally became separated from Drouillard while out hunting and was unable to find his way back to the expedition. Although Shannon had two horses with him, he ran out of ammunition, so he had no way of defending himself or hunting for food. Shannon decided to move upriver in hopes of locating the boats, but he misjudged the distance they had traveled. Although he was actually ahead of the expedition, he thought he was behind and raced along the river frantically trying to catch up. By the time the group overtook him on September 11, Shannon had been missing for two weeks and was weak from hunger. "Thus a man had like to have starved to death in a land of plenty for the want of bullets or something to kill his meat,"[6] Clark wrote.

As they moved into present-day South Dakota, Lewis and Clark marveled at the variety of wildlife they encountered on the Great Plains. They saw a number of species that were previously unknown to scientists in the United States, including coyotes, pronghorn antelopes, mule deer, jackrabbits, and badgers. One of the unfamiliar animals that the men found most interesting was the prairie dog, which Lewis called a "barking squirrel" because of the sound it made to warn of approaching danger. Large colonies of these burrowing rodents lived in complex networks of tunnels that extended for miles under the plains. The Corps of Discovery tried various methods to capture one—such as pouring water, blowing smoke, or sticking poles into burrows—but the prairie dogs confounded them by escaping through other entrances. The men eventually managed to collect a live specimen, however, which they sent back to President Thomas Jefferson.

To fulfill his duty as the leader of a scientific expedition, Lewis carefully described each new species of plant or animal the Corps discovered in his journal. He included physical descriptions, observations about behavior and habitat, and pictures and diagrams. In many cases he preserved hides, antlers, bones, leaves, flowers, or roots to ship back to Washington. Fortunately for American

40

scientists of the Enlightenment, Lewis took his work seriously and was very good at it. "He did have the naturalist's ability to describe objects with almost photographic fidelity," said historian James Ronda. "Lewis brought to ethnography the practiced eye of one who delighted in describing and cataloging the creatures of the natural world."[7]

Meeting with the Plains Indians

Another important mission of the Lewis and Clark Expedition involved making contact with Native American groups as representatives of the U.S. government. To carry out Jefferson's orders, the captains made a point of seeking out as many Indian tribes as possible. Since their goal was to establish friendly relations, they also took precautions to reduce their risk of coming under attack. They camped on islands or in other protected locations whenever possible, for instance. They also posted a sentry and kept their weapons secured at all times.

In each meeting with Native American leaders, Lewis and Clark followed the same basic script (see "Indian Diplomacy," p. 44). They started out by making a speech—using a rough form of sign language or an interpreter who spoke that Indian language—informing the Indians that the United States now owned their land. The captains explained that Jefferson was the "great chief" of a powerful nation, and that he had sent them to make peace with the Indians. Then they showed off the military strength and technological achievements of the United States by firing an air gun and demonstrating such newfangled gadgets as a compass and a magnifying glass. Finally, they expressed the U.S. government's desire to become the primary trading partners of the Indians. To reinforce their interest in trade, the captains offered each Native American group a package of gifts, including beads, cloth, fish hooks, combs, tobacco, and silver peace medals featuring Jefferson's image.

On August 2 the captains met with a group of Otoe and Missouri Indians near present-day Council Bluffs, Iowa. Although the Indians were friendly, they did not understand why Lewis and Clark would not give them more of the trade goods that were piled in the expedition's boats. On August 27 the Corps made contact with the Yankton Sioux at the mouth of the James River in present-day South Dakota. Sergeant Nathaniel Pryor visited their camp and became the first American to describe the tepee dwelling that was common among the Plains Indians. "Their camps formed of a conic form containing about twelve or fourteen persons each," he reported, "made of buffalo skins painted different color, all compact and handsomely arranged."[8] Although Lewis and Clark's meeting with Yankton Sioux leaders went relatively well, Chief Half Man warned them that the Sioux nations further upriver would not be as friendly.

The chief's warning proved true when the expedition encountered the Teton Sioux, or Lakota, in late September near present-day Pierre, South Dakota. The powerful Lakota warriors arrived at the meeting dressed in painted buffalo robes, feathered headdresses, and moccasins decorated with porcupine quills. Chief Black Buffalo informed the captains that his people controlled trade on the Missouri River. He then demanded one of the pirogues loaded with trade goods in exchange for allowing the American group to pass through Teton Sioux territory. When one of the Lakota warriors grabbed onto a rope attached to the boat, Clark drew his sword. Describing the tense confrontation in his journal, Sergeant John Ordway recalled that Clark "told them that we must and would go on ... that we were not squaws, but warriors. The chief said he had warriors too and if we were to go on they would follow us and kill and take the whole of us by degrees."[9]

The Corps of Discovery raised their guns at the chief's threat, which prompted the Lakota warriors to notch their arrows in response. As the two

This sketch from the journal of Sergeant Patrick Gass shows the captains holding a council with a group of Plains Indians.

groups stood ready to fight, however, the chief backed down and invited Lewis and Clark to visit his village. "The captains had been exceedingly lucky," Ambrose noted. "Had a fire fight broken out, they and their men would almost certainly have been wiped out. They would have taken a goodly number of Sioux with them, thus making the most powerful tribe on the Missouri River the implacable enemy of the United States. It would have been years, perhaps decades, before the United States would become strong enough to send trading parties up the river against the active opposition of the Sioux. The entire timetable of westward expansion would have been slowed."[10]

Lewis and Clark accepted the chief's invitation and spent two uneasy evenings with the Lakota. As they ate roasted dog meat and watched traditional dancing, they worried that the Sioux might have delayed them in order to plan an attack. Once the visit ended, however, the Corps were allowed to continue their journey upriver. Anxious to get away from Teton Sioux territory, the captains proceeded as quickly as possible. Clark came away with a very negative impression of the Lakota, calling them "the vilest miscreants of the savage race" and the "pirates of the Missouri."[11]

On October 8 the expedition reached the Arikara nation in northern South Dakota. In contrast to the Sioux, who ranged over a wide area in pursuit of buffalo herds, the Arikara lived in permanent earth lodges and subsisted by growing crops. The Arikara had once numbered 30,000, but a smallpox epidemic had reduced their population by 75 percent. As a result, they felt intimidated by their powerful neighbors to the south and hoped to acquire weapons through trade. They welcomed the explorers to their village, and Lewis and Clark enjoyed their hospitality. When the captains offered to help the Arikara forge an alliance with the Mandan and Hidatsa peoples further north, tribal leaders supported the idea.

Winter at Fort Mandan

By late October, the Lewis and Clark Expedition had been traveling up the Missouri for six months. Although the men had covered 1,600 miles since leaving Fort Wood, they still had not reached the headwaters of the river. Moreover, half a continent still remained between them and the Pacific Ocean. Nevertheless, the captains knew the arrival of autumn meant that they could not proceed much further before they had to stop for the winter. As they encountered migrating birds, falling leaves, and cold nighttime temperatures,

Indian Diplomacy

An important part of Lewis and Clark's mission involved establishing friendly relations with the Native American peoples of the West. Although President Jefferson wanted the captains to gather information about Indian populations, traditions, and cultures, he also ordered them to inform Indian leaders that the United States now owned their land and expected to control trade throughout the region. "The expedition, we must always keep in mind, was not simply one of pure exploration for the sake of scientific knowledge," explained Native American author William Least Heat-Moon. "Whether we like it or not, it was also one of imperialism: Thomas Jefferson and a majority of the Congress wanted to take unchallenged possession in all ways of the new and huge country just purchased from France."

The speech excerpted below, which Lewis and Clark delivered to each of the Native American peoples they encountered, shows how the promise of friendship was tempered by warnings about the power and influence of the United States:

Children. Your old fathers the French and the Spaniards have gone beyond the great lake toward the rising sun, from whence they never intend returning to visit their former red children.

Children. The great chief of the seventeen great nations of America, impelled by his parental regard for his newly adopted children on the troubled waters, has sent us out to clear the road ... and make it a road of peace.

Children. Know that the great chief who has ... offered you the hand of unalterable friendship is the great chief of the seventeen great nations of America, whose cities are as numerous as the stars of the heavens, and

they decided to make camp among the Mandan Indians north of present-day Bismarck, North Dakota.

The Mandan people tended to be very accepting of outsiders. They had been meeting with French and Spanish traders for decades by the time Lewis and Clark arrived, and their villages served as the central marketplace for an Indian trade network that stretched for hundreds of miles in every direction.

whose people like the grass of your plains cover ... the wide extended country ... to where the land ends and the sun rises from the face of the great waters.... He will serve you and not deceive you.

Children. You are to live in peace with all the white men; neither wage war against the red men your neighbors.... Injure not the persons of any traders ... who visit you under the protection of your great father's flag.

Children. Do these things which your great father advises and be happy ... lest by one false step you should bring down upon your nation the displeasure of your great father ... who could consume you as the fire consumes the grass of the plains.

Children. Follow [his] counsels and you will have nothing to fear, because the Great Spirit will smile upon your nation and in future ages will make you outnumber the trees of the forest.

Many Indian leaders responded to Lewis and Clark's overtures positively and offered the explorers food, hospitality, and assistance. Yet most were not swayed by the captains' message about the U.S. government owning the land and controlling the flow of trade. Since the United States had not yet established forts or trading posts in the West, the Native Americans knew that the "Great Chief" Jefferson had no way of protecting them from their enemies or meeting their needs. They remained determined to look out for their own interests and trade with whatever supplier offered them the best goods at the lowest prices.

Source

Quoted in Duncan, Dayton, and Ken Burns. *Lewis and Clark: The Journey of the Corps of Discovery.* New York: Knopf, 1997, pp. 49-52, 65.

Given their strong interest in commerce, the Mandan welcomed the Corps of Discovery and their boats full of merchandise with open arms. Clark described them as "the most friendly, well disposed Indians inhabiting the Missouri. They are brave, humane, and hospitable."[12]

Although the Mandan conducted annual buffalo hunts, they relied mostly on agriculture, growing corn, beans, squash, and other food crops. The Man-

Artist Charles M. Russell painted this scene, in which a puzzled Indian chief tries to rub off what he thinks must be dirt or paint from York's dark skin.

dan lived in large, circular, earth-covered lodges near the mouth of the Knife River. Together with the Hidatsa (also known as Minitaris or Gros Ventre), who lived a short distance upstream, they numbered around 4,000. The Mandan and Hidatsa peoples were related linguistically and culturally, and they formed an alliance for mutual protection against the Teton Sioux.

On November 2 the Corps of Discovery began building a winter camp on the east side of the Missouri River, opposite the Mandan village. "This morning early we fixed on the site for our fortification which we immediately set about," Lewis wrote. "This place we have named Fort Mandan in honor of our neighbors."[13] Gass, an accomplished carpenter, oversaw construction of the structure. He described it as roughly triangular in shape, with 56-foot-long sides and 18-foot-high walls. Along the insides of the walls were rows of huts with sloped roofs that served as quarters for the men, as well as a shed to hold their equipment and supplies.

The Corps of Discovery lived at Fort Mandan for five months. During that time, they endured snowstorms, high winds, and bitterly cold temperatures. Some nights were so bad that the sentries could only remain on duty for half-hour shifts or else they would get frostbite. Still, the men found some enjoyable ways to pass the time. They celebrated Christmas and New Year's Eve with music, dancing, and toasts with whiskey. They also socialized frequently with their Indian neighbors and observed their ceremonies and rituals. Some members of the Corps of Discovery engaged in sexual liaisons with Mandan and Hidatsa women, which resulted in the captains being forced to treat venereal diseases.

The Mandan and Hidatsa peoples were particularly fascinated by York, Clark's enslaved African-American servant. Since they had never seen a black person before, they "flocked around him & examined him from top to toe,"[14] according to Clark. The Hidatsa chief, Le Borgne, was so puzzled by York's appearance that he moistened his finger and rubbed it on York's skin to try to remove what he thought must be dirt or paint. When the pigment did not come off, Le Borgne said that York must possess spiritual powers and gave him the nickname "Big Medicine." York enjoyed entertaining the Indian children by pretending to be a wild animal and threatening to eat them. "All the nation made a great deal of him," Ordway wrote. "The children would follow after him, & if he turned towards them, they would run from him & holler as if they were terrified."[15]

Sacagawea Joins the Team

Over the course of the winter, the captains made several adjustments to the composition of the permanent party that would push onward to the Pacific Ocean. They dropped another private, John Newman, for not following orders and disrespecting authority. He would return to St. Louis on the keelboat with Reed, the deserter, and the French boatmen. Lewis and Clark also added Jean Baptiste Lepage, a French trader who was familiar with areas further up the Missouri River. At Fort Mandan he consulted with Clark and helped him fill in missing details on his map of the region.

The expedition also gained two other people who had been living among the Hidatsa: a French Canadian trader named Toussaint Charbonneau (see biography, p. 117) and one of his two young Indian wives, Sacagawea (see biography, p. 146). Charbonneau spoke several languages and joined the group as an interpreter. Sacagawea originally came from the Shoshone nation further west. She had been captured by a Hidatsa war party around 1800, when she was twelve or thirteen years old. Now in her late teens, Sacagawea would serve as an interpreter and guide for Lewis and Clark. She knew several Indian languages, had some basic knowledge of the region, and possessed strong outdoor survival skills.

Once Sacagawea joined the expedition as an interpreter and guide, her presence helped reassure the Indians they met of the group's friendly intentions.

The final member of the expedition was a baby boy, Jean Baptiste Charbonneau, who was born to Sacagawea and her husband on February 11, 1805. The infant would ride on his mother's back for the duration of the journey. He became a special favorite of Clark, who called him by the nickname Pomp or Pompey. Although it may seem strange that the captains allowed a woman with a newborn baby to become part of their expedition, Sacagawea proved to be very helpful. Her presence made the group appear much less threatening to the Indians they encountered, which helped them avoid conflict. She would become especially valuable in negotiations with Shoshone leaders when the expedition reached the Rocky Mountains.

When the spring thaw began breaking up the ice on the Missouri River, Lewis and Clark prepared to continue their journey. They also packed the keelboat full of scientific samples and geographic information for the return trip to St. Louis. Sending a shipment back to civilization helped lighten the load for the expedition's overland trip through the mountains. In addition, the captains wanted to ensure that the specimens they had collected so far reached Jefferson in case something happened to prevent them from completing their mission.

The shipment included seeds and dried specimens of sixty plants— including big bluestem, buffalo berry, and cottonwood—along with sixty-seven soil and mineral samples. It also included skins, bones, or horns from antelopes, elk, mule deer, bighorn sheep, coyotes, and other animals, as well as cages containing live magpies and prairie dogs. Other crates contained Indian artifacts, such as buffalo robes, pottery, and a bow and arrows. The captains also sent copies of their journals up to that point and letters to their families. Finally, Clark added the map of the West he had worked on all winter. The most accurate sections were based on the twenty-nine separate, detailed maps he had drawn along the way as the expedition made its way up the Missouri. But it also included more speculative sections based on information he had gathered from Indian hunting parties, French fur traders, and other people the group encountered.

On April 7, 1805, Corporal Richard Warfington led a squad of six soldiers, several French engages, and the expelled members Reed and Newman on the return trip to St. Louis in the keelboat. At the same time, Lewis and Clark embarked with the permanent party in the other direction—toward their ultimate goal, the Pacific Ocean. "Our vessels consisted of six small canoes, and two large pirogues," Lewis wrote. "This little fleet, although not quite so respectable as those of Columbus or Captain Cook, were still viewed by us with as much pleasure as those deservedly famed adventurers ever beheld theirs; and I dare say with quite as much anxiety for their safety and preservation."[16]

Notes

[1] Clark, William. July 6, 1804, entry in *The Journals of the Lewis and Clark Expedition,* ed. Gary Moulton. Lincoln: University of Nebraska Press/Electronic Text Center, 2005. Retrieved from http://lewisand clarkjournals.unl.edu/read/?_xmlsrc=1804-07-06&_xslsrc=LCstyles.xsl.

[2] Clark, July 4, 1804, entry in *The Journals of the Lewis and Clark Expedition.* Retrieved from http://lewis andclarkjournals.unl.edu/read/?_xmlsrc=1804-07-04.xml&_xslsrc=LCstyles.xsl.

[3] Lewis, Meriwether. September 17, 1804, entry in *The Journals of the Lewis and Clark Expedition.* Retrieved from http://lewisandclarkjournals.unl.edu/read/?_xmlsrc=1804-09-17.xml&_xslsrc=LCstyles.xsl.

[4] Gass, Patrick. September 3, 1804, entry in *The Journals of the Lewis and Clark Expedition.* Retrieved from http://lewisandclarkjournals.unl.edu/read/?_xmlsrc=1804-09-03&_xslsrc=LCstyles.xsl.

[5] Clark, August 20, 1804, entry in *The Journals of the Lewis and Clark Expedition.* Retrieved from http://lewisandclarkjournals.unl.edu/read/?_xmlsrc=1804-08-20&_xslsrc=LCstyles.xsl.

[6] Clark, September 11, 1804, entry in *The Journals of the Lewis and Clark Expedition.* Retrieved from http://lewisandclarkjournals.unl.edu/read/?_xmlsrc=1804-09-11&_xslsrc=LCstyles.xsl.

[7] Quoted in Duncan, Dayton, and Ken Burns. *Lewis and Clark: The Journey of the Corps of Discovery.* New York: Knopf, 1997, p. 50.

[8] Quoted in Ambrose, Stephen E. *Lewis and Clark: Voyage of Discovery.* Washington, DC: National Geographic Society, 1998, p. 60.

[9] Quoted in Duncan and Burns, p. 56.

[10] Ambrose, p. 68.

[11] Quoted in Ronda, James P. *Lewis and Clark among the Indians: The Teton Confrontation.* Lincoln: University of Nebraska Press, 1984. Retrieved from http://lewisandclarkjournals.unl.edu/read/?_xmlsrc= lc.ronda.01.02&_xslsrc=LCstyles.xsl.

[12] Clark, William. *Estimate of the Eastern Indians,* 1804-05. Retrieved from http://lewisandclarkjournals .unl.edu/read/?_xmlsrc=1804-1805.winter.part2&_xslsrc=LCstyles.xsl.

[13] Lewis, November 2, 1804, entry in *The Journals of the Lewis and Clark Expedition.* Retrieved from http://lewisandclarkjournals.unl.edu/read/?_xmlsrc=1804-11-02&_xslsrc=LCstyles.xsl.

[14] Clark, October 10, 1804, entry in *The Journals of the Lewis and Clark Expedition.* Retrieved from http://lewisandclarkjournals.unl.edu/read/?_xmlsrc=1804-10-10&_xslsrc=LCstyles.xsl.

[15] Ordway, John. October 15, 1804, entry in *The Journals of the Lewis and Clark Expedition.* Retrieved from http://lewisandclarkjournals.unl.edu/read/?_xmlsrc=1804-10-15&_xslsrc=LCstyles.xsl.

[16] Lewis, April 7, 1805, entry in *The Journals of the Lewis and Clark Expedition* Retrieved from http:// lewisandclarkjournals.unl.edu/read/?_xmlsrc=1805-04-07&_xslsrc=LCstyles.xsl.

Chapter Four

ACROSS THE CONTINENT TO THE PACIFIC, 1805

—◁◁◁◁◖◗▷▷▷▷—

We were now about to penetrate a country at least two thousand miles in width, on which the foot of civilized man had never trodden; the good or evil it had in store for us was for experiment yet to determine.... Entertaining as I do, the most confident hope of succeeding in a voyage which had formed a darling project of mine for the last ten years, I could but esteem this moment of my departure as among the most happy of my life.

—Meriwether Lewis, April 7, 1805

When Lewis and Clark left Fort Mandan on April 7, 1805, they launched the most challenging and uncertain part of their expedition. They still had to cross half a continent of unexplored territory in order to achieve their goal of reaching the Pacific Ocean. They had no maps and very little word-of-mouth information about the route that lay ahead. They knew that they would have to cross at least one mountain range, however, and they anticipated facing danger and hardship along the way.

Encountering Fearsome Beasts

The permanent party of the Corps of Discovery consisted of thirty-three people, including the two captains, three sergeants, twenty-three privates, two interpreters (George Drouillard and Toussaint Charbonneau), York, Sacagawea, and her two-month-old baby, Jean Baptiste. As they continued up the Missouri River in the two pirogues and six small canoes, Lewis felt great confidence in his crew. "The party are in excellent health and spirits, zealously attached to the enterprise, and anxious to proceed," he wrote. "Not a whisper or murmur of discontent to be heard among them, but all act in unison, with the most perfect harmony. With such men I have everything to hope, and but little to fear."[1]

As the Corps of Discovery entered the wilderness of present-day Montana, though, they encountered a fearsome new predator: the grizzly bear. The Mandan Indians had warned Lewis and Clark about the large, strong, and ferocious bears that lived further west. They advised the explorers to avoid the beasts, which they considered too dangerous to hunt except with large groups of warriors.

The expedition's first encounter occurred on April 29, when Lewis and a companion ran into a pair of grizzlies near the Yellowstone River. They fired their guns and wounded the bears, which caused one of the animals to run away. The other one began chasing the men, but Lewis managed to reload his rifle and kill it. Although the experience was frightening, Lewis expressed confidence that American weapons could meet the challenge. "The Indians may well fear this animal, equipped as they generally are with their bows and arrows," he noted, "but in the hands of a skillful rifleman they are by no means as formidable or dangerous as they have been represented."[2]

On May 5 the expedition got a clearer idea of how tough and resilient grizzlies could be. Upon encountering a large bear near the Milk River, they shot

The Corps of Discovery had many dangerous encounters with grizzly bears, as this sketch from Gass's journal shows.

it multiple times. Still, the wounded bear managed to swim across the river to a sandbar before it finally succumbed. A week later, Private William Bratton shot another grizzly while hunting on shore. He only managed to anger the bear, however, and it chased him for half a mile while he screamed in terror. Bratton finally escaped by leaping off a high bank into the Missouri River. Other expedition members tracked the dangerous creature back to its den, where it continued to fight until they shot it several more times.

> *"I must confess that I do not like the gentlemen," Lewis wrote after a frightening grizzly encounter, "and had rather fight two Indians than one bear."*

By this time, Lewis admitted that he found grizzlies intimidating. "I must confess that I do not like the gentlemen and had rather fight two Indians than one bear," he wrote. "I find that the curiosity of our party is pretty well satisfied with respect to this animal."[3] He ordered his men to avoid the bears whenever possible and only shoot them in self-defense. When grizzlies prowled around the group's camp at night, Seaman the dog helped keep them safe by growling or barking in warning.

In addition to bears, the expedition encountered a wide variety of other wildlife as they continued up the Missouri, including buffalo, elk, and bighorn sheep. Many of the animals had not yet developed a fear of humans, and some even showed curiosity toward the explorers. Lewis noted that they were "so gentle that we pass near them while feeding, without appearing to excite any alarm among them; and when we attract their attention, they frequently approach us more nearly to discover what we are."[4] In one spot they were surprised to discover dozens of dead buffaloes at the base of a cliff. They guessed that an Indian hunting party must have herded the beasts over the edge in order to harvest the meat. A pack of wolves was feasting on the remains, and Lewis commented that they were fat and gentle.

Approaching the Rocky Mountains

As the group moved further into Montana, the terrain gradually became dry and rugged. The lush, grassy prairies turned into rocky hills dotted with sagebrush, juniper, and other drought-tolerant plant species. The spring weather was unpredictable, and storms and strong winds sometimes occurred with little warning. A squall that blew in on May 14 nearly spelled disaster for the expedition. It was an unusual day because both Lewis and Clark were on shore, and they left Charbonneau—an inexperienced boatman who did not know how to swim—in charge of the white pirogue. A sudden gust of wind ripped the boat's sail and caused Charbonneau to lose hold of the rudder. The small craft tipped onto its side and started taking on water.

The captains watched helplessly as the pirogue floundered in the waves. The vessel contained "our papers, instruments, books, medicine, a great part of our merchandise [Indian gifts], and in short almost every article indispensably necessary to further the views, or ensure the success of the enterprise,"[5] according to Lewis. Fortunately, Pierre Cruzatte quickly took charge of the situation and got the boat upright. He confronted the terrified Charbonneau, who was "crying to his god for mercy,"[6] and threatened to shoot him if he did not resume his place at the rudder. Then he ordered the other expedition members on board to begin bailing water.

Lewis got his first glimpse of snow-capped mountains in the distance on May 26, 1805.

In contrast to her husband, Sacagawea remained calm throughout the ordeal. She collected floating gear with one hand while holding her baby's head above water with the other. The crew managed to guide the pirogue to shore, where the captains were relieved to find most of their equipment still salvageable. "The Indian woman, to whom I ascribe equal fortitude and resolution with any person,... caught and preserved most of the light articles which were washed overboard," Lewis wrote, and as a result "the loss we sustained was not so great as we had at first apprehended."[7]

As the expedition continued moving westward, the Missouri narrowed and flowed more swiftly. Although the captains were thrilled to be nearing the river's headwaters, the strong current and frequent rapids slowed their progress. The members of the Corps of Discovery were often forced to disembark and trudge along the rocky shoreline, using towropes to drag the boats upstream.

On May 26 Lewis climbed a tall bluff and saw snowcapped mountains in the distance. Assuming they were the fabled Rocky Mountains that divided the eastern and western halves of the continent, he was filled with a combination of excitement and apprehension. "While I viewed these mountains I felt a secret pleasure in finding myself so near the head of the heretofore conceived boundless Missouri; but when I reflected on the difficulties which this snowy barrier would most probably throw in my way to the Pacific," he admitted, "it in some measure counterbalanced the joy I had felt in the first few minutes I gazed at them."[8] In reality, though, Lewis was gazing upon the Bears Paw Mountains, one of many smaller ranges in western Montana.

In late May the expedition entered a landscape filled with incredible rock formations. They saw sheer cliffs of white sandstone, outcroppings of black volcanic rock, and red sandstone that had been carved by wind and water into elaborate shapes. The stunning scenery prompted several members of the crew to include poetic descriptions in their journals. "As we passed on it seemed as if those scenes of visionary enchantment would never have an end," Lewis wrote. "So perfect indeed are those walls that I should have thought that nature had attempted here to rival the human art of masonry had I not recollected that she had first begun her work."[9] Gass agreed that "they seem as if built by the hand of man, and are so numerous that they appear like the ruins of an ancient city."[10]

The Great Falls Portage

In mid-June the expedition members became the first white men to view another natural wonder: the Great Falls of the Missouri River (see "Lewis Scouts the Great Falls of the Missouri River," p. 182). Upon reaching the spectacular waterfall, Lewis called it the "grandest sight I ever beheld" and wished he "might be enabled to give to the enlightened world some just idea of this truly magnificent and sublimely grand object, which has from the commencement of time been concealed from the view of civilized man."[11]

Based on information they had gathered from Native American hunters, Lewis and Clark expected to be able to carry their boats around the falls and put them back into the river within a day. They soon realized, however, that the initial, eighty-seven-foot-high waterfall was only the first in a series of five major drops that extended upstream for more than ten miles. The expedition members ended up spending the next month portaging around these obstacles. They

Lewis described the Great Falls of the Missouri River as the "grandest sight I ever beheld," but portaging the boats around the falls was a month-long ordeal.

built crude wagons out of cottonwood trees and the masts of the pirogues. Then they placed their boats onto the wagons and loaded them with equipment and supplies.

Without horses to pull the heavy, unwieldy loads, the men had to haul the wagons upstream for eighteen miles by themselves. It was backbreaking labor, made worse by the thick brush that lined the riverbank and the blazing heat of summer. "They are obliged to halt and rest frequently," Lewis noted. "At every halt these poor fellows tumble down and are so much fatigued that many of them are asleep in an instant.... Some are limping from the soreness of their feet, others faint and [are] unable to stand for a few minutes, with heat and fatigue, yet no one complains."[12] Many of the men suffered cuts and puncture wounds from brushes with prickly pear cactus. They also endured a terrible hailstorm that left team members bruised and bloody, and a flash flood that nearly swept away Clark, Charbonneau, and Sacagawea.

The Great Falls portage turned into such a long, difficult ordeal that Lewis grew worried. Upon first setting out from Fort Mandan, he had hoped that the expedition would make it all the way to the Pacific and back to the Mandan villages that year. When it took an entire month to portage around the falls, however, he wondered whether they would even make it through the mountains to the Pacific before winter descended upon them once again.

Lewis's impatience and disappointment only increased when the crew finally completed the portage on July 15 and prepared to launch their boats above the falls. It was finally time to try out the collapsible, iron-framed boat that Lewis had carried all the way from Pittsburgh. He named it the *Experiment* and covered it with stretched buffalo skins. Without access to pine tar to waterproof the hides, however, the seams leaked and the boat would not float. The crew tried a number of different sticky substances—such as beeswax, tallow, and charcoal—but none of them worked, and Lewis was forced to abandon his plan. Instead, members of the Corps had to spend five more days building two additional dugout canoes out of cottonwood trees.

A Lucky Reunion

As the expedition continued moving up the Missouri from the Great Falls, they noticed the terrain becoming steeper and more mountainous. Near present-day Helena, Montana, they passed through a beautiful canyon with cliffs soaring 1,200 feet above them. At this point Sacagawea began recognizing famil-

Places Named by Lewis and Clark

In their exploration and mapping of previously unknown parts of North America, Lewis and Clark named hundreds of different geographical features, including mountains, rivers, lakes, valleys, and trails. Clark's published map of the area that eventually became Montana, for instance, contained 148 place names. Some of these names had been used by Native American inhabitants of the region for generations, but many others were coined by the captains themselves.

The explorers had to be creative to come up with distinctive names for so many landmarks. "They were predictably direct and simple in their choices," historian Donald Jackson noted. "They usually went straight to the heart of the matter and chose a sound, reasonable name." The captains named many places after people. For instance, they named the three forks of the Missouri River after prominent political figures of their day. Clark named one particularly beautiful, clear river the Judith after Julia "Judith" Hancock, the woman whom he later married. Many other place names recognized members of the Corps of Discovery, including York's Dry Fork, Shannon's Creek, and Pompey's Tower. Lewis even named one creek after his dog, Seaman.

Some of the most interesting place names came from memorable events that happened to the Corps of Discovery in that spot. During their ordeal in the Bitterroots, for instance, they chose Hungry Camp for a place

iar landmarks from her childhood among the Shoshone Indians. "The Indian woman recognizes the country and assures us that this is the river on which her relations live,"[13] Lewis wrote on July 22. The captains were eager to meet with Shoshone leaders in order to purchase horses to help carry their gear overland through the Rocky Mountains.

On July 25 the expedition came to a point known as Three Forks, where three smaller rivers converged to form the Missouri. The captains named the forks Jefferson, Madison, and Gallatin after the president and two of his cabinet secretaries, James Madison and Albert Gallatin, who had helped win approval for the Louisiana Purchase (see "Places Named by Lewis and Clark," p. 58). This spot—2,500 miles from where their journey began in St. Louis—

where they had nothing to eat, and Colt Killed Creek for a place where they were forced to eat one of their horses. When an angry buffalo stampeded around their campsite, they named the spot Bull Creek. Many other names described characteristics of the land. When Lewis said a stream looked like tea with milk, it became the Milk River. Big Dry Creek got its name because there was no water in it, while Teapot Creek was so named because it had only enough water to fill a teapot.

The vast majority of the names Lewis and Clark bestowed upon the West were eventually replaced with different ones. People who arrived later—such as fur traders, gold miners, surveyors, steamship captains, railroad builders, and settlers—updated the expedition's place names with others that reflected their own preferences and experiences. By 1892, only twenty-seven of Lewis and Clark's original names remained on the map of Montana. Of course, several new place names were later created to honor the first American explorers of the region. The twin towns of Lewiston, Idaho, and Clarkston, Washington, for instance, are located at the junction of the Clearwater and Snake Rivers, near where the captains camped with the Nez Perce in 1805.

Sources

Jackson, Donald. *Among the Sleeping Giants: Occasional Pieces on Lewis and Clark.* Champaign: University of Illinois Press, 1987.

Mussulman, Joseph. "Place Names." *Discovering Lewis and Clark,* September 2011. Retrieved from http://www.lewis-clark.org/article/3141.

turned out to be the place where Sacagawea's people had been camped when she was captured by the Hidatsa five years earlier.

After resting for a few days, Lewis set off overland with a few men in search of the Shoshone. He had heard from other tribes that the westernmost fork led to a short portage over the Continental Divide. This imaginary line, running from north to south through North America along the spine of the Rocky Mountains, marked the western boundary of the Louisiana Territory, and thus the United States. It also marked the dividing line between rivers that flowed eastward to the Atlantic Ocean and rivers that flowed westward to the Pacific Ocean. The captains hoped that upon reaching the headwaters of the eastward-flowing Missouri, they would discover the fabled Northwest Passage—a water route connecting it to the westward-flowing Columbia River. From there, they thought it would be an easy, downstream trip across gentle plains to the Pacific.

On August 12 Lewis followed an Indian trail to the top of a ridge near the current Montana-Idaho border and found what he believed to be "the most distant fountain of the waters of the Mighty Missouri, in search of which we have spent so many toilsome days and restless nights." Looking westward from Lemhi Pass, he eagerly anticipated seeing the source of the Columbia. But his dream of finding an easy route to the Pacific was shattered. Instead, Lewis saw "immense ranges of high mountains ... with their tops partially covered with snow,"[14] extending all the way to the horizon. He faced the troubling realization that the most difficult and perilous part of the journey still lay ahead.

The very same day that a discouraged Lewis learned that the Northwest Passage did not exist, a delighted Jefferson received the shipment of items the captains had sent back on the keelboat from Fort Mandan. The president was thrilled to read the journals and study the maps that chronicled the achievements of the Corps of Discovery so far. He also enjoyed examining the plant

Sacagawea had a joyous reunion with her Shoshone people on August 17, 1805.

and animal specimens and Indian artifacts the expedition had collected. Jefferson took some items back to Monticello, where he planted Indian corn in his garden, hung a set of antlers on his wall, and displayed a decorated buffalo robe in a room full of Indian artifacts. He sent the live magpie and prairie dog to a natural history museum at Independence Hall in Philadelphia.

Meanwhile, Lewis and his companions made contact with a party of sixty Shoshone warriors. Since they were the first white people the Indians had ever met, it took some time for the expedition members to convey their good intentions. They were finally allowed to visit the Shoshone encampment, and then they convinced Shoshone leaders to accompany them back to the Jefferson fork to meet Clark and the rest of the Corps of Discovery. When the two groups got together on August 17, Clark noted that "every article about us appeared to excite astonishment in [the Indians'] minds; the appearance of the men, their arms, the canoes, our manner of working them, the black man York and the sagacity [intelligence] of my dog were equally objects of admiration."[15]

As they prepared to discuss business, the captains asked Sacagawea to serve as an interpreter. To her amazement, she recognized the Shoshone chief as her brother Cameahwait. Sacagawea had not seen her family for many years, so the siblings had a joyous reunion. "She instantly jumped up, and ran and embraced him, throwing over him her blanket, and weeping profusely,"[16] Clark reported. Sacagawea's presence in the negotiations increased the level of trust between the explorers and the Shoshone. The captains learned that the Shoshone had been forced to abandon their former lifestyle of hunting buffalo on the plains when neighboring tribes acquired guns from French traders. Now the Shoshone people lived in the mountains, where they struggled with poverty and food shortages. They still possessed a large herd of horses, though, and the Americans managed to acquire thirty of them in exchange for rifles and other goods. Recognizing that the horses would greatly increase their chances of getting through the mountains, the captains named the lucky meeting spot Camp Fortunate.

The Shoshone also warned the Corps of Discovery not to attempt to navigate the Salmon River through the mountains. They explained that the river was full of large, dangerous rapids that were impassable in canoes, and that the water flowed through deep canyons with sheer walls that made portaging impossible. Clark decided to investigate the situation for himself on August 23. After scouting from shore, he noted that "the water runs with great violence from one rock to the other on each side, foaming and roaring through rocks in every direction."[17] The captains determined that the expedition would have to proceed over the Continental Divide on foot and on horseback. After stashing their canoes and extra equipment at Camp Fortunate, the expedition got underway again on September 1. They took along a Shoshone guide named Old Toby to help them follow the Native American route through the mountains.

The expedition made their way northward into "mountains far more difficult to pass than any American had ever attempted—steep and massive peaks … thickly timbered in pine,"[18] historian Stephen Ambrose noted. Crossing over the divide was only the first step in getting through the Rockies, which included several more mountain ranges to the west. On September 3 the Corps of Discovery reached the Bitterroot Valley and made contact with the Salish (also known as Flathead) Indians. The Salish language was the most complex they had encountered on their expedition. Communicating with tribal leaders required a five-step translation from Salish to Shoshone to Hidatsa to French to English. With the help of Sacagawea and Old Toby, however, the captains managed to purchase a dozen more horses to help carry their supplies through the Bitterroot Mountains.

The Lolo Trail

On September 9 the expedition made camp near present-day Missoula, Montana, at a spot they called Travelers Rest. Old Toby informed the captains that it was possible to reach the Great Falls of the Missouri from that location in only four days of overland travel. The water route the expedition had followed, by contrast, had taken eight weeks. The Corps of Discovery repacked their equipment and rested up for the difficult journey through the Bitterroots. Looking west toward the massive, snow-covered peaks, Sergeant Patrick Gass described them as "the most terrible mountains that I ever beheld."[19] Sergeant John Ordway added that "the mountains continue as far as our eyes could extend. They extend much further than we expected."[20]

The Lewis and Clark Expedition began climbing into the Bitterroots on the treacherous Lolo Trail on September 11 (see "Sergeant Patrick Gass Crosses Treacherous Mountain Passes," p. 186). By that time, winter had already arrived in the high elevations at which they traveled. The men mostly proceeded on foot, leading horses heavily laden with equipment and supplies. As if the narrow, rocky paths were not difficult enough to negotiate, they often had to trudge through cold rain, hail, and blinding snowstorms. Several horses lost their footing on the steep, slippery trail and fell to their deaths, taking their loads of gear with them. The horse carrying Clark's field desk tumbled downhill more than one hundred feet until it got caught on a tree. Although the desk was destroyed, the horse managed to avoid injury. The men also struggled to make headway in the snow while wearing thin leather moccasins. "I have been wet and as cold in every part as I ever was in my life,"[21] Clark wrote on September 16.

To make matters worse, wild game was scarce in the mountains, and the men became desperately hungry. "Most of the party is weak and feeble suffering with hunger,"[22] Joseph Whitehouse recalled. They made up batches of portable soup by combining it with melted snow, but it was not enough to sus-

The most treacherous part of the journey came when the expedition members crossed through the Bitterroot Mountains on the steep, narrow, icy Lolo Trail.

tain them through the heavy exertion. "We were compelled to kill a colt for our men & selves to eat for the want of meat,"[23] Clark explained. They named the small stream where they had eaten the horse Colt Killed Creek.

In need of food and shelter, the captains decided to send a small scouting party ahead to try to make contact with the Nez Perce Indians. These people of the western Rockies got their name, meaning "pierced nose," from French traders. Clark and a few men broke off from the main group September 18. After descending for two days, they reached the open country known as Weippe Prairie near present-day Orofino, Idaho. To their relief, they soon found a Nez Perce settlement, and tribal members offered them dried salmon and camas lily roots. Private Reubin Field then headed back up the trail with a supply of food to help the rest of the expedition make it down to the Indian village.

Lewis and the others finally arrived on September 23. "The pleasure I now felt in having triumphed over the Rocky Mountains," he wrote, "and descending once more to a level and fertile country where there was every rational hope of finding a comfortable subsistence for myself and party, can be more readily conceived than expressed."[24]

As it turned out, though, the danger was not over yet. Upon seeing the quantities of Indian gifts, rifles, and other supplies the Americans had carried over the mountains, Chief Twisted Hair considered ordering his warriors to kill the weak and exhausted strangers. He knew that these items held great value in trade and would make the Nez Perce the wealthiest tribe in the region. Fortunately for the expedition, an elderly woman named Watkuweis—which meant "Returned from a Faraway Country"—intervened on their behalf. She explained that when she was captured by a rival tribe as a girl, white men in Canada had helped her return home. To pay back their kindness, she asked Twisted Hair not to harm the expedition members.

Lewis and Clark camped among the Nez Perce on the Clearwater River at a spot they named Canoe Camp. The Indians had informed them that it was possible to travel by water from that location all the way to the Pacific. Excited at the prospect of completing their mission, the expedition members built five dugout canoes for the downstream journey. On October 7 they left their horses with the Nez Perce for safekeeping and loaded their gear into boats once again. For the first time since they had left St. Louis, however, the group traveled in the same direction as the current.

The expedition made quick progress down the Clear-water and Snake Rivers, with occasional portages around rapids. They soon entered an open desert landscape with few trees and no wild game for hunting. "The country is barren and broken," Ordway noted. "We can scarcely get wood enough to cook a little victuals."[25] Along the way they met the Yakima Indians, who lived in mat houses near the river and subsisted on fish and roots.

"The pleasure I now felt in having triumphed over the Rocky Mountains," Lewis wrote, "can be more readily conceived than expressed."

On October 16 the expedition finally reached the Columbia River. Two days later they were delighted to see the snowcapped peak of Mount Hood looming in the distance. This landmark near present-day Portland, Oregon, had been mentioned by coastal explorers, so the captains knew that they were leaving uncharted territory and nearing the Pacific. The Wanapam Indians lived along this section of the Columbia. They warned the explorers that they would encounter a series of large rapids downstream. They also sold the Americans forty dogs to serve as a food source on the last leg of their journey.

Within a week the Columbia narrowed between steep cliffs and sped over a series of treacherous rapids and waterfalls known as the Dalles. Although the expedition managed to portage around a few of the hazards, the high canyon walls combined with their eagerness to reach the ocean convinced them to take the boats through some rough stretches of water. "I determined to pass through this place," Clark stated, "notwithstanding the horrid appearance of this agitated gut, swelling, boiling & whirling in every direction, which from the top of the rock did not appear as bad as when I was in it."[26]

By early November the river's character changed again. It became wider and slower, and it entered a dense rainforest filled with huge trees and noisy birds. The expedition encountered the Wishram and Wasco Indians, who lived in plank houses along the banks of the river and subsisted by fishing from elaborately carved wooden canoes. The captains soon learned that these Native American nations stood at the center of an extensive trade network that stretched from the present-day American Southwest to Alaska.

Winter at Fort Clatsop

On November 7 the Columbia widened into a large bay. Believing it to be part of the Pacific, Clark triumphantly wrote, "Ocean in View! O, the joy!"[27]

In reality, though, the expedition was still twenty miles from the river's mouth on the coast. The Corps of Discovery remained tantalizingly close to their goal for the next three weeks, as they became socked in by weather. A combination of torrential rain, high waves, thick fog, and giant, floating piles of driftwood prevented them from crossing the bay.

With the onset of winter at hand, the captains realized that they had no chance of returning to the Mandan villages that year and would be stuck on the west side of the Rockies until spring. Forced to come up with a plan, they considered three main options. First, they thought about heading back up the Columbia to where they had left their horses and camping among the Nez Perce. Second, they contemplated moving on to the coast in hopes of meeting a ship that could transport the expedition's findings back east by water. Third, they considered building winter quarters near their current location on the Columbia, either with the Chinook Indians on the north side of the bay (present-day Washington) or with the Clatsop Indians on the south side (present-day Oregon).

Rather than making the decision for the entire group, Lewis and Clark took a vote of all its members on November 24. Remarkably, the nonmilitary members of the expedition were allowed to participate as well, including Sacagawea and York. Historians have noted that it would be another sixty years before African-American men received voting rights in the United States, and more than a century before women or Native Americans were allowed to vote. Within the expedition, however, all members were considered equal. "What the captains do not say in their journals becomes noteworthy," said historian Erica Funkhouser. "Neither one makes a point about including Sacagawea and York in the vote, apparently taking for granted their right to participate equally in this first truly democratic moment in American history."[28]

The expedition members voted to build a winter camp on the south side of the Columbia estuary. They chose a location on the Netul River near present-day Astoria, Oregon (see "William Clark Searches for Winter Quarters on the Pacific Coast," p. 192). According to their estimates, they had traveled a total of 4,162 miles from Fort Wood. The captains celebrated their accomplishment by carving their names into the trunks of trees. Clark's note imitated the one left near Vancouver by Canadian explorer Alexander Mackenzie: "William Clark. By land from the U. States in 1804 & 1805."

The expedition members constructed Fort Clatsop out of balsam pine. It was a square-shaped compound with fifty-foot-long sides. They built eight rooms along the sides and left a twenty-foot-wide open space in the middle. Lewis and Clark shared one of the rooms, while Sacagawea shared another with her husband and son. Two more rooms were used for storage, and the other twenty-eight men crammed into the remaining three rooms.

The group struggled to maintain their good spirits during the long, dreary winter at Fort Clatsop. The cold, wet weather and cloudy skies did not improve their moods. In fact, they only had a dozen days without rain for the duration of their stay. In addition, the expedition was running low on food and other supplies, so the captains grew concerned about their ability to last through the winter. Although they managed to hunt some elk, deer, and birds, game was relatively scarce and difficult to find in the dense forest.

Finally, the Corps of Discovery did not particularly like or trust the coastal Indians. The Chinook and Clatsop peoples had long traded with Europeans who reached the Pacific Coast by ship, and they were tough and demanding negotia-

This drawing by western artist Frederic Remington depicts the explorers and their crew at the mouth of the Columbia River.

tors. When they were unable to make a bargain, they sometimes simply made off with the items they wanted. "The persons who usually visit the entrance of this river for the purpose of traffic or hunting, I believe, are either English or American," Clark wrote. "The Indians inform us they speak the same language with ourselves and give up proofs of their veracity by repeating many words of English, as musket, powder, shot, knife, file, damned rascal, son of a bitch, etc."[29] The expedition members described the Chinook and Clatsop peoples as greedy and unattractive, and they marveled at their strange custom of fastening angled boards across babies' cradles in order to flatten the front of their heads.

The men spent the winter months cleaning and repairing their equipment, gathering roots and herbs, and sewing 338 pairs of moccasins and other clothing for the return trip. They occasionally trekked to the ocean in order to boil seawater to obtain salt for preserving food. Clark spent much of his downtime adding details to his maps of the region. He also helped Lewis prepare a report called *Estimate of Western Indians*, which provided extensive information about the populations, locations, and cultures of the tribes they had encountered.

Lewis took the opportunity to update and expand the information in his journals. Although he had been less diligent about recording daily events on the final legs of the westward journey, he continued to note scientific discoveries. Lewis became the first American to describe a number of plant species found west of the Rocky Mountains, including common snowberry, western trumpet honeysuckle, mountain huckleberry, Douglas fir, lodgepole and ponderosa pine, Sitka alder, western larch, and western red cedar. He also described a number of bird species native to the region, such as varied thrush, Oregon ruffled grouse, Steller's Jay, and Lewis's woodpecker, which was named after him.

The group found a few enjoyable or interesting ways to pass the time. They exchanged token gifts for Christmas, for instance, and celebrated New Year's Eve with a rifle salute, singing, and dancing. In January the captains heard that a huge whale had washed up on the beach a short distance from where they prepared salt. Clark decided to lead a small group to see it, catalog it, and perhaps gather some meat or oil. He was surprised when Sacagawea insisted that she be included in the party. "The Indian woman was very impatient to be permitted to go with me, and was therefore indulged," he wrote. "She observed that she had traveled a long way with us to see the great waters, and that now that a monstrous fish was also to be seen, she thought it very hard that she could not be permitted to see either."[30] Clark measured the length of the whale carcass at 105 feet.

The winter seemed even longer to the Corps of Discovery because now that they had finally reached the Pacific, the men felt homesick and grew eager to return to civilization. They longed to see their loved ones, share their discoveries with Jefferson, and receive the acclaim and rewards that would come from the successful completion of their mission. Lewis noted that he looked forward to returning home "in the bosom of our friends" and enjoying "the repast which the hand of civilization has prepared for us."[31]

Notes

[1] Lewis, Meriwether. April 7, 1805, entry in *The Journals of the Lewis and Clark Expedition,* ed. Gary Moulton. Lincoln: University of Nebraska Press/Electronic Text Center, 2005. Retrieved from http://lewisandclarkjournals.unl.edu/read/?_xmlsrc=1804-04-07&_xslsrc=LCstyles.xsl.

[2] Lewis, April 29, 1805, entry in *The Journals of the Lewis and Clark Expedition.* Retrieved from http://lewisandclarkjournals.unl.edu/read/?_xmlsrc=1805-04-29&_xslsrc=LCstyles.xsl.

[3] Lewis, May 11, 1805, entry in *The Journals of the Lewis and Clark Expedition.* Retrieved from http://lewisandclarkjournals.unl.edu/read/?_xmlsrc=1805-05-11&_xslsrc=LCstyles.xsl.

[4] Lewis, April 25, 1805, entry in *The Journals of the Lewis and Clark Expedition.* Retrieved from http://lewisandclarkjournals.unl.edu/read/?_xmlsrc=1805-04-25&_xslsrc=LCstyles.xsl.

[5] Lewis, May 14, 1805, entry in *The Journals of the Lewis and Clark Expedition.* Retrieved from http://lewisandclarkjournals.unl.edu/read/?_xmlsrc=1805-05-14&_xslsrc=LCstyles.xsl.

[6] Lewis, May 14, 1805, entry in *The Journals of the Lewis and Clark Expedition.*

[7] Lewis, May 16, 1805, entry in *The Journals of the Lewis and Clark Expedition.* Retrieved from http://lewisandclarkjournals.unl.edu/read/?_xmlsrc=1805-05-16&_xslsrc=LCstyles.xsl.

[8] Lewis, May 26, 1805, entry in *The Journals of the Lewis and Clark Expedition.* Retrieved from http://lewisandclarkjournals.unl.edu/read/?_xmlsrc=1805-05-26.xml&_xslsrc=LCstyles.xsl.

[9] Lewis, May 31, 1805, entry in *The Journals of the Lewis and Clark Expedition.* Retrieved from http://lewisandclarkjournals.unl.edu/read/?_xmlsrc=1805-05-31&_xslsrc=LCstyles.xsl.

[10] Gass, Patrick. May 31, 1805, entry in *The Journals of the Lewis and Clark Expedition.* Retrieved from http://lewisandclarkjournals.unl.edu/read/?_xmlsrc=1805-05-31&_xslsrc=LCstyles.xsl.

[11] Lewis, June 13, 1805, entry in *The Journals of the Lewis and Clark Expedition.* Retrieved from http://lewisandclarkjournals.unl.edu/read/?_xmlsrc=1805-06-13&_xslsrc=LCstyles.xsl.

[12] Lewis, June 23, 1805, entry in *The Journals of the Lewis and Clark Expedition.* Retrieved from http://lewisandclarkjournals.unl.edu/read/?_xmlsrc=1805-06-23&_xslsrc=LCstyles.xsl.

[13] Lewis, July 22m, 1805, entry in *The Journals of the Lewis and Clark Expedition.* Retrieved from http://lewisandclarkjournals.unl.edu/read/?_xmlsrc=1805-07-22&_xslsrc=LCstyles.xsl.

[14] Lewis, August 12, 1805, entry in *The Journals of the Lewis and Clark Expedition.* Retrieved from http://lewisandclarkjournals.unl.edu/read/?_xmlsrc=1805-08-12&_xslsrc=LCstyles.xsl.

[15] Quoted in "Inside the Corps: York." *Lewis and Clark: The Journey of the Corps of Discovery.* PBS, 1997. Retrieved from http://www.pbs.org/lewisandclark/inside/york.html.

[16] Clark, William, August 17, 1805, entry in *The Journals of the Lewis and Clark Expedition.* Retrieved from http://lewisandclarkjournals.unl.edu/read/?_xmlsrc=1805-08-17.xml&_xslsrc=LCstyles.xsl.

[17] Clark, August 23, 1805, entry in *The Journals of the Lewis and Clark Expedition.* Retrieved from http://lewisandclarkjournals.unl.edu/read/?_xmlsrc=1805-08-23&_xslsrc=LCstyles.xsl.

[18] Ambrose, Stephen E. *Lewis and Clark: Voyage of Discovery.* Washington, DC: National Geographic Society, 1998, p. 140.

[19] Gass, September 16, 1805, entry in *The Journals of the Lewis and Clark Expedition.* Retrieved from http://lewisandclarkjournals.unl.edu/read/?_xmlsrc=1805-09-16&_xslsrc=LCstyles.xsl.

[20] Ordway, John. September 18, 1805, entry in *The Journals of the Lewis and Clark Expedition*. Retrieved from http://lewisandclarkjournals.unl.edu/read/?_xmlsrc=1805-09-18&_xslsrc=LCstyles.xsl.

[21] Clark, September 16, 1805, entry in *The Journals of the Lewis and Clark Expedition*. Retrieved from http://lewisandclarkjournals.unl.edu/read/?_xmlsrc=1805-09-16&_xslsrc=LCstyles.xsl.

[22] Whitehouse, Joseph. September 19, 1805, entry in *The Journals of the Lewis and Clark Expedition*. Retrieved from http://lewisandclarkjournals.unl.edu/read/?_xmlsrc=1805-09-19&_xslsrc=LCstyles.xsl.

[23] Clark, September 14, 1805, entry in *The Journals of the Lewis and Clark Expedition*. Retrieved from http://lewisandclarkjournals.unl.edu/read/?_xmlsrc=1805-09-14&_xslsrc=LCstyles.xsl.

[24] Lewis, September 23, 1805, entry in *The Journals of the Lewis and Clark Expedition*. Retrieved from http://lewisandclarkjournals.unl.edu/read/?_xmlsrc=1805-09-23&_xslsrc=LCstyles.xsl.

[25] Ordway, October 11, 1805, entry in *The Journals of the Lewis and Clark Expedition*. Retrieved from http://lewisandclarkjournals.unl.edu/read/?_xmlsrc=1805-10-11&_xslsrc=LCstyles.xsl.

[26] Clark, October 24, 1805, entry in *The Journals of the Lewis and Clark Expedition*. Retrieved from http://lewisandclarkjournals.unl.edu/read/?_xmlsrc=1805-10-24&_xslsrc=LCstyles.xsl.

[27] Clark, November 7, 1805, entry in *The Journals of the Lewis and Clark Expedition*. Retrieved from http://lewisandclarkjournals.unl.edu/read/?_xmlsrc=1805-11-07&_xslsrc=LCstyles.xsl.

[28] Funkhouser, Erica. "Finding Sacagawea." In Duncan, Dayton, and Ken Burns. *Lewis and Clark: The Journey of the Corps of Discovery*. New York: Knopf, 1997, p. 181.

[29] Clark, January 9, 1806, entry in *The Journals of the Lewis and Clark Expedition*. Retrieved from http://lewisandclarkjournals.unl.edu/read/?_xmlsrc=1806-01-09&_xslsrc=LCstyles.xsl.

[30] Clark, January 6, 1806, entry in *The Journals of the Lewis and Clark Expedition*. Retrieved from http://lewisandclarkjournals.unl.edu/read/?_xmlsrc=1806-01-06&_xslsrc=LCstyles.xsl.

[31] Lewis, January 1, 1806, entry in *The Journals of the Lewis and Clark Expedition*. Retrieved from http://lewisandclarkjournals.unl.edu/read/?_xmlsrc=1806-01-01&_xslsrc=LCstyles.xsl.

Chapter Five

THE RETURN JOURNEY, 1806

⟨⟨⟨⟩⟩⟩

Never did a similar event excite more joy through the United States. The humblest of its citizens had taken a lively interest in the issue of this journey, and looked forward with impatience for the information it would furnish.

—Thomas Jefferson, recalling the return of
the Lewis and Clark Expedition, 1813

In early 1806 the Lewis and Clark Expedition launched its return journey across the continent and back to civilization. Midway through their trip, the captains decided to split up in order to explore more areas of the Louisiana Territory. While Clark enjoyed a relatively uneventful trip down the Yellowstone River, Lewis had a deadly encounter with Blackfeet Indians and was accidentally shot by one of his own men. The Corps of Discovery was eventually reunited, however, and returned to a hero's welcome in St. Louis. Over the course of their remarkable journey, they mapped large sections of the unexplored West and described 200 previously unknown species of plants and animals.

Heading Home

As the long winter at Fort Clatsop came to a close, the members of the Lewis and Clark expedition were eager to head back home. The captains originally set a departure date of April 1, 1806, but they ended up getting underway a week earlier. Before they took off, they prepared a set of documents to leave behind. These documents listed the names of the members of the Corps of Discovery and summarized the expedition's achievements on the journey westward. The captains asked local Indian leaders to present these papers to any

English-speaking sea captain who might arrive on the Pacific Coast. They wanted to preserve some record of their experiences in case something happened to prevent the expedition from reaching St. Louis.

Before starting the return journey, the captains also needed to secure additional boats. Only three of the five dugout canoes they had built at Canoe Camp near the Nez Perce village had survived the winter. They tried to buy two more canoes from the Clatsop, but the Indians placed a high value on their intricately carved wooden boats, and the expedition had few trade items remaining. They managed to acquire one more boat in exchange for Lewis's laced uniform coat, but they were unable to afford a second one. Anxious to get underway, the captains reluctantly decided to let George Drouillard steal a Clatsop canoe. They

In the spring of 1806, members of the Lewis and Clark Expedition loaded their gear in canoes and started their return journey up the Columbia River.

excused this violation of military policy by noting that the Clatsop had stolen six elk that had been shot by Corps hunters over the winter.

On March 23, 1806, the Corps of Discovery loaded its gear into the canoes and headed for home. Whenever they followed the same route they had taken westward the previous year, the captains did not spend much time taking readings and recording the distances they traveled. Clark still added new details to his maps, however, while Lewis described several more bird species, including the mountain quail. The group also stopped to explore a few areas they had skipped past on their hurried trip downriver. For instance, they spent two days in early April checking out the Willamette River near Portland, Oregon.

In mid-April they reached the Dalles, the series of waterfalls and rapids that they had negotiated fairly quickly the previous fall. This time, traveling up the Columbia River, the Corps of Discovery spent two weeks portaging their boats and equipment around the obstacles. The steep, rocky canyons offered little opportunity for hunting, and fishing was not an option because the annual salmon run had not yet arrived. As a result, the hungry explorers were forced to buy dried fish, roots, and dogs from the Native Americans who lived along the river.

After the long winter among the coastal Indians, the expedition members had little patience remaining for the Columbia River tribes. They complained about their behavior and expressed their preference for dealing with the tribes who lived further east. "All the Indians from the Rocky Mountains to the falls of Columbia are an honest, ingenious and well disposed people," Patrick Gass declared, "but from the falls to the seacoast, and along it, they are a rascally, thieving set."[1]

The captains lost their tempers on several occasions when they caught Indians trying to make off with the expedition's belongings. Lewis slapped one man for stealing a piece of metal from a canoe. When a couple of Indians stole Lewis's Newfoundland, he sent three armed men to retrieve the dog with orders to shoot the thieves if necessary. Luckily, they managed to get Seaman back without bloodshed. Clark angrily confronted another group of Indians who crowded around and started handling his equipment, warning them "that I had it in my power at that moment to kill them all and set fire to their houses, but it was not my wish to treat them with severity provided they would let my property alone."[2]

Frustrating Delays

Once the expedition completed the portage around the falls, their relations with the Native Americans improved. On April 27 they met with the Wallawalla Indians and were honored with a feast and a display of traditional dancing. By this time the captains had grown frustrated with the slow progress of their boats against the strong current, which was being fed by melting snow from the mountains. They made arrangements with Chief Yelleppit of the Wallawalla to exchange their canoes for horses in order to continue their journey overland. The chief also told the captains about a shortcut to the Nez Perce village on the Clearwater River. On April 29 the Indians ferried the expedition members, horses, and supplies across to the south side of the Columbia, where they proceeded overland on the recommended route.

This 1807 portrait shows Lewis wearing traditional clothing that was presented to him by the Shoshone Indians.

Although they covered the distance between the Columbia and the Clearwater more quickly than they had on the westward journey, they soon learned that it was impossible to cross the Bitterroot Mountains at that time of year. The treacherous Lolo Trail was buried under deep snow, and the explorers had no choice but to wait for it to melt. Beginning on May 14, they camped on the east side of the Clearwater, at the site of present-day Kamiah, Idaho, for more than a month. Lewis felt very impatient at being stuck on the west side of "that icy barrier which separates us from my friends and country, from all which makes life esteemable."[3]

The expedition ran low on food during their forced stay at Camp Chopunnish. With few material goods remaining to offer the local Indians in trade, they came up with an ingenious scheme to obtain the needed supplies. When the explorers had passed through the Nez Perce village the previous year, Clark had treated a few people with minor injuries or common illnesses and provided some relief from their problems. To the captains' surprise, word of Clark's abilities as a medicine man had spread far and wide by the time they returned. Native Americans from surrounding tribes came to see him with various complaints, so Clark arranged to trade medical care for food. "I was busily employed for several hours this morning in administering eye water to a crowd of applicants," he wrote. "We once more obtained a plentiful meal, much to the comfort of all the party."[4] Although Clark's simple remedies were not necessarily effective, Lewis did not feel bad about taking advantage of his reputation. "In our present situation I think it pardonable to continue this deception for they will not give us any provision without compensation,"[5] he noted.

Although the Indians insisted that Lolo Pass would not be open until July, the Corps of Discovery was so anxious to get home that they decided to start earlier. On June 10 they left Camp Chopunnish and began climbing into the Bitterroots. After a week of slogging through twelve-foot-deep snow, however, they were forced to turn back and return to the Nez Perce village. "This is the first time since we have been on this long tour that we have ever been compelled to retreat,"[6] Lewis lamented in his journal.

After another frustrating week of waiting, the Corps of Discovery set out again on June 24. They were accompanied by three Nez Perce guides who agreed to take them over the mountains to the Great Falls of the Missouri in exchange for two rifles. The high price was worth it, as this time the expedition made it over the pass without incident in only six days. Once again they camped at Travelers Rest, near present-day Missoula, Montana, for a few days to recover their strength. It was at this point that Lewis and Clark divided the expedition into two groups. They had come up with this plan during the winter months at Fort Clatsop. Although separating the team involved some risks, they felt that it would enable them to explore more of the vast Louisiana Territory.

The Corps Is Divided

The group led by Lewis, which included Sergeant Gass and eight other men, planned to proceed directly to the Missouri River. Their mission was to explore the shortcut that the Indians claimed would reduce their eight-week river journey to four days overland. The new route would take them east along the Blackfoot River and over the Continental Divide at what is now known as Lewis and Clark Pass. Once they reached the Great Falls, part of the team would stay and build carts for transporting the boats and gear over the portage. Lewis and the others would explore up the Marias River, which ran northward from its confluence with the Missouri for 200 miles. When the expedition had passed through the area in 1805, they had briefly mistaken it for the main channel of the Missouri, and Lewis had named it for his cousin, Maria Wood.

In the meantime, the group led by Clark—which included Sergeant John Ordway, Toussaint Charbonneau, Sacagawea, and York, among others—planned to travel south through the Bitterroot Valley and across the Continental Divide to Camp Fortunate, where they had obtained horses from the Shoshone and stashed their canoes and supplies the previous year. Then they would take the boats down the Jefferson River to Three Forks. At that point, Clark's group planned to divide into smaller groups. Ordway and nine men would continue down the Missouri in canoes to rejoin Lewis's group at the Great Falls. Clark and seven others would take the horses up the Gallatin Valley to the Yellowstone River, build canoes, and follow the river eastward in hopes of finding a more direct route from the Rockies to the Missouri. If all went well, they would meet up with Lewis and the others at the junction of the Yellowstone and Missouri Rivers, near the present-day border of Montana and North Dakota.

After traveling together for two years and sharing both adventures and hardships, the men felt some sadness and worry when the Corps of Discovery was divided. Parting was especially difficult for Lewis and Clark, who had held joint command and consulted on all major decisions up to this point. Yet the captains had tremendous confidence in each other and in their men. They also felt secure in their general knowledge of the landscape that lay ahead. Determined to fulfill their mission and explore as much territory as possible, the two groups went their separate ways on July 3, 1806. "I took leave of my worthy friend and companion, Capt. Clark, and the party that accompanied him," Lewis wrote. "I could not avoid feeling much concern on this occasion although I hoped this separation was only temporary."[7]

Five days later, Clark reached Camp Fortunate and retrieved the expedition's boats and supplies. The men were especially pleased to find the cache of tobacco they had stored there, because they had run out several months earlier. After floating down the Jefferson River to Three Forks, the group divided again. Ordway and nine men continued down the Missouri in canoes toward the Great Falls, while Clark and twelve others traveled east on horseback toward the Yellowstone River. The Shoshone people had frequented this area in Sacagawea's youth, so she was able to guide the party to its destination. They arrived at the Yellowstone on July 15 and began hollowing out large cottonwood trees to make canoes. A few days later, they awoke in the morning to find most of their horses missing. Clark suspected that the local Indians may have stolen them, and scouts he sent out in search of the animals found evidence to confirm his suspicions.

Once the boats were ready, Clark and his group began making their way down the Yellowstone River. On July 25 the captain came across a large, distinctive sandstone outcropping with a flat top. He described it as "a remarkable rock" and noted that he climbed to the top and "had a most extensive view in every direction."[8] He named the formation Pompey's Tower, after his nickname for Saca-

Clark's signature, engraved on Pompeys Pillar in Montana, is the only physical evidence remaining of the journey of the Corps of Discovery.

gawea's toddler son, Jean Baptiste. Upon seeing that Native Americans had engraved symbols and pictures of animals on the stone, Clark added his name and the date. This inscription is still visible today in what is now known as Pompeys Pillar National Monument near Billings, Montana. It is the only physical evidence remaining on the landscape from the journey of the Corps of Discovery.

Meanwhile, Lewis's group had reached the Missouri on July 11. They found thousands of buffalo gathered on the plains around the river, as well as swarms of mosquitoes. "The mosquitoes continue to infest us in such manner that we can scarcely exist," Lewis wrote. "My dog even howls with the torture he experiences from them."[9] Leaving a few men behind to prepare for the Great Falls portage, the captain then continued up the Marias River on horseback with the rest of the group. They tried to mark the geographic coordinates of the northern reach of the river, but cloudy skies prevented them from getting good readings with their instruments.

Lewis Encounters the Blackfeet

During his exploration of the Marias, Lewis remained alert for signs of the much-feared Blackfeet Indians. He knew that he was close to territory controlled by this powerful tribe, which possessed guns and was the sworn enemy of the Shoshone and Nez Perce peoples. He was also well aware that he was 300 miles away from Clark and the rest of the Corps of Discovery, which put his small party in a vulnerable position. On July 26 he saw a group of eight Blackfeet warriors with horses on a hilltop in the distance. "This was a very unpleasant sight," he admitted. "However, I resolved to make the best of our situation and to approach them in a friendly manner."[10]

Lewis calculated that running away would only convince the Indians that he was their enemy. Instead, he decided to advance slowly toward them and hope the Blackfeet would not attack. As the two parties met cautiously, Lewis presented the Blackfeet leaders with a peace medallion and other gifts. They discussed the possibility of trading with the United States, but the Indians were not pleased to hear that the Americans also planned to trade with their enemies. Since it was nearly nightfall, the two parties agreed to make camp together. After a restless and watchful night, the expedition members awoke the next morning to find the Blackfeet stealing their guns.

Reubin Field chased the man who had taken his gun. Upon catching up, Field fought to regain his weapon and stabbed the Indian in the chest with his knife. Back

Gass's drawing depicts the deadly encounter between Lewis and the Blackfeet Indians that occurred while the captains were traveling separately in 1806.

by the campfire, Lewis drew his pistol and threatened to shoot the Indian who had taken his rifle, but the man dropped it and walked away. Meanwhile, Drouillard managed to wrestle his rifle away from another Blackfoot warrior.

Then the expedition members noticed that the retreating Blackfeet were trying to drive away their horses. They ran after the Indians and prevented them from taking some of the animals. Lewis chased the men who had taken his horse into a niche in a bluff and demanded that they return his mount. When one of the Indians brandished a gun at him, Lewis was forced to defend himself. "I shot him through the belly," the captain recalled. "He fell to his knees and on his right elbow, from which position he partly raised himself up and fired at me, and turning himself about crawled in behind a rock which was a few feet from him. He overshot me, [but] being bareheaded I felt the wind of his bullet very distinctly."[11] The deaths of the two Blackfeet warriors were the only acts of bloodshed that occurred during the Lewis and Clark Expedition.

Concerned that the Blackfeet might return in greater numbers to take revenge, Lewis and his companions quickly packed up their camp. They burned the bows and arrows that the Indians had left behind and took one of their guns with them. They decided to leave the peace medal "about the neck of the dead man that they might be informed who we were,"[12] according to Lewis. Using four of their own horses that they had recaptured plus four Indian horses that had been left behind, the group rushed back toward the mouth of the Marias River.

After traveling overland for nearly twenty-four hours straight, they reached the confluence with the Missouri on July 28. A short time later, they heard the sound of rifles firing on the river. "We quickly repaired to this joyful sound and on arriving at the bank of the river had the unspeakable satisfaction to see our canoes coming down,"[13] Lewis wrote. It was Sergeant Ordway and his men from Clark's group, who had met up with the rest of Lewis's group at the Great Falls. The combined group was delighted to find Lewis, Drouillard, and the others. They joined together and continued moving quickly downstream, sometimes logging up to seventy miles per day, toward their meeting with Clark at the confluence with the Yellowstone River.

On August 11 the expedition nearly lost one of its leaders. Lewis was on shore hunting when a rifle discharged from the brush nearby and a bullet passed through his upper thigh and buttock. He ran back toward the canoes, raising the alarm that hostile Indians were in the area. As it turned out, though, Lewis had been shot by one of his own men. Pierre Cruzatte, who had lost one eye and was nearsighted in the other, had mistaken the captain's buckskin pants for an elk in the bushes.

> *"I was alarmed on the landing of the canoes to be informed that Capt. Lewis was wounded by an accident," Clark wrote. "I found him lying on the pirogue."*

The next day Lewis and his crew arrived at Clark's camp. The captains were delighted to see each other again, although Clark expressed concern about Lewis's wound. "At meridian Capt. Lewis hove in sight," Clark wrote. "I was alarmed on the landing of the canoes to be informed that Capt. Lewis was wounded by an accident. I found him lying in the pirogue. He informed me that his wound was slight and would be well in twenty or thirty days. This information relieved me very much."[14]

On August 14 the reunited expedition arrived at the Mandan villages, where they had spent the first winter of their westward journey. At this point the group that had faced so many challenges together began to disperse. John Colter (see biography, p. 125) was invited to join some trappers who were heading back up the Missouri. Since his services were no longer needed on the downstream journey to St. Louis, the captains agreed to release him from duty. Colter went on to become a legendary "mountain man" of the West and the first white person to see the famous geysers of Yellowstone National Park.

The expedition also parted ways with Sacagawea, Toussaint Charbonneau, and their son, Jean Baptiste. The captains paid the couple $500 for their services as interpreters and guides. Clark, who had grown fond of little Pomp, offered to take the boy back to civilization and raise him as his own son. Although the couple refused the offer, they agreed to reconsider it in a year or two, and they did eventually send Jean Baptiste to live with Clark. Before departing, the expedition also added Sheheke, a Mandan chief who agreed to accompany them east to meet President Jefferson.

The Triumphant Return

Traveling with the current of the Missouri River, the expedition made good progress, averaging nearly fifty miles per day. The captains' main concern on this final leg of the journey was getting through the territory controlled by the Lakota or Teton Sioux. They had no desire to repeat their tense first encounter with the tribe, when Lakota warriors had "attempted to detain us in the fall of 1804 as we ascended this river and ... we were near coming to blows,"[15] according to Clark. When three young Lakota men appeared on August 30 and invited the captains to meet with Chief Black Buffalo, Clark refused. "I told those Indians that they had been deaf to our councils and ill treated all the whites who had visited them since ... and directed them to return with their band to their camp, that if any of them come near our camp we should kill them certainly."[16] As the expedition's boats floated past the Teton encampment, Black Buffalo stood on a hilltop and cursed them.

A few days downriver, the explorers began encountering boats full of traders going in the other direction. The Corps of Discovery excitedly asked for news from the United States and inquired about the health of President Jefferson. In exchange, the traders eagerly gathered information about their explorations of the wilderness. The captains were able to obtain whiskey from one of the traders, which provided the men with their first drink in over a year. The Americans who encountered the returning expedition were shocked to see them and reported that most people had given up hope of their safe return long ago. They said rumors had circulated that the explorers had been killed or captured by Spanish troops.

At the conclusion of a remarkable journey lasting two and a half years and covering 7,689 miles, the explorers made a triumphant return to St. Louis on September 23, 1806.

As it turned out, the rumors had some basis in fact. The king of Spain had been upset to learn of Jefferson's plans to explore the West, with possible incursions into Spanish-held territory. Although Jefferson had tried to keep his plans secret, the king learned of them from people who had met Lewis and Clark in St. Louis at the official ceremony transferring control of the Louisiana Territory in 1804. He viewed the American expedition as a threat to Spanish control of the lucrative trade with the region's Native American tribes. He recognized that the Corps of Discovery was not just a scientific expedition, but also a military force that "represented a rising American empire, one built on aggressive territorial expansion and commercial gain,"[17] as a Library of Congress exhibition put it.

Spanish authorities in Santa Fe sent a military expedition into Nebraska with orders to capture Lewis and Clark. Although the Spanish expedition came within one hundred miles of the American explorers in the fall of 1804, they could not locate Lewis and Clark's group and decided to turn back. But two other American expeditions commissioned by Jefferson—one led by Zebulon Pike to explore the Rocky Mountains in present-day Colorado, and one led by Thomas Freeman and Peter Custis to explore the headwaters of the Red River in present-day Texas—were later intercepted by Spanish military patrols.

Having avoided potential clashes with Spanish troops, the Lewis and Clark expedition began seeing even more signs of civilization. On September 20 they rejoiced to see the first domestic cows grazing along the banks of the river. The following day they passed by St. Charles and saluted the residents of the town by firing their rifles. Finally, on September 23, the Corps of Discovery arrived back in St. Louis (see "Sergeant John Ordway Returns to Civilization," p. 195). Their remarkable journey had lasted two and a half years and covered a total distance of 7,689 miles. "Drew out the canoes, then the party all considerable much rejoiced that we have the expedition completed," Ordway wrote. "We intend to return to our native homes to see our parents once more, as we have been so long from them."[18]

A swarm of townspeople gathered on shore to greet the weary travelers. Many people expressed astonishment upon hearing that they had traveled all the way to the Pacific Ocean and returned safely. Some observers commented on the wild, rugged appearance of the explorers and compared them to the fictional castaway Robinson Crusoe, who spent thirty years marooned on a deserted tropical island.

One of Lewis's first acts upon returning to civilization was to write a letter to Jefferson (see "Lewis Informs Jefferson That He Completed His Mission," p. 197). "It is with pleasure that I announce to you the safe arrival of myself and party," he wrote. "In obedience to your orders we have penetrated the Continent of North America to the Pacific Ocean.... The whole of the party who accompanied me from the Mandans have returned in good health, which is not, I assure you, to me one of the least pleasing considerations of the voyage."[19] Jefferson received the letter a month later and immediately sent a reply expressing his feelings of joy and relief. "I received, my dear Sir, with unspeakable joy your letter of September 23 announcing the return of yourself, Captain Clark, & your party in good health to St. Louis," the president wrote. "The unknown scenes in which you were engaged, & the length of time without hearing of you had begun to be felt awfully.... I salute you with sincere affection."[20]

Word of Lewis and Clark's homecoming appeared in the St. Louis newspaper, and from there it traveled quickly from town to town across the United States. The captains became national heroes, and dozens of balls were held in their honor as they made their way east—accompanied by a delegation of Man-

The Epic Story of the
Publication of the Expedition's Journals

Shortly after the Lewis and Clark Expedition returned to a hero's welcome, the captains began thinking about publishing the story of their epic journey. They knew that the American people would be fascinated to read about their adventures and discoveries. They also believed that publishing their findings would help justify President Jefferson's decision to mount the expedition. Only one day after their arrival in St. Louis, Lewis wrote a long letter describing the major achievements of the expedition. Clark then affixed his signature to the letter and sent it to his brother, George Rogers Clark, in Louisville. As expected, the elder Clark proudly passed it along to his local newspaper, and from there it quickly spread to other papers across the country.

Recognizing the potential for financial gain, however, several other members of the Corps of Discovery began considering publishing deals for their own accounts of the journey. At least seven members of the crew kept journals, including Sergeants John Ordway, Patrick Gass, and Charles Floyd. Lewis bought the rights to Ordway's journal for $150, but he soon heard that Gass had sold his journal to a publisher. This unwelcome news prompted him to post a notice in the *National Intelligencer* on March 18, 1807, warning people to wait for the official version of events. Nevertheless, Gass's book appeared in print a short time later, and it sold well.

Although Lewis promised to produce his own story of the expedition, he proved to be unequal to the task. His busy social calendar, along with his

dan and Osage Indians—to meet with Jefferson. The president was delighted to see Lewis when he reached Washington, D.C. Lewis spread out the maps Clark had created on the floor of the White House, and Jefferson examined them with great interest and asked lots of questions. After hearing some of Lewis's stories from the epic journey, the president encouraged him to prepare a formal report for Congress and to publish the journals for the benefit of the American people (see "The Epic Story of the Publication of the Expedition's Journals," p. 84).

At every turn, Lewis pointedly gave Clark equal credit for the expedition's success. He also continued his campaign to convince U.S. military officials to cor-

responsibilities as governor of the Louisiana Territory, prevented him from working on the manuscript. Likewise, Clark never seemed able to find the time and energy to condense their thousands of pages of journal entries into a printed book. Finally, after Lewis died in the fall of 1809, Clark hired a well-known Philadelphia editor named Nicholas Biddle to edit the expedition papers. Biddle, succeeded by Paul Allen, used the captains' original journals and those of Ordway and Gass to produce an official, two-volume *History of the Expedition under the Command of Captains Lewis and Clark* in 1814. By this time, though, public interest in the expedition had faded.

Following publication, the editors sent the original journals to the American Philosophical Society in Philadelphia. After gathering dust for nearly a century, they wound up in the hands of Reuben Gold Thwaites, an accomplished editor of historical documents. Thwaites uncovered previously unknown journals and scientific notebooks. His eight-volume edition of the expedition papers appeared in 1904—exactly 100 years after the explorers launched their journey—and provided many new insights into Lewis and Clark. The most complete and accurate edition of the journals, however, is the thirteen-volume version prepared by Gary Moulton for the University of Nebraska Press in 1985, which is available online at http://lewis andclarkjournals.unl.edu/index.html.

Source

Jackson, Donald. "The Race to Publish Lewis and Clark." Lincoln: University of Nebraska Press, 2005. Retrieved from http://lewisandclarkjournals.unl.edu/read/?_xmlsrc=lc.jackson.01&_xslsrc=LCstyles.xsl.

rect the rank assigned to his partner. "With respect to the exertions and services rendered by that esteemable man Capt. William Clark in the course of our voyage I cannot say too much," he wrote. "If sir any credit be due for the success of the arduous enterprise in which we have been mutually engaged, he is equally with myself entitled to your consideration and that of our common country."[21]

Although Clark never did get his captain's commission, he and the other members of the group did receive generous payments for their services and other forms of recognition for their achievements. Congress granted Lewis and Clark each 1,600 acres of land, while all of the other expedition members received 320 acres each. Everyone was also awarded double the usual pay for their military rank for the duration of the journey. Jefferson appointed Lewis as governor of the Louisiana Territory and Clark as its superintendant of Indian affairs, making them the leading federal officials in the West. The president also commissioned a statue of the expedition leaders to be placed in Independence Hall in Philadelphia.

Although the total cost of the expedition came to $38,722—more than fifteen times the $2,500 Lewis had originally budgeted—Congress readily approved the additional expenses. Lewis's careful planning and acquisition of supplies enabled the Corps of Discovery to accomplish their mission and return home safely. Although the expedition ran out of some luxury items, like tobacco and whiskey, they had more than enough of such necessities as gunpowder, ammunition, paper, and ink.

Accomplishments and Discoveries

Jefferson had hoped that the Lewis and Clark Expedition would discover the fabled Northwest Passage, but this aspect of their exploration of the West proved disappointing. They concluded that no easy water route crossed the continent. Instead, they found that going from the Missouri to the Columbia involved a 340-mile overland trek through rugged, snow-covered mountains. Nevertheless, the expedition identified many opportunities for American trade and commerce.

As a scientific undertaking, the expedition was a tremendous success. The captains took this aspect of their work very seriously and spent a significant amount of time on it. As a result, the expedition catalogued 178 plants and 122 animals that were unknown to American science at that time. Some of the major species of mammals they were the first to formally describe include the coyote, pronghorn antelope, mountain goat, bighorn sheep, grizzly bear, and prairie dog. They also discovered dozens of new species of birds, fish, and reptiles, including the trumpeter swan, mountain plover, least tern, western meadowlark, western rattlesnake, and channel catfish. A few of the species they discovered were later named after the explorers, including Clark's nutcracker, Lewis's woodpecker, and the cutthroat trout (scientific name *Oncorhynchus clarki lewisi*). The captains were also the first Americans to catalog some of the iconic plant species of the West, such as the lodgepole and ponderosa pine, Pacific yew, Sitka spruce, and Mariposa lily. Even when Lewis was suffering from an

the feathers about its head pointed and stiff some hairs the base of the beak. feathers fine and stiff about the ears, This is a faint likeness of the of the plains or Heath the first of those fowls we met with was Missouri below in the neighbour- of the Rocky and from which pass between and Rapids Gorges and make

Mountain Columbia real falls 30 in large ularly

hide remarkably close when pursued, flights &c Large Black & white Pheasant is peculiar portion of the Rocky Mountains watered by Columbia River. at least we did not see them untill

This page from Clark's journal describes the sage grouse, one of 122 animal species the expedition catalogued that were previously unknown to science.

accidental gunshot wound and rushing to stay ahead of hostile Blackfeet Indians, he took time out to draw and describe a small prairie plant.

In addition to describing and sending back samples of new species, however, the Corps of Discovery also killed and ate a large number of animals during their long journey. With all the hard, physical labor the men had to perform, they consumed up to nine pounds of meat per person, per day when it was available. "We eat an immensity of meat," Clark acknowledged in his journal. "It requires four deer, or an elk and a deer, or one buffalo to supply us plentifully twenty-four hours."[22]

One historian went through the journals of the expedition members and compiled a list of the wild game they killed. It included at least 1,000 deer, 227 bison, 113 beavers, 62 antelope, 43 grizzly bears, 35 elk, 23 black bears, 18 wolves, 16 otters, and more than 250 geese, ducks, turkeys, grouse, and other birds. Although Lewis and Clark's meat consumption had little impact on the vast wildlife population of the West at that time, within a few generations human hunters and settlers would begin to create problems. "This level of resource exploitation marked the beginning of a century of unrestrained wildlife slaughter in America," noted historian Paul A. Johnsgard, "ending in the elimination of the bison, elk, gray wolf, and grizzly bear from the Great Plains, and the complete extinction of the passenger pigeon, Carolina parakeet, and Eskimo curlew."[23] Today, several of the animals first encountered by Lewis and Clark are extinct, thirteen appear on the federal endangered species list, and many others are considered threatened.

The expedition also succeeded in its mission of documenting "the face of the country," as Jefferson put it in his instructions. Clark gathered vast amounts of information about the geography of the West—both from his own observations and from his contact with Native Americans—and recorded it on maps. He sketched field maps along the route and pieced them together into larger, more detailed versions at Fort Mandan, Fort Clatsop, and other stopovers. Upon his return to civilization, Clark prepared a large "track map" showing the entire route taken by the expedition. It was the first published map to display reasonably accurate geographic information about the area west of the Mississippi River. "Lewis and Clark put the world into a new order," historian Stephen Dow Beckham declared. "They gave form and substance to the complex geography of a vast continent."[24] Jefferson and his colleagues in the American Philosophical Society thus learned that the region was far more topographically diverse than they had imagined.

Lewis and Clark also accomplished their mission to open diplomatic and trade relations with the Native American peoples of the West. They encountered nearly fifty different tribes over the course of their journey, and they made an effort to observe and record information about their various lifestyles and customs. They discovered a tremendous diversity in Native American life. The peoples they encountered ranged from farmers and traders who lived in permanent villages, to nomadic hunters who rode horses in pursuit of wild game and lived in portable tepees, to fishermen who carved elaborate canoes and lived in houses made of wooden planks. They compiled all of this information, along with location data and population figures, in their volumes *Estimate of Eastern Indians* and *Estimate of Western Indians*. They also shipped hundreds of artifacts back to Jefferson and his ethnographer friends, including buffalo robes, headdresses, bow and arrows, pipes, clay pots, and woven baskets.

Lewis and Clark managed to establish peaceful relations with the majority of the tribes they met. They even convinced a delegation of Indian chiefs to travel to Washington, D.C., to meet with Jefferson (see "Jefferson Meets with an American Indian Delegation," p. 202). When the Mandan chief Sheheke accompanied the captains back east at the conclusion of their journey, the president entertained the group at Monticello and showed them the "Indian Hall" he had established to hold all of the artwork and artifacts from the expedition. Although the visiting Indians spoke fondly of Lewis, they were already growing wary of the white traders and settlers who had followed in their wake. "We have seen the beloved man [Lewis], we shook hands with him and we heard the words you put in his mouth. We wish him well," they told Jefferson. "[But when] you tell us that your children of this side of the Mississippi hear your word, you are mistaken, since every day they raise their tomahawks over our heads.... Tell your white children on our lands to follow your orders and to do not as they please, for they do not keep your word."[25]

Notes

[1] Gass, Patrick. May 7, 1806, entry in *The Journals of the Lewis and Clark Expedition*, ed. Gary Moulton. Lincoln: University of Nebraska Press/Electronic Text Center, 2005. Retrieved from http://lewisandclarkjournals.unl.edu/read/?_xmlsrc=1806-05-07&_xslsrc=LCstyles.xsl.

[2] Clark, William. April 21, 1806, entry in *The Journals of the Lewis and Clark Expedition*. Retrieved from http://lewisandclarkjournals.unl.edu/read/?_xmlsrc=1806-04-21&_xslsrc=LCstyles.xsl.

[3] Lewis, Meriwether. May 17, 1806, entry in *The Journals of the Lewis and Clark Expedition*. Retrieved from http://lewisandclarkjournals.unl.edu/read/?_xmlsrc=1806-05-17&_xslsrc=LCstyles.xsl.

[4] Clark, May 6, 1806, entry in *The Journals of the Lewis and Clark Expedition*. Retrieved from http://lewisandclarkjournals.unl.edu/read/?_xmlsrc=1806-05-06&_xslsrc=LCstyles.xsl.

[5] Lewis, May 6, 1806, entry in *The Journals of the Lewis and Clark Expedition*.

[6] Lewis, June 17, 1806, entry in *The Journals of the Lewis and Clark Expedition*. Retrieved from http://lewisandclarkjournals.unl.edu/read/?_xmlsrc=1806-06-17&_xslsrc=LCstyles.xsl.

[7] Lewis, July 3, 1806, entry in *The Journals of the Lewis and Clark Expedition*. Retrieved from http://lewisandclarkjournals.unl.edu/read/?_xmlsrc=1806-07-03&_xslsrc=LCstyles.xsl.

[8] Clark, July 25, 1806, entry in *The Journals of the Lewis and Clark Expedition*. Retrieved from http://lewisandclarkjournals.unl.edu/read/?_xmlsrc=1806-07-25&_xslsrc=LCstyles.xsl.

[9] Lewis, July 15, 1806, entry in *The Journals of the Lewis and Clark Expedition*. Retrieved from http://lewisandclarkjournals.unl.edu/read/?_xmlsrc=1806-07-15&_xslsrc=LCstyles.xsl.

[10] Lewis, July 26, 1806, entry in *The Journals of the Lewis and Clark Expedition*. Retrieved from http://lewisandclarkjournals.unl.edu/read/?_xmlsrc=1806-07-26&_xslsrc=LCstyles.xsl.

[11] Lewis, July 27, 1806, entry in *The Journals of the Lewis and Clark Expedition*. Retrieved from http://lewisandclarkjournals.unl.edu/read/?_xmlsrc=1806-07-27&_xslsrc=LCstyles.xsl.

[12] Lewis, July 27, 1806, entry in *The Journals of the Lewis and Clark Expedition*.

[13] Lewis, July 28, 1806, entry in *The Journals of the Lewis and Clark Expedition*. Retrieved from http://lewisandclarkjournals.unl.edu/read/?_xmlsrc=1806-07-28&_xslsrc=LCstyles.xsl.

[14] Clark, August 12, 1806, entry in *The Journals of the Lewis and Clark Expedition*. Retrieved from http://lewisandclarkjournals.unl.edu/read/?_xmlsrc=1806-08-12&_xslsrc=LCstyles.xsl.

[15] Clark, August 30, 1806, entry in *The Journals of the Lewis and Clark Expedition*. Retrieved from http://lewisandclarkjournals.unl.edu/read/?_xmlsrc=1806-08-30&_xslsrc=LCstyles.xsl.

[16] Clark, August 30, 1806, entry in *The Journals of the Lewis and Clark Expedition*.

[17] Quoted in "Rivers, Edens, Empires: Lewis and Clark and the Revealing of America." Library of Congress, n.d. Retrieved from http://www.loc.gov/exhibits/lewisandclark/lewis-landc.html.

[18] Ordway, John. September 23, 1806, entry in *The Journals of the Lewis and Clark Expedition*. Retrieved from http://lewisandclarkjournals.unl.edu/read/?_xmlsrc=1806-09-23&_xslsrc=LCstyles.xsl.

[19] Lewis, Meriwether. Letter to Thomas Jefferson, September 23, 1806. Thomas Jefferson Papers, Library of Congress. Retrieved from http://www.loc.gov/resource/mtj1.036_0912_0917/?sp=1&st=text.

[20] Jefferson, Thomas. Letter to Meriwether Lewis, October 26, 1806. Retrieved from http://www.monticello.org/site/return-lewis-and-clark.

[21] Lewis, Letter to Thomas Jefferson, September 23, 1806.

[22] Clark, July 13, 1805, entry in *The Journals of the Lewis and Clark Expedition*. Retrieved from http://lewisandclarkjournals.unl.edu/read/?_xmlsrc=1805-07-13&_xslsrc=LCstyles.xsl.

[23] Johnsgard, Paul A. "Lewis and Clark on the Great Plains." *The Journals of the Lewis and Clark Expedition*. Lincoln: University of Nebraska Press, 2003. Retrieved from http://lewisandclarkjournals.unl.edu/read/?_xmlsrc=lc.johnsgard.01.01&_xslsrc=LCstyles.xsl.

[24] Beckham, Stephen Dow. *Lewis and Clark: From the Rockies to the Pacific*. Portland, OR: Graphic Arts Center, 2011, p. 7.

[25] Quoted in Duncan, Dayton, and Ken Burns. *Lewis and Clark: The Journey of the Corps of Discovery*. New York: Knopf, 1997, p. 173.

Chapter Six

SETTLEMENT OF THE WEST

In the course of ten or twelve years a tour across the Continent … will be undertaken by individuals with as little concern as a voyage across the Atlantic is at present.

—Meriwether Lewis, letter to
President Thomas Jefferson, September 23, 1806

When President Thomas Jefferson purchased the Louisiana Territory from France in 1803, he took the first step toward achieving his vision of building an America that stretched from coast to coast. Yet even Jefferson could not foresee how quickly his dream would become a reality. He thought it would take more than one hundred generations to settle the vast lands west of the Mississippi. Less than five generations later, however, the region had been transformed in ways that he never imagined.

Armed with the maps and information brought back by the Lewis and Clark Expedition, people soon began flooding into the West, hoping to exploit its resources for their own personal gain. "Through their journals, field notes, and collections, [Lewis and Clark] planted the seeds of curiosity that nurtured commerce, colonization, and conquest,"[1] noted historian Stephen Dow Beckham. The white settlers who followed in their footsteps hunted animals for their valuable furs, turned grassy prairies into farmland, and crowded out or killed off the Native Americans who had lived there for generations.

Lewis and Clark were not directly responsible for the changes that took place in the West over the next century, of course, and many of them would have occurred anyway. But the expedition did help remove the air of mystery surrounding the region and encourage people to view it as a land of opportunity. "The West, once daunting and intimidating, was now a more familiar place to Americans," explained Sara Huyser and Janet Pearson of the University of Virginia. "Meriwether Lewis, William Clark, and the other explorers achieved an extraordinary feat. Because of their expedition, however, the West that they experienced would never be the same."[2]

Native Americans Forced onto Reservations

Part of Lewis and Clark's mission was to establish friendly relations with the Native American nations of the West. They promised the leaders of each tribe they encountered that the U.S. government would treat them fairly. Jefferson based his policy toward the Indians on the 1787 Northwest Ordinance, which opened the Great Lakes region to white settlement and specified how new states could be formed from these lands. In crafting this ordinance, the U.S. Congress declared that "the utmost good faith shall always be observed towards the Indians: their lands and property shall never be taken from them without their consent," and that "laws founded in justice and humanity, shall from time to time be made for preventing wrongs being done to them, and for preserving peace and friendship with them."[3]

Over the years following the Lewis and Clark Expedition, however, the U.S. government betrayed its promises to the Native Americans countless times by breaking treaties and stealing their land (see "Native Americans Offer Their Perspective on Westward Expansion," p. 205). The trouble began in the area east of the Mississippi River. As the U.S. population increased rapidly during the first half of the nineteenth century—from around 5 million in 1800 to more than 23 million by 1850—millions of Americans decided to leave the crowded, industrial cities of the East in search of new opportunities in the West. The open land on the nation's western frontier offered them the prospect of wealth, freedom, and self-determination.

As land speculators and surveyors poured over the Appalachian Mountains, U.S. government authorities pressured the tribes that made their homes in the region to hand over their traditional lands for white settlement. Some Indians managed to hang on to fragments of their once-vast territories—either by trying to assimilate into white society or by using various means of resistance—but others were swept entirely away from the lands of their ancestors.

Once Lewis and Clark completed their exploration of the Louisiana Territory, Indian removal proposals gained in popularity. Supporters of these

Between 1817 and 1850, more than 100,000 American Indians were deported from their ancestral homelands to reservations west of the Mississippi River.

schemes wanted to meet the rapidly growing demand for frontier land by forcing all the Native American communities to move west of the Mississippi River. "The hunter state [of the Indian] can exist only in the vast uncultivated desert," declared President James Monroe in his 1817 State of the Union address. "It yields to the more dense and compact form and greater force of civilized population; and of right it ought to yield, for the earth was given to mankind to support the greatest number of which it is capable, and no tribe or people have a right to withhold from the wants of others more than is necessary for their own support and comfort."[4]

Between 1817 and 1850, more than 100,000 American Indians from twenty-eight tribes were deported from their ancestral homelands to reservations west of the Mississippi River. These removals were carried out according to language contained in dozens of treaties that Native American leaders signed with heavy hearts. In cases where tribal leaders refused to sign despite the overwhelming pressure upon them, U.S. officials simply forged their names or

> *"Meriwether Lewis, William Clark, and the other explorers achieved an extraordinary feat. Because of their expedition, however, the West that they experienced would never be the same."*

expelled the bands at gunpoint. White negotiators also secured the cooperation of some tribal leaders through outright bribery.

America's campaign of officially sanctioned robbery opened large expanses of new land for white development. But it also ripped apart Indian cultures that had prospered for hundreds of years. "Generation after generation of Native American families came to know only the sorrows and terrors of exile," wrote historian Peter Nabokov. "All their worldly goods on their backs, the Indian refugees suffered harassment from unfriendly whites along the way. Starvation and disease were their constant companions as they walked along unfamiliar roads to country they had never seen. Sometimes friendly Indians gave them shelter; sometimes enemy tribes took the opportunity to attack them."[5]

Although many tribes suffered greatly during this period, the Cherokee nation almost certainly ranks as the best-known victim of U.S. Indian removal policies. Cherokee culture had thrived in the southeastern part of what eventually became the United States for thousands of years prior to European contact. When whites swept into their territories, the Cherokee agreed to turn over large tracts of land to the U.S. government. Members also adopted "civilized" ways—including European-style forms of farming, government, law, and religious practice—to stay in the good graces of the whites who surrounded them. In the end, though, all of these desperate efforts were not enough to stem white demands for their remaining lands.

Andrew Jackson—a Southern planter who possessed a deep well of hostility toward all Native Americans—made Indian removal a top priority when he became president of the United States in 1828. Two years later Congress passed the Indian Removal Act, a ruthless piece of legislation that formally authorized Jackson to relocate all eastern tribes to reservations west of the Mississippi. Although Cherokee leaders challenged the law in court, they ultimately lost the battle. On May 26, 1838, federal troops forcibly evicted thousands of Cherokee from their homes and marched them to official reservation land in eastern Oklahoma. An estimated 4,000 tribal members died from disease, exhaustion, or starvation during the thousand-mile journey. The ordeal became known among the Cherokee as the "Trail of Tears," and it ranks as one of the most shameful episodes in American history.

Westward Expansion and "Manifest Destiny"

In the half-century after the Louisiana Purchase was finalized, the United States continued to acquire new territory. U.S. leaders wanted to expand in order to satisfy the growing population's demands for land. They also believed that gaining control of more land and natural resources would increase the overall wealth and security of the nation. Instead of extending U.S. rule over new territory in a way that would create dependent colonies, however, they planned to organize it into new states that would be equal in status to those that already existed.

Many Americans held an idealistic view of territorial expansion. They felt that the United States had a national mission to spread freedom and democracy across the continent. They believed that the country would be serving God's purpose by extending its borders all the way to the Pacific Ocean. An influential New York journalist named John L. O'Sullivan coined the term "manifest destiny" to describe this sense of purpose. In an article published in

As the United States expanded westward, Americans rushed to settle the newly acquired land.

1845, he argued that it was "the fulfillment of our manifest destiny to overspread the continent allotted by Providence."[6]

The idea of manifest destiny caught on in newspapers and magazines of the era. Countless articles and books extolled the virtues of California, for instance, praising its sunny climate, abundant natural resources, and excellent ports for shipping goods across the Pacific. Before long, many Americans were pressuring U.S. leaders to purchase California from Mexico. Upon taking office in 1845, President James K. Polk made the acquisition of California one of his primary goals. He also aggressively pursued the annexation of Texas (which had declared its independence from Mexico in 1836) and the Oregon Country (which Great Britain considered part of Canada).

The dispute over Texas had begun in 1803, when Jefferson and other prominent Americans had insisted that the area was included as part of the Louisiana Purchase. But Spain continued to claim the territory until 1821, when Mexico gained its independence and Texas became part of Mexico. In 1836 Texas declared its independence from Mexico—although Mexico refused to recognize the newly created Republic of Texas—and asked to become part of the United States. A few days before Polk took office in 1845, the U.S. Congress finally granted this request by passing a joint resolution annexing Texas to the United States.

In the midst of the tension surrounding the annexation of Texas, Polk launched his plan to acquire California. He sent diplomat John Slidell to Mexico to offer up to $30 million for the purchase of California and New Mexico. Outraged that the United States would try to buy additional territory without offering any compensation for Texas or the disputed land along the Rio Grande, Mexican government officials refused to negotiate with Slidell.

In the meantime, Texas settlers approved the annexation measure and made a formal request of statehood. Even though Polk knew that doing so could lead to war with Mexico, he signed a bill admitting Texas as a state on December 29, 1845. In early 1846 Polk sent U.S. troops under General Zachary Taylor to defend Texas and put pressure on Mexico to negotiate. Mexican troops attacked Taylor's forces and killed sixteen American soldiers. Polk seized upon this incident to ask Congress for a declaration of war.

The Mexican-American War raged for two years. American forces achieved a series of victories over poorly equipped Mexican troops and quickly occupied California and northern Mexico. When Mexican leaders still refused to negotiate, Polk authorized a military invasion that culminated in General Winfield Scott's capture of Mexico City in August 1847. On February 2, 1848, the two sides officially ended hostilities by signing the Treaty of Guadalupe Hidalgo. Under the terms of the treaty, the United States took possession of 525,000 square miles of Mexican territory—an area encompassing present-day California, Nevada, Utah, and Arizona, as well as parts of New Mexico and Colorado—in exchange for $15 million in compensation for war damages. Mexico was also forced to accept the loss of Texas, which comprised another 225,000 square miles. The Mexican Cession thus expanded the boundaries of the United States south to the Rio Grande and west to the Pacific Ocean, while also reducing Mexico's total land area by more than half.

> *President James K. Polk proclaimed it his "duty to assert and maintain by all constitutional means the right of the United States to that portion of our territory which lies beyond the Rocky Mountains."*

In the meantime, Polk used a combination of threats and promises to reach an agreement with England regarding the Oregon Country. The president initially demanded that England give up territory extending northward through modern-day British Columbia all the way to the border of the Russian territory of Alaska. "Our title to the country of the Oregon is 'clear and unquestionable,'" he declared in his inaugural address. "[It is] my duty to assert and maintain by all constitutional means the right of the United States to that portion of our territory which lies beyond the Rocky Mountains."[7] After tensions between the United States and Great Britain mounted to the brink of war, Polk signed the Oregon Treaty of 1846, which established the U.S. border significantly further south, along the 49th Parallel. The newly acquired territory in the Pacific Northwest eventually became the states of Washington, Oregon, and Idaho, as well as small parts of Montana and Wyoming. Combined with the Mexican Cession, Polk's acquisitions increased the total land area of the United States by one-third.

The Oregon Trail and the Indian Wars

Although some people criticized the aggressive tactics Polk used to wrestle control of the West from Spain, Mexico, and Great Britain, many Americans believed that the president's expansionist policies had brought great prestige, wealth, and opportunity to the nation. As soon as the United States took control over the Pacific Coast, hopeful farmers, ranchers, miners, and settlers began traveling across the country to lay claim to the land. Many of these pioneers followed the Oregon Trail, a 2,200-mile overland route from the Missouri River to various destinations in the West.

Parts of the Oregon Trail followed the route mapped by the Lewis and Clark Expedition between 1804 and 1806. The main difference was that the main routes the explorers took through the Rocky Mountains, Lemhi Pass and Lolo Pass, were too steep and rough for the settlers' wagons to get through. The trappers, traders, and mountain men who followed in Lewis and Clark's footsteps found better ways to cross the Rockies further south. The expedition did map the eastern end of the Oregon Trail in present-day Kansas, Nebraska, and Wyoming, however, as well as the Platte and Snake River valleys on the trail's western end. After the first migrant wagon train departed from Independence, Missouri, in 1836, the Oregon Trail was gradually cleared and improved with bridges and ferries to allow for faster, safer, and easier travel. Offshoots were added in the 1840s to allow travelers to reach new destinations, such as California, Washington, and Utah.

The pace of westward migration increased rapidly in 1848, when a carpenter named James Wilson Marshall found gold flakes in the American River near Sacramento, California. His discovery launched the Gold Rush, a period when people flocked to California in hopes of making their fortune. The miners came from neighboring areas of the West, like the Oregon Territory, as well as the cities of the East, South America, and even China. Traffic on the Oregon Trail and its offshoots increased dramatically during this time, and the population of California grew from 14,000 at the time of the Mexican Cession to 200,000 only four years later. By 1850 an estimated four million Americans had surged across the continent to settle in the West.

The pace of settlement increased further with the completion of a coast-to-coast telegraph communication system in 1861 and of the first transcontinental railroad in 1869. This 1,900-mile railroad line connected the existing eastern U.S. rail network to the Pacific Coast in California. The Central Pacific Railroad Company built its way eastward from Sacramento, while the Union Pacific Railroad Company built its way westward from Council Bluffs, Iowa. The two lines met at Promontory Point, Utah, on May 10, 1869. With the driving of the last spike, a mechanized transportation system connected the United States from coast to coast. Use of the Oregon Trail declined as the railroad made the cross-country trip faster, safer, and less expensive than ever before.

By pushing westward and settling new territory on the frontier, many Americans believed that they were helping to spread the benefits of modern civilization to "backward" areas. In reality, though, westward expansion took place

One hundred years after Lewis and Clark struggled to cross the Bitterroot Mountains, a railroad line was built to carry passengers and freight through the rugged area.

at the expense of Native American peoples whose ancestors had lived in those areas for many generations. Just as it had happened in the East, countless Indian tribes were either tricked or forced into giving up their land and relocating to less desirable areas in order to make room for white settlements.

For much of the first half of the nineteenth century, white settlers and politicians saw the Great Plains region in the middle of the continent as unsuitable for farming or other development. They mostly regarded the region as an obstacle that had to be crossed to reach the booming mining and agricultural regions in California and Oregon. As a result, they were content to leave this flat, dry, and mostly treeless region to the Indians who had long resided there. In the 1830s, in fact, U.S. leaders treated the Great Plains as a convenient dumping ground for the Cherokee and other tribes that they removed from the East.

By the 1850s, however, white perspectives on the Great Plains began to change. People increasingly recognized that the oceans of grass covering the

The Extermination of the Buffalo

When Lewis and Clark traveled across the Great Plains, they found immense herds of American buffalo stretching as far as the eye could see. "The Missouri bottoms on both sides of the river were crowded with buffalo," Lewis wrote. "I sincerely believe that there were not less than ten thousand buffalo within a circle of two miles around that place." Scientists estimate that thirty million buffalo roamed the continent in the early nineteenth century.

The buffalo occupied a central place in the culture of the Great Plains Indians. Buffalo meat was the main staple of their diet, and the tough hides of the beasts were treated to make robes, blankets, moccasins, and tipi covers. Internal organs like the stomach and bladder were sometimes used as containers for water, and buffalo sinew was used as sewing thread. Horns, hooves, and bones, meanwhile, were used to make everything from arrowheads to toys. Given the buffalo's all-around importance to the existence of the Plains Indians, the animal also played a key role in the religious life of the tribes.

Over the course of the next hundred years, however, the American buffalo was virtually wiped out as white settlers took over the Great Plains. Diseases introduced by domestic cattle played a role in the population decline,

plains could be plowed up and turned into fertile farmland. They also noted that the advent of steam-powered railroads and riverboats allowed farmers and ranchers in remote parts of the country to deliver their goods to distant markets.

As white settlers, miners, railroad workers, and buffalo hunters poured across the Mississippi River into the Great Plains, however, they quickly ran into trouble with Indian nations that had thrived there for centuries—including some that had befriended Lewis and Clark. So-called "Indian Wars" flared up all across the West in the 1850s and 1860s, and in some cases these conflicts lasted for decades. In modern-day Arizona and New Mexico, U.S. Army troops and settlers battled fierce Navajo and Apache warriors. In present-day Oklahoma, Texas, Kansas, and Colorado, whites fought the Kiowa, Comanche, Cheyenne, and Arapaho nations for control of the southern Plains. California and the Pacific Northwest saw violent clashes between whites and the Nez Perce and Modoc tribes. The Rocky

as did habitat loss from the conversion of grazing lands to farms and towns. The single greatest destroyer of the buffalo, though, was the market hunter. These professional killers laid waste to the great herds in order to meet the demand for buffalo blankets and smoked buffalo tongue in the big cities of the East. As the railroads snaked ever deeper into the West, opening remote lands to the rifles of the hunters, the great herds vanished.

The decimation of the buffalo herds dealt a terrible blow to the Plains Indians. Without their main source of food and clothing, they could no longer resist the white invasion of their traditional territory. Although some whites mourned the loss of the great buffalo herds, others saw their falling numbers as a positive development in paving the way for American progress. "For the sake of a lasting peace, let them kill, skin, and sell until the buffaloes are exterminated," U.S. Army general Philip Sheridan proclaimed in 1875. "Then your prairies will be covered with speckled cattle and the festive cowboy."

Sources

Geist, Valerius. *Buffalo Nation: History and Legend of the North American Bison.* Stillwater, MN: Voyageur Press, 1998.

Lewis, Meriwether. July 11, 1806, entry in *The Journals of the Lewis and Clark Expedition*, ed. Gary Moulton. Lincoln: University of Nebraska Press/Electronic Text Center, 2005. Retrieved from http://lewisandclarkjournals.unl.edu/journals.php?id=1806-07-11.

Mountain region, meanwhile, was wracked by bloodshed between whites and members of the Shoshone, Ute, Bannock, and Paiute nations.

All of these wars ultimately ended in the same way: the Indian tribes were vanquished and herded onto reservations, and white Americans moved onto their old hunting grounds to seek gold and silver, cut timber, plant crops, and build railroads and towns. With the arrival of regular railroad service, white "market hunters" became an increasing problem. These hunters mowed down entire herds of bison—the cornerstone of the Great Plains Indian societies—for their valuable pelts, then left the skinned carcasses to rot on the plains (see "The Extermination of the Buffalo," p. 100). Lakota, Mandan, Hidatsa, and other northern Plains tribes also suffered from devastating outbreaks of "white man diseases" like smallpox, typhus, and cholera. "[The white man's] numbers were greater than blades of grass," summarized one American Indian elder.

"They took away the buffalo and shot down our best warriors. They took away our lands and surrounded us by fences."[8]

The Closing of the American Frontier

With the purchase of Alaska from Russia in 1867—which added nearly 600,000 square miles to the land area of the United States for the sum of $7.2 million—U.S. territory came close to assuming its final form. As the nation's population more than tripled in the second half of the nineteenth century—from 23 million in 1850 to 76 million in 1900—people continued to settle the newly acquired western lands. By 1880 the population of the city of San Francisco alone was nearly 250,000.

Following the 1890 U.S. Census, government analysts announced that the population figures no longer showed a clear line of advancing settlement across the continent. This announcement meant that the nation had achieved

San Francisco and other cities in the West grew so rapidly that America's western frontier was declared closed before the end of the nineteenth century.

its manifest destiny and tamed the West—less than one hundred years after Lewis and Clark had first explored the lands west of the Mississippi River. Although many people viewed the settling of the West as a monumental achievement, others lamented the closing of the frontier and wondered what impact it would have on the national character.

Historian Frederick Jackson Turner expressed this concern in a famous 1893 speech entitled "The Significance of the Frontier in American History." He said that the existence of a vast area of untamed land in the West, as well as the steady advancement of civilization across that land, had played a vital role in shaping American culture. "To the frontier the American intellect owes its striking characteristics," he noted. "That coarseness and strength combined with acuteness and inquisitiveness; that practical, inventive turn of mind, quick to find expedients; that masterful grasp of material things, lacking in the artistic but powerful to effect great ends; that restless, nervous energy; that dominant individualism, working for good and for evil, and withal that buoyancy and exuberance which comes with freedom."[9]

In what became known as his "Frontier Thesis," Turner suggested that the foundations of individual freedom and democracy in the United States were intimately connected to the development of the frontier. He concluded by wondering what impact the settlement of the West would have on the nation and its people. "And now, four centuries from the discovery of America, at the end of a hundred years of life under the Constitution, the frontier has gone," he declared, "and with its going has closed the first period of American history."[10]

Notes

[1] Beckham, Stephen Dow. *Lewis and Clark: From the Rockies to the Pacific.* Portland, OR: Graphic Arts Center, 2011, p. 7.

[2] Huyser, Sara, and Janet Pearson. "The Lewis and Clark Expedition Returns Safely to St. Louis in September 1806." *Medicine and Health on the Lewis and Clark Expedition.* Claude Moore Health Sciences Library, University of Virginia, 2007. Retrieved from http://exhibits.hsl.virginia.edu/lewisclark/return_home/.

[3] "Northwest Ordinance." Transcript. *Ohio History Central: An Online Encyclopedia of Ohio History.* Retrieved from http://www.ohiohistorycentral.org/entry.php?rec=1462&nm=Northwest-Ordinance-Transcript.

[4] Monroe, James. First Annual Message to Congress, December 12, 1817. *The American Presidency Project.* Retrieved from http://www.presidency.ucsb.edu/ws/?pid=29459.

[5] Nabokov, Peter. *Native American Testimony: A Chronicle of Indian-White Relations from Prophecy to the Present, 1492-2000.* 1978. Revised ed. New York: Penguin Books, 1999, p. 148.

[6] O'Sullivan, John L. "Annexation." *United States Magazine and Democratic Review,* July-August 1845, p. 5. Retrieved from http://web.grinnell.edu/courses/HIS/f01/HIS202-01/Documents/OSullivan.html.

[7] Polk, James K. "Inaugural Address," March 4, 1845. Retrieved from http://www.presidency.ucsb.edu/ws/index.php?pid=25814#ixzz1GbOzjSuV.

[8] Quoted in Wissler, Clark. *Indian Cavalcade.* New York: Sheridan House, 1938, p. 351.

[9] Turner, Frederick Jackson. "The Significance of the Frontier in American History." Paper read at the annual meeting of the American Historical Association, July 12, 1893. Retrieved from http://xroads.virginia.edu/~Hyper/TURNER/.

[10] Turner, "The Significance of the Frontier in American History."

Chapter Seven

LEGACY OF THE LEWIS AND CLARK EXPEDITION

◄━━◖∫◗━━►

I think that the nature of America, how it was born, how it grew up, sort of exemplified the idea of exploration. We were a young country, we grew, and I think this idea of being explorers is ingrained in our psyche.... I think we'll always be explorers.

—American astronaut James Lovell

The Lewis and Clark Expedition occupies a much more significant place in U.S. history than if it were an ordinary cross-country journey or scientific enterprise. It has come to represent a uniquely American tradition of exploration and discovery. "When Thomas Jefferson dispatched the Corps of Discovery toward the Pacific, he launched the nation on a trajectory of exploration that arcs all the way to the present," according to historian Dayton Duncan. "It began a tradition that links Lewis and Clark ... to the astronauts of the twentieth century."[1]

The adventures of the captains and their Corps of Discovery still hold tremendous appeal for Americans today. Although much of the western landscape has changed and been developed over the past two centuries, there are still wild places—like the Bitterroot Mountains or the Salmon River in Idaho—where intrepid travelers can see what Lewis and Clark did in 1804–1806. Each year, millions of people read the explorers' journals, retrace their route across the continent on the Lewis and Clark National Historic Trail, and visit the many parks and monuments throughout the West that mark important points in their journey. "We are a people in motion," wrote historian James P. Ronda. "The lure of the road and the promise of the journey still hold us. And it was Lewis and Clark who gave us our first great national road story."[2]

The American Tradition of Exploration and Discovery

Once Lewis and Clark pierced the veil of mystery surrounding the West, a legion of new explorers followed in their wake. "Lewis and Clark had the honor of being first," Duncan wrote. "They would not be disappointed—or surprised—to learn that they were not the last."[3] Each of the later expeditions provided additional details to help fill in the empty spaces on the captains' maps.

Zebulon Pike led a twenty-man military expedition up the Mississippi River in 1805, even before Lewis and Clark had made their triumphant return to St. Louis. Pike's slow progress left him no choice but to spend a harsh winter in Minnesota before returning the following spring. In 1806 Pike went on another mission to explore the headwaters of the Arkansas River in present-day Colorado, where he attempted to climb the mountain that became known as Pike's Peak. After wandering into Spanish territory, Pike was arrested by a Spanish patrol and taken to Mexico. Although he was eventually released at the border of the Louisiana Territory, he used his time in custody to gather more information about the Southwest.

> *"When Thomas Jefferson dispatched the Corps of Discovery toward the Pacific, he launched the nation on a trajectory of exploration that arcs all the way to the present," according to historian Dayton Duncan.*

Another famous explorer to follow in the footsteps of Lewis and Clark was John C. Frémont, who led a series of U.S. government-sponsored expeditions between 1842 and 1854. A colorful character who earned the nickname "The Pathfinder," Frémont explored and mapped large sections of the Oregon Trail. His *Report on an Exploration of the Country Lying between the Missouri River and the Rocky Mountains on the Line of the Kansas and Great Platte Rivers* was published in newspapers across the country, and it served as a guide for many pioneers who migrated westward. "Frémont became an instant celebrity, a champion of expansion, a conqueror wielding not a sword but a compass and a transit,"[4] noted historian Hampton Sides. Frémont also played a role in securing the Spanish territory of California for the United States during the Mexican-American War.

Although government-sponsored exploration of the West dropped off during the Civil War, it picked up again afterward. In 1869 John Wesley Pow-

This statue of Sacagawea, Lewis, and Clark in Kansas City, Missouri, is one of many monuments honoring the explorers and their place in American history.

Some historians place the Lewis and Clark Expedition within a tradition of American exploration and discovery that includes the 1969 Moon landing.

ell, a Union Army veteran who had lost an arm in combat, launched an expedition to explore one of the last remaining blank spaces on the map of the West: the Grand Canyon of the Colorado River. When his group of nine men set out from Green River, Wyoming, in four small boats, no one knew what they would encounter on their journey. As it turned out, their 900-mile route through the

Grand Canyon to the mouth of the Virgin River required them to negotiate some of the largest and most dangerous rapids in North America.

In the 1870s, as Americans continued to migrate westward, the U.S. government organized official surveys in order to create a detailed map of the West. In 1879 Congress created the U.S. Geographical Survey (USGS) to coordinate these efforts. The official mission of the agency included "classification of the public lands, and examination of the geological structure, mineral resources, and products of the national domain." The USGS still exists today, and its scientists continue to study and map the nation's climate, ecosystems, natural resources, and natural hazards.

"Mankind is drawn to the heavens for the same reason we were once drawn into unknown lands and across the open sea," declared President George W. Bush. "We choose to explore space because doing so improves our lives, and lifts our national spirit."

Once the territorial holdings of the United States had been explored, mapped, and settled, Americans increasingly turned their attention toward expanding human knowledge in new areas. One place that continued to be shrouded in mystery into the mid-twentieth century was outer space. On May 25, 1961, President John F. Kennedy made a speech before Congress in which he proposed that "this nation should commit itself to achieving the goal, before this decade is out, of landing a man on the Moon and returning him safely to the Earth."[5] He expanded upon this ambitious idea in a speech delivered at Rice University in Texas on September 12, 1962. Kennedy presented outer space as a new frontier waiting to be discovered and explored, and he challenged the American people to live up to their pioneer heritage by supporting the U.S. space program. "We set sail on this new sea because there is new knowledge to be gained, and new rights to be won, and they must be won and used for the progress of all people,"[6] he declared.

The astronauts of *Apollo 11*—Neil Armstrong, Edwin "Buzz" Aldrin Jr., and Michael Collins—achieved Kennedy's goal on July 20, 1969. The historic Moon landing was broadcast live on television to a worldwide audience. Upon becoming the first human to touch the lunar surface, Armstrong famously described it as "one small step for man, one giant leap for mankind."[7]

Many historians have drawn parallels between the Moon landing and the Lewis and Clark Expedition. Both missions were conceived by a president who was eager to expand the nation's frontiers, for instance, and promoted as a way to advance scientific knowledge. The men who risked their lives to fulfill both missions were members of the U.S. military, and upon their safe return they were welcomed as heroes. Lewis and Clark brought back Indian artifacts, plant and animal specimens, and other objects that generated public excitement, while the astronauts brought back moon rocks. Finally, both sets of explorers carried American flags and used them to lay claim to distant areas of conquest.

President George W. Bush maintained the comparison in announcing plans to resume the U.S. space program in 2004. "Mankind is drawn to the heavens for the same reason we were once drawn into unknown lands and across the open sea," he declared. "We choose to explore space because doing so improves our lives, and lifts our national spirit."[8] Some historians, on the other hand, have argued that Lewis and Clark actually had a more daunting mission than the astronauts. Very little was known about the West when they launched their expedition in 1804, whereas the Moon had been extensively studied by scientists on Earth. "In many respects, the expedition was like going to the moon," according to geographer and historian John Logan Allen, "with one remarkable exception that I think a lot of people forget about, and that is that when *Apollo 13* is having difficulty, those people are in constant contact with Earth. They're speaking with Houston, and they're getting advice on how to deal with problems. Lewis and Clark were on their own."[9]

The Lewis and Clark National Historic Trail

The American landscape has undergone transformative changes in the two centuries since Lewis and Clark traveled through the West. In the journals they kept during the journey, the captains predicted some of the changes that have taken place. Lewis noted the fertile soil and favorable climate of the Great Plains region along the Missouri River, for instance, and wrote that it held great potential for agriculture. Today, the region produces grains and other crops that feed millions of people across the United States and around the world. Likewise, Clark indicated many spots on his maps that he believed would be excellent locations for future forts and settlements. Large cities now occupy dozens of these locations, including Kansas City, Missouri; Omaha, Nebraska; and Portland, Oregon.

Some of the changes made in the name of "progress" have had negative impacts on the land, rivers, people, and animals of the West. Both of the major rivers that Lewis and Clark followed on their westward journey—the Missouri and the Columbia—have been significantly altered by the construction of dams.

Many of the waterfalls and rapids that slowed their progress or forced them to portage have been harnessed for power generation or buried under placid reservoirs. Some of the animals that were abundant in Lewis and Clark's day are rare or extinct today. Similarly, the Native American nations that they encountered on their journey were relocated from their ancestral lands and forced to find new ways to survive in a white-dominated world. "Lewis and Clark mark a turning point in the American past. They stand at a new beginning, but it is also the beginning of the end," wrote Anthony Brandt. "Behind them came steamboats and railroads, millions of acres of soybeans and feed corn, vast herds of cattle. They gave us our continent, but what have we done to it?"[10]

On the other hand, there are still some places in the West today that look much as they did when Lewis and Clark first saw them. The White Cliffs of the Missouri in Montana have been protected from development, for instance, and the Bitterroot Mountains on the Idaho border are surrounded by one of the

The Upper Missouri Breaks National Monument preserves a natural area traversed by Lewis and Clark for modern-day adventurers to explore.

The Lewis and Clark National Historic Trail ends at the mouth of the Columbia River, where the expedition reached the Pacific Ocean in 1805.

largest protected wilderness areas in the continental United States. The Salmon River still features many of the imposing rapids that frightened Lewis and Clark, and today they challenge whitewater adventurers in kayaks and rubber rafts.

Modern-day travelers can follow the explorers' historic route across the country. The Lewis and Clark National Historic Trail, which was established by Congress in 1978 and is administered by the National Park Service, starts near St. Louis and ends at the mouth of the Columbia River. The easternmost portion of the trail follows the Missouri River through Kansas, Nebraska, Iowa, North Dakota, and South Dakota into Montana. From the river's headwaters at Three Forks, the trail crosses over the Continental Divide at Lemhi Pass. It then climbs through the Bitterroot Valley to Lolo, Montana, which is near the spot Lewis and Clark called Travelers Rest. After following the Snake River between the twin cities of Lewiston, Idaho, and Clarkston, Washington, the trail meets the Columbia River. Finally, it parallels the Columbia Gorge to the Pacific Ocean. The historic trail also marks a few spots that the captains explored separately during the return journey, including the Yellowstone River and the Marias River.

Along the Lewis and Clark National Historic Trail, travelers can visit dozens of monuments, commemorative sites, and interpretive centers recognizing the explorers, as well as counties, towns, forests, rivers, schools, campgrounds, motels, and restaurants named after them. A few of the important locations that have been preserved for visitors to enjoy include:

- The Sergeant Floyd Monument near Sioux City, Iowa, which marks the spot where the Corps of Discovery buried their fallen comrade;

- The Big Hidatsa Village Site near Stanton, North Dakota, where Lewis and Clark spent the winter camped among the Mandan Indians;

- Missouri Headwaters State Park in Montana, where the expedition reached the Three Forks and searched for the Shoshone;

- Clark's Lookout near Dillon, Montana, which marks a scenic view that Clark sketched in his journal on August 13, 1805;

- The Sacagawea Interpretive, Cultural, and Education Center in Salmon, Idaho, near the spot where Sacagawea was reunited with her people;

- The Nez Perce National Historic Park near Spalding, Idaho, which commemorates the valuable assistance the American explorers received from the tribe;

- The Lewis and Clark National Historic Park near Astoria, Oregon, which includes the site of Fort Clatsop and the trail the explorers took to the Pacific Coast;

- Cape Disappointment State Park near Ilwaco, Washington, where Lewis and Clark reached the mouth of the Columbia; and

- Pompeys Pillar National Monument near Billings, Montana, where Clark's inscription from 1806 can still be viewed today.

Many people enjoy reading pertinent passages from the captains' journals while they drive, hike, ride, or paddle sections of the trail. Travelers are certain to experience some of the same conditions that the explorers wrote about, such as clouds of hungry mosquitoes on the prairie, rain and fog in the Pacific Northwest, and breathtaking views of snow-covered peaks in the Rocky Mountains. "Now, as we try to preserve what is left of America's wild lands, rivers, and their native species and attempt to restore fragmented and degraded landscapes, the journals of Lewis and Clark can serve as a guide to what that country once was,"[11] wrote guidebook author Elizabeth Grossman.

Many locations along the trail held special celebrations to mark the bicentennial of the expedition in 2004-2006 (see "Historian James Ronda Explores the Legacy of Lewis and Clark," p. 210). The continuing interest in Lewis and Clark has also generated conferences, films, books, Web sites, and clubs associated with the expedition. "In a time when America is finding its common purpose elusive, it is not surprising that the sense of mission that drove Lewis and Clark evokes nostalgia and admiration,"[12] historian Landon Y. Jones wrote.

Gary E. Moulton, who edited the most comprehensive version of the explorers' journals, argues that the written record left behind by the Corps of Discovery is their greatest legacy. "The journals of the Lewis and Clark expedition are one of our country's national treasures," he wrote. "On those records rest all the expedition's claims to greatness. The men set a standard of record-keeping for later expeditions and left a literary heritage for the ages. In large measure, the scope and quality of the documents account for much of the continuing fascination in the Lewis and Clark story."[13]

Notes

[1] Duncan, Dayton, and Ken Burns. *Lewis and Clark: The Journey of the Corps of Discovery.* New York: Knopf, 1997, p. 213.

[2] Ronda, James P. "Why Lewis and Clark Matter." *Smithsonian,* August 2003. Retrieved from http://www.smithsonianmag.com/history/why-lewis-and-clark-matter-87847931/?all.

[3] Duncan and Burns, p. 213.

[4] Sides, Hampton. *Blood and Thunder.* New York: Anchor Books, 2006, p. 82.

[5] Quoted in "NASA Moon Landing." John F. Kennedy Library and Museum, n.d. Retrieved from http:// www.jfklibrary.org/JFK/JFK-Legacy/NASA-Moon-Landing.aspx.

[6] Kennedy, John F. "Address at Rice University on the Nation's Space Effort," September 12, 1962. John F. Kennedy Presidential Library and Museum, n.d. Retrieved from http://www.jfklibrary.org/Research/Research-Aids/JFK-Speeches/Rice-University_19620912.aspx.

[7] Quoted in "NASA Moon Landing."

[8] Bush, George W. "A Renewed Spirit of Discovery: The President's Vision for Space Exploration." NASA, January 14, 2004. Retrieved from http://www.nasa.gov/pdf/55583main_vision_space_exploration2.pdf.

[9] Quoted in Duncan and Burns, p. 213.

[10] Brandt, Anthony. "My Year with Lewis & Clark: Two Hundred Years On, Lewis and Clark's Expedition Is More Popular Than Ever." *National Geographic Adventure,* May 2003, p. 76.

[11] Grossman, Elizabeth. *Adventuring along the Lewis and Clark Trail.* San Francisco: Sierra Club Books, 2003, p. 14.

[12] Jones, Landon Y. *The Essential Lewis and Clark.* New York: Ecco Press, 2000, p. xviii.

[13] Moulton, Gary E. "The Missing Journals of Meriwether Lewis." *Montana: The Magazine of Western History,* Summer 1985, p. 28. Retrieved from http://lewisandclarkjournals.unl.edu/read/?_xmlsrc=lc.missing.

BIOGRAPHIES

Toussaint Charbonneau (c. 1760-1843)
Fur Trader and Translator for the Lewis and Clark Expedition

Toussaint Charbonneau was born some-time between 1758 and 1768 near Montreal, Canada. At the time of his birth, Montreal was a major center of the North American fur trade. Hunters and trappers brought furs from the Canadian wilderness to Montreal for shipment across the Atlantic Ocean to Great Britain and France. As a young man, the French-speaking Charbonneau began working as a fur trapper for the British-owned North West Company. His job took him to the western frontier of Canada and the United States, where he encountered many different Native American nations.

In 1795 Charbonneau was involved in a violent altercation during a North West expedition. According to a report filed by the company clerk, he was stabbed "in the act of committing a Rape upon her Daughter by an old [Chippewa Indian] woman with a Canoe Awl." Although Charbonneau was not seriously injured, the clerk noted that "it was with difficulty he could walk back over the portage."[1]

During the course of his travels as a fur trapper, Charbonneau came to the Mandan and Hidatsa Indian villages on the Upper Missouri River in present-day North Dakota. By 1797 he began living in an earth lodge among the Indians. He continued trapping for fur companies that operated in the region and also served as an interpreter for French traders who visited the villages. Around 1800 a Hidatsa war party raided a Shoshone Indian encampment near Three Forks, Montana, and kidnapped several young Shoshone women. When the Hidatsas returned with the captives, Charbonneau bought two teenaged girls—Sacagawea and Otter Woman—and made them his wives.

Joins the Lewis and Clark Expedition

In the late fall of 1804, a group of American explorers arrived at the Mandan village near where Charbonneau lived with his wives. The leaders, Captains Meriwether Lewis and William Clark, explained that they were on a scientific expedition sponsored by the U.S. government. They planned to continue up the

117

Missouri River to its source, cross over the Rocky Mountains, and then follow the Columbia River all the way to the Pacific Ocean. Since the arrival of winter was near, however, they asked to camp among the Indians for a few months before resuming their journey. The expedition members erected their winter quarters, Fort Mandan, just outside the village. They exchanged regular visits with the Indians and traded for food and other items they needed.

During that winter, Charbonneau offered to accompany the Lewis and Clark Expedition and serve as a translator. Although the captains were not overly impressed with Charbonneau, they believed that his pregnant wife, Sacagawea, might be helpful to them. Lewis and Clark had heard that her Shoshone people lived near the headwaters of the Missouri and had large herds of horses. They knew that they would need to acquire horses to carry their equipment and supplies over the mountains. The explorers believed that Sacagawea could help them locate and communicate with the Shoshone. They hired both Charbonneau and his young wife to serve as interpreters and guides for the expedition. Two months before they embarked, Sacagawea gave birth to a son, Jean Baptiste Charbonneau.

As they prepared to leave in the spring of 1805, Charbonneau decided that he was unhappy with the terms of his employment. When he informed the captains that he was not willing to perform all the same duties as the twenty-eight enlisted men on the U.S. military expedition, such as standing guard and carrying gear, they dismissed him. "Charbonneau determines on not proceeding with us as an interpreter under the terms mentioned yesterday, he will not agree to work let our situation be what it may," Clark wrote on March 12. "We suffer him to be off the engagement which was only verbal." A few days later, though, Charbonneau changed his mind and asked to be reinstated. "He was sorry for the foolish part he had acted and if we pleased he would accompany us agreeably to the terms we had proposed and do everything we wished him to do,"[2] Clark explained. Charbonneau became the oldest member of the Corps of Discovery, while his infant son became the youngest.

"A Man of No Peculiar Merit"

As the group made its way up the Missouri River, it quickly became clear that Charbonneau's skills did not include handling a boat. In May 1805 he was at the helm of a pirogue when a storm suddenly blew in. He lost control of the craft in the wind and waves, and it tipped onto its side and began filling with water. While Sacagawea calmly bailed water and collected documents, equipment, and supplies that washed overboard, her husband panicked. Charbonneau refused to take action until another crew member threatened to shoot him if he did not resume his place at the rudder. Lewis, who often found Charbonneau irritating, wrote that he "cannot swim and is perhaps the most timid waterman in the world."[3]

Charbonneau performed better in his role as an interpreter. Both he and Sacagawea helped Lewis and Clark communicate with the Native Americans they encountered. At times the process of translation became very complicated. Communicating with the Salish Indians of the Bitterroot Valley, for instance, required Sacagawea to translate the complicated Salish language to Hidatsa, which Charbonneau understood. He then translated the Hidatsa to French, and another crew member translated the French to English for Lewis and Clark. They used a similar process to negotiate with the Shoshone Indians to acquire horses to transport the expedition's supplies over the Rocky Mountains.

Charbonneau received praise in the captains' journals for his cooking skills. He occasionally prepared *boudin blanc,* a French dish that consisted of stuffed sausage made from buffalo intestine, which the crew considered a special treat. On the other hand, Clark mentioned disciplining Charbonneau for neglecting his duties. He also felt the need to intervene in a marital dispute when Charbonneau hit Sacagawea.

The Lewis and Clark Expedition succeeded in reaching the Pacific Ocean in late 1805. After spending the winter near the coast, they launched their return journey eastward across the continent in the spring of 1806. On August 14 they arrived back at the Hidatsa-Mandan villages. This marked the end of the journey for Charbonneau and his family. Although Lewis described Charbonneau as "a man of no peculiar merit,"[4] the captains paid him $500 for his services as an interpreter. Clark had grown fond of little Jean Baptiste and offered to take him home and raise him. Charbonneau and Sacagawea refused the offer, but they agreed to reconsider it when the boy got a little older.

Life after the Expedition

Along with other expedition members, the U.S. government granted Charbonneau title to 320 acres of land. In 1810 he and Sacagawea moved to St. Louis to claim the property. Charbonneau did not enjoy the farming lifestyle, however, so the family did not remain in St. Louis for long. In 1811 Charbonneau sold the land to Clark for $100 and, leaving Jean Baptiste behind to receive an education, moved back west with Sacagawea to Fort Manuel Lisa in South Dakota.

Sacagawea gave birth to a daughter, Lisette, at Fort Manuel Lisa. A short time later, she died of typhus at the age of twenty-five. Charbonneau continued working as a trapper and trader in the West for another thirty years. Thanks to Clark, who became governor of the Missouri Territory in 1813, he also served as an interpreter for the U.S. government's Indian Bureau. In 1833 Charbonneau accompanied an expedition led by Prince Maximilian, a German explorer and naturalist. In 1837 he survived a smallpox epidemic that wiped out 90 percent of the population of the Mandan villages, including an Indian woman he had taken as a wife. Charbonneau, who was in his seventies, married a fourteen-year-old Assiniboine girl later that year.

Records indicate that Toussaint Charbonneau died at Fort Mandan in 1843. He is best remembered as the comparatively less helpful and less likeable husband of Sacagawea, who is widely admired as a brave and resourceful young woman who provided valuable assistance to the Lewis and Clark Expedition. Their son Jean Baptiste Charbonneau went on to live a long, full life. He traveled to Europe and throughout the West before he died in 1866.

Sources

Fifer, Barbara. "Toussaint Charbonneau." Discovering Lewis and Clark, May 2006. Retrieved from http://www.lewis-clark.org/article/2664.

Hunter, Frances. "A Man of No Peculiar Merit: Toussaint Charbonneau." American Heroes Blog, May 16, 2011. Retrieved from https://franceshunter.wordpress.com/2011/05/16/a-man-of-no-peculiar-merit-toussaint-charbonneau/.

"Inside the Corps: Toussaint Charbonneau." *Lewis and Clark: The Journey of the Corps of Discovery.* PBS, 1997. Retrieved from http://www.pbs.org/lewisandclark/inside/tchar.html.

Nelson, W. Dale. *Interpreters with Lewis and Clark: The Story of Sacagawea and Toussaint Charbonneau.* University of North Texas Press, 2003.

"Toussaint Charbonneau." Jefferson National Expansion Memorial. U.S. National Park Service, n.d. Retrieved from http://www.nps.gov/jeff/learn/historyculture/toussaint-charbonneau.htm.

Notes

[1] Quoted in Hunter, Frances. "A Man of No Peculiar Merit: Toussaint Charbonneau." American Heroes Blog, May 16, 2011. Retrieved from https://franceshunter.wordpress.com/2011/05/16/a-man-of-no-peculiar-merit-toussaint-charbonneau/.

[2] Quoted in Hunter.

[3] Quoted in Hunter.

[4] Quoted in Fifer, Barbara. "Toussaint Charbonneau." Discovering Lewis and Clark, May 2006. Retrieved from http://www.lewis-clark.org/article/2664.

William Clark (1770-1838)
Co-Captain and Primary Mapmaker of the Corps of Discovery

William Clark was born on August 1, 1770, on his family's plantation in Caroline County, Virginia. William was the ninth of ten children born to John and Ann Clark. All of his older brothers served in the military during the Revolutionary War, including George Rogers Clark, who became famous as the commander of American forces in Kentucky. Although William was only a boy during the war, he followed in their footsteps by joining the U.S. military later in his life.

In 1784, when Clark was fourteen years old, his family moved from Virginia to Kentucky. At that time, Kentucky had not yet become a state, and it was considered to be on the western frontier of the newly established nation. His family built a new plantation called Mulberry Hill near present-day Louisville, and Clark quickly developed a deep love for the hills and forests that surrounded his home. Growing up on a farm, Clark did not receive an extensive formal education. However, he had many opportunities to learn practical skills that would prove useful both in his military career and in his later explorations, such as riding, hunting, and surveying.

Military Life

In 1789, at the age of nineteen, Clark joined the militia to help protect white settlers from Native Americans who resented their efforts to take control of the Ohio Valley. Three years later he enlisted in the U.S. Army and was quickly commissioned as an officer, eventually rising to the rank of captain. During his military service, Clark gained valuable leadership experience. The tall, strongly built redhead also developed skills in construction, topography, engineering, and survival in the wilderness. Clark "learned how to build forts, draw maps, lead pack trains through enemy country, and fight Indians on their ground,"[1] according to historian Irving W. Anderson.

Clark also became acquainted with a young ensign from Virginia named Meriwether Lewis during his time in the army. He was Lewis's commanding officer in the Chosen Rifle Company. The two men became close friends and formed deep bonds of mutual respect and trust. In 1796, upon learning that his father's health was failing, Clark retired from the army in order to run the family plantation. When his father died in 1799, Clark inherited the Mulberry Hill estate as well as York, an enslaved African-American man who had been his companion and servant since childhood.

In 1803 Clark received an unexpected letter from Lewis inviting him to sign on as co-captain of the Corps of Discovery. This military unit had been specially commissioned by President Thomas Jefferson to explore, map, and study the Louisiana Territory—a vast wilderness on the west side of the Mississippi River that the United States had just purchased from France. "In this enterprise," Lewis wrote, "its fatigues, its dangers, and its honors, believe me there is no man on earth with whom I should feel equal pleasure in sharing them as with yourself."[2] Clark happily accepted Lewis's offer and sold the plantation to his brother Jonathan. Before setting off on the adventure of a lifetime, Clark undertook additional study in astronomy and cartography, for he was to serve as the main navigator and mapmaker for the expedition.

The Journey of a Lifetime

After recruiting a crew of rugged outdoorsmen to form the Corps of Discovery, Clark was ready to join Lewis when he traveled past Kentucky on the Ohio River in the fall of 1803. Also embarking on the journey was York, who quickly came to be regarded as an equal member of the crew. The captains spent the winter conducting military training exercises at Camp Wood near St. Louis.

On May 14, 1804, the group set off on their historic journey. Their plan involved taking small boats up the Missouri River to its source, then proceeding on foot or on horseback over the Rocky Mountains. When they reached the other side, they hoped to find a westward-flowing river that would take them all the way to the Pacific Ocean. According to Jefferson's instructions, the goals of the expedition included recording scientific data about the plants, animals, weather, and landscape of the West; creating detailed maps of the region and identifying opportunities for commercial development; and establishing friendly relations with the Native American nations they encountered.

With his steady nature and firm leadership, Clark proved to be an excellent choice as co-captain. Throughout the trip, "Clark continued to keep careful compass records, measure distances, and produce detailed maps for areas between major landmarks,"[3] according to Anderson. He eventually combined his smaller field maps to complete the most accurate map of the Louisiana Territory available at that time. He also wrote descriptive notes indicating the locations of mineral deposits, plants, and animals that had potential commercial value. This information helped U.S. leaders in Washington understand what resources were contained in the land they had recently purchased.

Clark also proved to be highly skilled at Indian diplomacy. He observed and kept accurate records of Indian cultural and religious practices. He became close friends with Sacagawea, a young Shoshone woman who served as an interpreter and guide for the Corps of Discovery, and took an interest in her toddler son. At one point in the journey, when wild game was scarce, Clark even provided medical services to tribal members in exchange for food for his men. One of Clark's most significant contributions to the expedition was documenting their progress through letters and journals. Lewis was not terribly diligent with his correspondence, but Clark made up for it. Although his lack of formal education showed in his writing, he still provided invaluable insights into the experiences of the Corps of Discovery.

The Lewis and Clark Expedition succeeded in reaching the Pacific Ocean in late 1805. After spending the winter on the coast, they returned safely to St. Louis in September 1806. Their epic journey spanned two and a half years and covered 7,689 miles. Over the course of their travels, they mapped large sections of the unexplored West and described 200 previously unknown species of plants and animals.

After the Expedition

After returning from their expedition, Lewis and Clark received many honors and rewards for their service as captains of the Corps of Discovery. Jefferson gave both men 1,600 acres of land and double pay, and he appointed Clark as the superintendent of Indian Affairs for the territory of Louisiana. The Indian Department was plagued by poor administration, and Jefferson believed that Clark's proficiency in Indian diplomacy made him the perfect man to fill the position.

On January 5, 1808, Clark married Julia Hancock. The couple had five children before Julia died at the age of twenty-eight. Clark married Harriet Kennerly Radford shortly thereafter, and they had two more children. Upon the death of Sacagawea in 1812, Clark fulfilled a promise to her by adopting her two children and ensuring that her son, Jean Baptiste Charbonneau, received an education.

In 1813 Clark was appointed governor of the Missouri Territory. He served in this position until Missouri became a state in 1820. Although Clark's campaign to be elected governor was unsuccessful, he continued to serve as superintendent of Indian Affairs in St. Louis. In this position, Clark was largely responsible for maintaining a long peace between the United States and many Indian tribes. He negotiated treaties and helped warring tribes settle their disputes peacefully. The Indians respected "the red-haired chief" and trusted him to keep their best interests in mind. At the same time, though, Clark helped carry out the U.S. government's policy of removing Indians from land that was needed for white settlement. Clark died of natural causes on September 1, 1838, at the age of sixty-nine. His funeral procession stretched for more than a mile through the streets of St. Louis.

Sources

Anderson, Irving W. "Captain William Clark." *Lewis and Clark: The Journey of the Corps of Discovery*, PBS, 1997. Retrieved from http://www.pbs.org/lewisandclark/inside/wclar.html.

Buckley, Jay H. *William Clark: Indian Diplomat.* Norman: University of Oklahoma Press, 2008.

Foley, William E. *Wilderness Journey: The Life of William Clark.* Columbia: University of Missouri Press, 2004.

Jones, Landon Y. *William Clark and the Shaping of the West.* New York: Hill and Wang, 2004.

"William Clark." Lewis and Clark National Historic Trail, U.S. National Park Service, n.d. Retrieved from http://www.nps.gov/lecl/learn/historyculture/william-clark.htm.

Notes

[1] Anderson, Irving W. "Captain William Clark." *Lewis and Clark: The Journey of the Corps of Discovery*, PBS, 1997. Retrieved from http://www.pbs.org/lewisandclark/inside/wclar.html.

[2] Quoted in "William Clark." Lewis and Clark National Historic Trail, U.S. National Park Service, n.d. Retrieved from http://www.nps.gov/lecl/learn/historyculture/william-clark.htm.

[3] Anderson, "Captain William Clark."

John Colter (c. 1774-1813)
Explorer, Trapper, and Member of the Corps of Discovery

John Colter was born around 1774 in Augusta County, Virginia, to Joseph Colter and Ellen Shields Colter. Very little is known about his early life. The exact date of his birth is uncertain, and even the year is somewhat disputed by historians. In 1779, when Colter was approximately five years old, his family moved from Virginia to what is now Maysville, Kentucky. At that time, Kentucky had not yet become a state, and it was considered to be the western frontier of the United States. Colter's family built a home on the Ohio River, and Colter spent the rest of his childhood exploring the area's forests, hills, and streams. He developed skills as a woodsman and hunter and learned how to survive on his own in the wilderness.

Recruited for the Lewis and Clark Expedition

In 1803 Captain Meriwether Lewis traveled down the Ohio River from Pittsburgh on a keelboat. Lewis was on his way to meet his partner, Captain William Clark, near Louisville, Kentucky. The two men had been specially commissioned by President Thomas Jefferson to mount a U.S. military expedition to explore, map, and study the Louisiana Territory—a vast wilderness on the west side of the Mississippi River that the United States had just purchased from France. Lewis happened to come across Colter on his way to Louisville, and the young man expressed an interest in joining the group of rugged outdoorsmen that would become known as the Corps of Discovery. After Colter proved himself worthy in a brief trial period, Lewis signed him up for the mission.

Colter quickly emerged as one of the best hunters and scouts on the Lewis and Clark Expedition. The captains often relied on him to lead hunting parties into the wilderness to bring back game to feed the crew. They also called upon him to join special scouting missions. In August 1805, for instance, Colter was one of the men Clark chose to help him scout a trail through the Rocky Moun-

125

tains. They attempted to descend the Salmon River, but they discovered large rapids that proved to be impassable. Clark then trusted Colter to carry a message back to the main party describing their findings and warning Lewis to take a different route through the mountains.

In November 1805, when the Corps of Discovery successfully reached the Pacific Ocean, Colter was again chosen as a member of Clark's scouting team. They set off from their camp on the Columbia River and walked for miles along the coastline of present-day Washington. Clark wrote down details of the landscape to add to his maps and reports. After spending the winter on western edge of the continent, the Corps of Discovery began their return journey eastward in the spring of 1806. When the captains split up to explore different areas, Colter joined the group led by Lewis that ended up killing two Blackfeet Indians who attempted to steal their guns and horses.

As the expedition neared the Mandan villages on the Upper Missouri River, most of the crew was eager to return to civilization. Colter instead wanted to join Forrest Hancock and Joseph Dixon, a pair of trappers who were heading in the other direction to begin a wilderness journey of their own. "Colter, one of our men expressed a desire to join some trappers ... who offered to become shares with him and furnish traps etc.," Clark wrote on August 15, 1806. "The offer was a very advantageous one to him."[1] The captains agreed to grant Colter an early discharge from his military service on the condition that the rest of the crew promised to accompany them back to St. Louis. The other men agreed, and Colter turned around and headed back into the western wilderness.

Hunting, Trapping, and Running from the Blackfeet

Colter trapped with Hancock and Dixon along the Yellowstone River. The trapping was not terribly successful, however, and the Indians in the area were unfriendly toward the trio. Recurring disagreements among the three men finally convinced Colter to return to St. Louis in 1807. On his way back to civilization, though, Colter met Manuel Lisa, who was leading a trapping party to the Yellowstone River for the Missouri Fur Company. Colter joined this party and helped them erect a trading post at the mouth of the Bighorn River.

Lisa then sent Colter on a solo mission to track down the Crow Indians at their winter camp to inform them about the new trading post. This 500-mile trek took Colter through modern-day Yellowstone National Park. Colter is believed to have been the first white man to see Yellowstone's famous geysers and hot springs, as well as the Teton Mountains and Jackson Hole, Wyoming. When he returned and told the other trappers about his journey, however, they did not believe him and jokingly called the steaming valley he described "Colter's Hell."

In 1808 Colter joined the Crow and Flathead Indians on a trapping journey to Three Forks in Montana. The group was attacked by a hostile band of Blackfeet Indians. Colter's leg was injured during this battle, and he subsequently returned to Fort Manuel Lisa to heal. As it turned out, Colter would have more dangerous encounters with the Blackfeet in which he barely made it out alive. Once Colter's leg healed, he set off on a beaver trapping mission along the Jefferson Fork with another former member of the Corps of Discovery, John Potts. The Blackfeet found them, killed Potts in a shootout, and captured Colter.

The Blackfeet stripped Colter of his clothing, shoes, and other possessions and sent him running through the woods, while they pursued him as part of a deadly game. After approximately six miles, only one Indian still managed to keep up the chase. In a shrewd attempt to save his own life, Colter suddenly swung around to face his startled pursuer and wrestled away his spear. Colter then killed the Indian, took his blanket, and scrambled into a river. He hid in the water beneath a pile of driftwood until nightfall, when the other Blackfeet gave up the search. It took him eleven days to make the 200-mile trek back to Fort Manuel Lisa. His unrivaled wilderness skills enabled him to survive with only an Indian blanket for clothing and roots for food.

A Legendary Mountain Man

By 1810 Colter decided he was tired of being attacked by Indians and having to fight for his life. It had been six years since he had last experienced civilization, so he decided to move to St. Louis. While there, Colter met with Clark, who was serving as the superintendent of Indian affairs for the Louisiana Territory. Colter was able to give his former captain valuable new information about the West to include in his maps and journals from the expedition, which Clark was still preparing for publication.

With earnings from his work as an explorer and trapper, Colter bought a plot of land near present-day Dundee, Missouri. He built a cabin and worked his farm. He married a woman named Sally, and the couple had one son, Hiram. Colter still felt a longing for adventure, however, so he enlisted in the army when the United States declared war on Great Britain in 1812. He fell ill during his military service, and the legendary outdoorsman died of jaundice on November 22, 1813. Bernard DeVoto, a well-known historian of the West, described Colter as "the first of the mountain men."[2]

Sources

Harris, Burton. *John Colter: His Years in the Rockies.* New York: Scribner's, 1952.

"Inside the Corps: Private John Colter." *Lewis and Clark: The Journey of the Corps of Discovery.* PBS, 1997. Retrieved from http://www.pbs.org/lewisandclark/inside/jcolt.html.

Weiser, Kathy. "John Colter, Fearless Mountain Man." Legends of America, 2015. Retrieved from http://www.legendsofamerica.com/we-johncolter.html.

Yater, George H. "John Colter." Lewis and Clark in Kentucky, n.d. Retrieved from http://www.lewisand clarkinkentucky.org/people/colter_bio.shtml.

Notes

[1] Quoted in Yater, George H. "John Colter." Lewis and Clark in Kentucky, n.d. Retrieved from http://www.lewisandclarkinkentucky.org/people/colter_bio.shtml.

[2] Quoted in Yater.

George Drouillard (c. 1774-1810)
Interpreter and Hunter for the Lewis and Clark Expedition

George Drouillard was born near Windsor, Ontario, around 1774. His father was Pierre Drouillard, a French Canadian, and his mother was Asoundechris Flat Head, a Shawnee Indian. Although Drouillard was christened Pierre after his father, he was called George for his entire life. When Drouillard was a boy, he and his mother moved west to be near Shawnee family in Cape Giradeau, Missouri. Except for a few visits to his father's family in Detroit, Michigan, he spent the rest of his childhood in Missouri, which was considered the western frontier of the United States at that time.

Drouillard did not receive a formal education while he was living among the Shawnee Indians, but he did learn some very useful skills. He became fluent in several languages, including Shawnee, French, English, and Plains Indian Sign. He also became an excellent hunter and learned to live off the land and survive in the wilderness. As he grew up, Drouillard was described as being courageous, with good judgment and common sense. All of these skills and characteristics would prove very valuable when he met Captains Meriwether Lewis and William Clark in 1803.

Recruited to Join the Corps of Discovery

In November of that year, Drouillard was working as a translator at Fort Massac on the Ohio River in Illinois. Lewis arrived at the fort seeking recruits for a military expedition that had been specially commissioned by President Thomas Jefferson to explore, map, and study the Louisiana Territory—a vast wilderness on the west side of the Mississippi River that the United States had just purchased from France. Lewis was immediately impressed by Drouillard's hunting skills, as well as his knowledge of Indian customs and the sign language typically used by Plains Indians to communicate with members of other Native

American nations. Lewis was not sure how many languages or Indian nations the expedition would encounter, so he promptly offered Drouillard a position on his team as an interpreter.

Drouillard's first assignment involved transporting eight volunteers for the Corps of Discovery from Tennessee to Camp Wood near St. Louis, where the expedition would train during the winter of 1803-1804. Drouillard received a thirty-dollar advance in his pay for completing this task, which immediately showed Lewis that he was trustworthy. Drouillard also proved his value to the expedition as a tracker and scout. Whenever Lewis left the main party to explore or scout ahead, he always made sure that Drouillard was assigned to his team. When a member of the crew deserted his post in August 1804, Drouillard tracked him down and returned him to camp. In the process, he also located the Otoe Indians and brought back nine representatives of the tribe looking to make peace with the Americans.

During the winter of 1804-1805, Drouillard played an important role in establishing friendly relations with the Mandan Indians of the Upper Missouri River. His sign language skills helped the captains communicate with Mandan leaders, who were persuaded to allow the Corps of Discovery to camp among them. Throughout that frigid winter, Drouillard often led hunting groups into the wilderness. The game he brought back not only helped feed the crew, but also provided the captains with extra meat to trade with the Mandans for other provisions and supplies. In February 1805 Drouillard led a group of hunters downriver to collect some buffalo meat they had previously stored there. Along the way, his group was attacked by approximately 100 Sioux Indians. The badly outnumbered hunting team wisely decided not to fire upon the Sioux. While they escaped the encounter unharmed, however, the Indians made off with several horses and weapons.

To the Pacific and Back

As the Lewis and Clark Expedition continued westward to the Rocky Mountains in 1805, the captains realized that they needed to acquire horses to carry their gear over the steep mountain passes. In hopes of fulfilling this need, Drouillard accompanied Lewis on an advance scouting mission to locate the Shoshone Indians. When they found the Shoshone people in August, Drouillard's skills as an interpreter proved valuable once again. "The means I had of communicating with these people was by way of Drewyer," Lewis wrote on

August 14, "who understood perfectly the common language of gesticulation or signs which seems to be universally understood by all the Nations we have yet seen."[1] (Throughout their journey across the continent, Lewis and Clark were unable to spell Drouillard's last name correctly and referred to him in their journals as Drewyer.) Thanks to Drouillard and Sacagawea, who arrived later and recognized relatives among the Shoshone, the expedition obtained the horses they needed to cross the mountains.

Drouillard did not manage to establish friendly relations with every Native American group he met, though. On the return journey in 1806, he joined Lewis on a mission to explore the Marias River. While they were separated from the main group, they encountered some Blackfeet Indians. When the Blackfeet tried to steal the Americans' guns and horses, a skirmish ensued and two Indians were killed. Lewis and Drouillard recovered their own horses, and the other men in their group took a few more that belonged to the Blackfeet. Some historians point to this incident as one that made the Blackfeet hostile toward white men in the future.

When the Corps of Discovery returned safely to St. Louis in the fall of 1806, the captains trusted Drouillard to transport Lewis's initial report to the postmaster, so it could be forwarded to President Thomas Jefferson in Washington, D.C. Drouillard received a stipend of twenty-five dollars per month for his time with the expedition, making him the highest-paid member aside from Lewis and Clark. Lewis described Drouillard as "a man of much merit; he has been peculiarly useful from his knowledge of the common language of gesticulations, and his uncommon skill as a hunter and woodsman; those several duties he performed in good faith, and with an ardor which deserves the highest commendation. It was his fate also to have encountered, on various occasions, with either Captain Clark or myself, all the most dangerous scenes of the voyage, in which he uniformly acquitted himself with honor."[2]

Killed by the Blackfeet

Drouillard remained in the West after the expedition ended. In the spring of 1810, he accompanied a trapping crew led by Manuel Lisa to Three Forks, where Lisa wanted to construct a fur-trading post. While trapping in the area, Drouillard and his fellow hunters had several hostile encounters with the Blackfeet. While these incidents convinced the other men to stay close to camp, Drouillard refused to be intimidated and continued trapping beaver. "One of our company, a Shawnee half-breed named Druyer, the principal hunter of Lewis & Clark's party, went up the river one day and set his traps about a mile from the camp," recalled Thomas James, another member of the hunting party. "In the morning he returned alone and brought back six beavers. I warned him of his danger. 'I am too much of an Indian to be caught by Indians,' said he."[3]

In early May Drouillard and two other men set out once again to trap beaver. They were ambushed by the Blackfeet not long after leaving camp. Drouillard attempted to ward off his attackers, but he was outmatched. The rest of the trapping party found his dead body, along with those of his two companions, later that day. Drouillard was "mangled in a horrible manner," as James described the gruesome scene. "His head was cut off, his entrails torn out and his body hacked to pieces."[4]

The violent demise of Drouillard deprived the West of one of its most skilled outdoorsmen. "With the exception of Lewis and Clark themselves, perhaps no other member of the Corps of Discovery was more important to the success of the Lewis and Clark Expedition," wrote historian James J. Holmberg. "What further role George Drouillard would have played in the opening of the West will never be known. It is possible that he would have assumed a place beside those trappers and traders who are recorded in the annals of history as the most famous of the mountain men."[5]

Sources

Fifer, Barbara, and Joseph Mussulman. "George Drouillard." Discovering Lewis and Clark, 2006. Retrieved from http://www.lewis-clark.org/article/2708.

Holmberg, James J. "A Man of Much Merit." Lewis and Clark in Kentucky, 2000. Retrieved from http://www.lewisandclarkinkentucky.org/people/drouillard_bio.shtml.

"Inside the Corps: George Drouillard." *Lewis and Clark: The Journey of the Corps of Discovery*. PBS, 1997. Retrieved from http://www.pbs.org/lewisandclark/inside/gdrou.html.

Skarsten, M.O. *George Drouillard: Hunter and Interpreter for Lewis and Clark and Fur Trader, 1807-1810.* 2nd ed. Spokane, WA: Arthur H. Clark, 2003.

Notes

[1] Quoted in "Inside the Corps: George Drouillard." *Lewis and Clark: The Journey of the Corps of Discovery*. PBS, 1997. Retrieved from http://www.pbs.org/lewisandclark/inside/gdrou.html.

[2] Quoted in Holmberg, James J. "A Man of Much Merit." Lewis and Clark in Kentucky, 2000. Retrieved from http://www.lewisandclarkinkentucky.org/people/drouillard_bio.shtml.

[3] Quoted in Holmberg, "A Man of Much Merit."

[4] Quoted in Holmberg, "A Man of Much Merit."

[5] Holmberg, "A Man of Much Merit."

Patrick Gass (1771-1870)
Sergeant, Carpenter, and Journal Keeper for the Corps of Discovery

Patrick Gass was born on June 12, 1771, in Falling Springs, Pennsylvania. His parents, Benjamin and Mary McLene Gass, moved the family around a lot while Patrick was growing up and eventually settled in Maryland. Like many others of his day, Gass made up for his lack of formal education by developing extensive practical knowledge. During his youth, he often had to traverse the wilderness to reach the nearest town in order to buy food or other supplies. Since there were no roads, Gass learned to navigate through the hills, valleys, and forests by other means. He also gained experience in hunting, fishing, and other outdoor skills.

Joins the Army and Becomes a Carpenter

In 1789, when Gass was eighteen years old, he enlisted in the army. This marked the beginning of a military career that would extend, off and on, over twenty-five years. In 1792 Gass joined a unit that was assigned to protect white settlers from attacks by Native Americans who resented their growing presence on the western frontier. After receiving a discharge in 1794, Gass moved to Mercersberg, Pennsylvania, and began training as a carpenter. He served a two-year apprenticeship under an experienced carpenter, then worked on his own for three more years. In 1799, with the threat of a war with France looming, Gass enlisted in the army once more. He served under General Alexander Hamilton until 1800, when the tension with France eased and he was discharged.

Eager to resume his military career, Gass enlisted again the following year. This time he was stationed at Kaskaskia, Illinois, under Captain Russell Bissell. In 1803 President Thomas Jefferson commissioned a special U.S. military expedition to explore, map, and study the Louisiana Territory—a vast wilderness on the west side of the Mississippi River that the United States had just purchased from France. The leaders of this expedition, Captains Meriwether

Lewis and William Clark, recruited a company of rugged outdoorsmen with wilderness skills to form their Corps of Discovery.

The secretary of war ordered Bissell to select qualified volunteers from Fort Kaskaskia to join the Lewis and Clark Expedition. Gass immediately volunteered for the exciting yet dangerous mission to explore the western frontier. Reluctant to lose one of his best soldiers, though, Bissell initially denied Gass permission to join the expedition. Gass appealed to Lewis, who interceded on his behalf. On January 3, 1804, Gass reported for training at Camp Wood and officially became a member of the Corps of Discovery.

Promoted to Sergeant

Although Gass initially joined the expedition as a private, it was not long before he was promoted. On August 20, 1804, only a few months after the group launched their journey up the Missouri River, Sergeant Charles Floyd died from a ruptured appendix. Two days later, Lewis and Clark took a vote among the remaining crew members to elect a sergeant to take Floyd's place. The men elected Gass by a wide margin, and Lewis made his promotion official on August 26, 1804.

Gass's carpentry skills proved very valuable during the expedition. He led the construction of the three winter forts used by the Corps of Discovery: Camp Wood in Illinois; Fort Mandan in North Dakota; and Fort Clatsop in Oregon. His ability to build these structures properly helped protect the expedition members and their supplies from the harsh winter weather. Gass also demonstrated his woodworking skills by hollowing out tree trunks to make dugout canoes for the river portions of their journey. When the group reached the Great Falls of the Missouri River in 1805, Gass built wagons to haul the boats and gear over an eighteen-mile land portage.

The Lewis and Clark Expedition succeeded in reaching the Pacific Ocean in late 1805. The following spring, they launched their return journey eastward across the continent. When the captains decided to split the group into smaller parties in order to explore additional territory, they entrusted Gass to lead one of the crews. He successfully negotiated the Great Falls Portage in the opposite direction, then met up with the rest of the Corps of Discovery at the junction of the Yellowstone River. By the time the expedition made its triumphant return to St. Louis in September 1806, Gass was a tough and hardy frontiersman. He survived the twenty-eight month, 8,000-mile journey in good health and without any major accidents or injuries.

Publishes First Book about the Expedition

Gass was one of seven members of the Lewis and Clark Expedition who kept a journal of his experiences when exploring the West. After his return to civilization, many of Gass's friends and family members encouraged him to publish his journals. Recognizing the strong public interest in the epic journey, Gass went along with the idea. Gass knew that his writing skills were not well developed, however, so he asked David McKeehan, a bookstore proprietor, to help edit and prepare his journals for publication. "I have arranged and transcribed it for the press, supplying such geographical notes and other observations as I supposed would render it more useful and satisfactory to the reader,"[1] McKeehan said after the work was finished.

Lewis, who was preparing a report for Congress on the results of the expedition, was not pleased when he heard that Gass planned to publish his journals. On March 18, 1807, the captain posted a notice in the *National Intelligencer* warning people to wait for the official version of events and not accept "spurious" and "unauthorized" accounts of the journey. Nevertheless, Gass's book appeared in print a short time later. As the first work to satisfy the American people's desire for more details about the explorers' adventures, it sold well.

Most historians believe that Gass's book provides a fairly accurate account of the expedition. The main complaints about it involve the elegant, flowery writing style that was imposed by the editor. Although the changes made the text more accessible for readers, it differed dramatically from Gass's original journals and those of the other expedition members. As it turned out, Gass's book was the only account of the expedition that was available for many years. Lewis and Clark did not manage to publish their journals until 1814, by which time public interest in the expedition had faded.

Outlives Other Members of the Expedition

After publishing his journals, Gass returned to Fort Kaskaskia. He fought in the War of 1812 and was wounded in action when a splinter from a falling tree impaled one of his eyes. Although he received an honorable discharge and was sent home to recover, Gass was not yet ready to give up his military career. Despite having only one eye, in 1814 he fought at the Canadian border to protect the United States from a possible British invasion.

In the spring of 1815, at the age of forty-four, Gass left the army for the last time and settled in Mansfield, Pennsylvania. He held many different jobs over the years, including working at a brewery, hunting stray horses, and doing carpentry. In 1831, when Gass was sixty years old, he married twenty-year-old Maria Hamilton. The couple had seven children, although one died in infancy. In 1846 Gass's wife died of measles, leaving him to raise young children alone at the age of seventy-five.

Gass often struggled to keep his family fed on his military pension. Although he received 160 acres of land as a reward for his services with the Corps of Discovery, he lost the land due to his failure to pay taxes on it. At that point, he moved his family to Wellsburg, West Virginia, where he lived out the rest of his days. Gass died in April 1870 at the age of ninety-nine. He was the last surviving member of the historic Lewis and Clark Expedition.

Sources

Fifer, Barbara. "Patrick Gass." Discovering Lewis and Clark, 2006. Retrieved from http://www.lewis-clark
.org/article/2653.

"Inside the Corps: Sergeant Patrick Gass." Lewis and Clark: The Journey of the Corps of Discovery. PBS,
1997. Retrieved from http://www.pbs.org/lewisandclark/inside/pgass.html.

MacGregor, Carol Lynn, ed. *The Journals of Patrick Gass, Member of the Lewis and Clark Expedition.*
Missoula, MT: Mountain Press, 2000.

"Sergeant Patrick Gass." Virginia Center for Digital History, n.d. Retrieved from http://www2.vcdh.vir
ginia.edu/lewisandclark/biddle/biographies_html/gass.html.

Note

[1] Quoted in "Inside the Corps: Sergeant Patrick Gass." Lewis and Clark: The Journey of the Corps of Discovery. PBS, 1997. Retrieved from http://www.pbs.org/lewisandclark/inside/pgass.html.

Thomas Jefferson (1743-1826)
President Who Organized the Lewis and Clark Expedition

Thomas Jefferson was born on April 13, 1743, on Shadwell Plantation in Albemarle County, Virginia. He was the third of ten children born to Peter Jefferson, a successful planter and surveyor, and Jane Randolph Jefferson, who came from a wealthy family of high social standing. As a boy, Thomas learned to ride horses and enjoyed exploring the forests and countryside of the nearby Blue Ridge Mountains.

Throughout his youth, Jefferson received a first-class education from private tutors and boarding schools. Filled with intellectual curiosity, he studied Latin, Greek, history, science, mathematics, philosophy, literature, and violin. At the age of sixteen Jefferson enrolled in the College of William and Mary in Williamsburg, Virginia. He studied law and read a wide variety of political works. Jefferson graduated with honors in 1762, and he was admitted to the Virginia bar five years later.

By this time Jefferson had inherited 5,000 acres of land and dozens of enslaved African Americans upon the death of his father. He designed and built a home, Monticello, on a scenic hilltop and filled its library with books. In 1772 Jefferson married Martha Wayles Skelton, a young widow. The marriage produced six children, only two of whom survived to adulthood. Jefferson was distraught when, after ten happy years together, his beloved wife died. He never remarried.

Author of the Declaration of Independence

As a practicing attorney, Jefferson quickly gained respect for his sharp legal mind and outstanding writing skills. He also became involved in local politics, representing Albemarle County in the Virginia House of Burgesses. By this time the relationship between Great Britain and its thirteen American colonies had been deteriorating for years. Colonial leaders resented the high taxes imposed by the British parliament and wanted greater freedom to govern themselves. In 1775 the longstanding disputes erupted into the Revolutionary War.

137

Jefferson represented Virginia in the Continental Congress, a group of prominent colonial leaders who met to discuss options for handling the conflict with Great Britain. When the group decided that the American colonies should formally withdraw from the British Empire and form a separate nation, they called upon Jefferson to draft the Declaration of Independence. This historic document, which was issued on July 4, 1776, expressed the political philosophy of the United States. It famously proclaimed "that all men are created equal, that they are endowed by their Creator with certain unalienable Rights, that among these are Life, Liberty and the pursuit of Happiness."

Jefferson returned to Virginia and served as governor for two years during the Revolution. After the United States won its independence in 1783, he went to France as a representative of the new nation. While there, he studied European culture and sent books, statues, plants, and other objects of intellectual interest back to Monticello. Jefferson also corresponded with his close friend James Madison and other U.S. leaders who were forging the U.S. Constitution. Jefferson sought to balance the power of the federal government by protecting the individual liberties of citizens. He pushed Madison to add the Bill of Rights, a series of ten amendments that guaranteed such fundamental rights as freedom of speech, religion, and assembly.

Third President of the United States

Jefferson returned from France to serve as secretary of state under President George Washington from 1790 to 1793. In 1796 he became the presidential candidate of the Democratic-Republican Party, which opposed a strong central government and supported the rights of states. Although Jefferson lost a close election to Federalist candidate John Adams, he became vice president under his political rival according to constitutional rules that were later changed. In 1800 he defeated Adams in a bitterly contested election to become the third president of the United States.

Upon taking office, Jefferson took several steps to minimize the influence of the federal government, such as reducing the number of government employees, cutting military spending, and eliminating an unpopular tax on whiskey. In 1803, however, he overstepped the powers granted to the federal government in the Constitution by purchasing the vast Louisiana Territory from France for $15 million. Jefferson had a lifelong fascination with the unexplored lands west of the Mississippi River, and he longed to expand the fledgling nation's territorial holdings across the continent of North America. He believed that laying claim to these western lands would increase national security, promote economic development, and establish the United States as a world power. These factors helped Jefferson overcome his concerns about the legality of the Louisiana Purchase, which doubled the size of the United States and shifted the nation's western border all the way from the Mississippi River to the Rocky Mountains.

Jefferson immediately commissioned a scientific expedition to explore and map the new territory. He chose Captain Meriwether Lewis, his personal secretary and protégé, to lead the mission. Lewis invited William Clark, a military officer and Kentucky frontiersman, to serve as co-captain. Between 1804 and 1806, the Lewis and Clark Expedition took small boats up the Missouri River to its source, crossed over the Rocky Mountains, followed the Columbia River westward to the Pacific Ocean, and then returned safely to St. Louis, Missouri. In accordance with Jefferson's instructions, the captains and their Corps of Discovery recorded scientific data about the plants, animals, weather, and landscape of the West; created detailed maps of the region and identified opportunities for commercial development; and established friendly relations with many of the Native American nations they encountered. The successful expedition answered many of Jefferson's questions about the West and helped open the region for American settlement.

Jefferson easily won reelection in 1804. During his second term in office, he struggled to prevent the United States from becoming involved in a war between England and France. Remaining neutral became more difficult when the European powers interfered with American shipping on the Atlantic Ocean. Jefferson attempted to solve the problem by suspending trade with both of the warring nations. This policy had devastating effects on the U.S. economy, however, and was deeply unpopular with the American people.

A Controversial Personal Life

In 1809 Jefferson left office and retired to Monticello, where he spent his time pursuing intellectual interests in science, natural history, philosophy, and literature. A lifelong proponent of public education, Jefferson also devoted himself to founding the University of Virginia. He organized its charter, obtained land for its campus, designed its buildings, and planned its curriculum. Late in his life, Jefferson sold his extensive collection of books to the federal government, which provided the foundation for the Library of Congress.

For modern-day scholars, however, a shadow hangs over Jefferson's remarkable contributions as a Founding Father of the United States. From the time he reached the age to legally inherit property, Jefferson owned slaves. In addition to Monticello and other estates, his "property" included around 200 human beings. He only freed two enslaved people during his lifetime, and five others upon his death. Although the enslavement of African Americans was legal in Virginia at that time, critics find it difficult to reconcile Jefferson's private behavior with his public support for freedom, equality, and individual rights. Complicating the debate over Jefferson's slave ownership are questions concerning his relationship with Sally Hemings, one of his enslaved African-American servants. Many historians believe that Jefferson had a long-term sexual relationship with Hemings after his wife's death. Recent DNA evidence suggests that he fathered several children by her, and records indicate that these children were also enslaved.

Jefferson died on July 4, 1826, at the age of eighty-three. His death came exactly fifty years after the signing of the Declaration of Independence and on the same day that John Adams died. Late in life, the former political rivals had become close friends and carried on a lively correspondence. "A philosopher and a scientist, a naturalist and a historian, Jefferson was a man of the Enlightenment, always looking forward, consumed by the quest for knowledge," biographer Jon Meacham wrote. "More than any of the other early presidents … Jefferson believed in the possibilities of humanity. He dreamed big but understood that dreams become reality only when their champions are strong enough and wily enough to bend history to their purposes. Broadly put, philosophers think; politicians maneuver. Jefferson's genius was that he was both and could do both, often simultaneously."[1]

Sources

Freidel, Frank, and Hugh Sidey. "The Presidents of the United States of America: Thomas Jefferson." WhiteHouse.gov, 2006. Retrieved from https://www.whitehouse.gov/1600/presidents/thomas jefferson.

Malone, Dumas. *Jefferson and His Time* (6 vols.). Charlottesville: University of Virginia Press, 2006.

"Thomas Jefferson." Miller Center of Public Affairs, University of Virginia, n.d. Retrieved from http://millercenter.org/president/jefferson.

"Thomas Jefferson: A Brief Biography." Monticello.org, n.d. Retrieved from .

"Thomas Jefferson and the West." Library of Congress, n.d. Retrieved from http://www.loc.gov/exhibits/jefferson/jeffwest.html.

Note

[1] Meacham, Jon. *Thomas Jefferson: The Art of Power*. New York: Random House, 2012, p. xx.

Meriwether Lewis (1774-1809)
Explorer, Naturalist, and Co-Captain of the
Corps of Discovery

Meriwether Lewis was born on August 18, 1774, in Albemarle County, Virginia. His parents, William Lewis and Lucy Meriwether Lewis, owned the Locust Hill plantation, where Lewis spent his childhood years. When Lewis was five years old, his father died in an accident. William Lewis was away serving in the colonial army during the American Revolution. While traveling home to see his family on a military leave, he and his horse fell into a frigid stream. Future president Thomas Jefferson, a friend of the family who owned a neighboring estate, took the fatherless boy under his wing at that time.

Lewis's mother soon married a retired military officer by the name of John Marks. Marks relocated the family to Georgia, and Lewis spent several formative years of his childhood there. He loved exploring the wilderness around his new home. By the age of eight he would often hunt alone, even at night and during the winter months. He also developed a strong interest in the plants common to that area. From his mother, Lewis learned how to recognize different herbs and use them as medicine. He also had his first encounters with Native Americans during his time in Georgia. He met Cherokee Indians who lived nearby and became fascinated by their language and culture. Even as a young man, Lewis found himself acting as spokesman for the interests of the Cherokee among white settlers.

When Lewis was in his teens, he elected to return to his family home at Locust Hill to pursue a formal education. He received instruction from several prestigious tutors, including one man who had taught Jefferson and two other future presidents. After completing his education, Lewis managed his family plantation for a few years. He also borrowed books from Jefferson to learn more about natural history and other subjects. Lewis came to share his mentor's thirst for knowledge and fascination with the West. He also learned many scientific skills, such as how to preserve plant and animal specimens and how to navigate by the stars.

Chosen to Lead Expedition

When Lewis was twenty years old, he enlisted in the army to help suppress an anti-tax protest known as the Whiskey Rebellion. Lewis's military service brought him into further contact with Native Americans, which deepened his interest in and understanding of them. In 1795 Lewis was assigned to a frontier rifle company commanded by Captain William Clark. The two men developed a high level of trust and respect for one another. By 1800 Lewis had been promoted to captain.

The following year, when Jefferson took office as president of the United States, he invited Lewis to Washington, D.C., to serve as his personal secretary. Lewis quickly accepted the prestigious position. Although Lewis's poor spelling and grammar and stiff manners made him a less-than-ideal secretary, he soon learned that Jefferson had a much larger role in mind for him. The president believed that Lewis possessed many of the qualities needed to lead an expedition into the unexplored territory of the West, including courage, wisdom, outdoor skills, frontier experience, and good health. Jefferson described his protégé as "brave, prudent, habituated to the woods and familiar with Indian manners and character."[1]

In 1803 the Jefferson administration made a deal to purchase the vast Louisiana Territory from France. The Louisiana Purchase doubled the size of the United States and shifted the nation's western border from the Mississippi River to the Rocky Mountains. The president immediately began organizing a scientific expedition to explore and map the newly acquired lands. He asked Lewis to lead it, and the young captain jumped at the opportunity. According to Jefferson's instructions, the goals of the expedition included recording scientific data about the plants, animals, weather, and landscape of the West; creating detailed maps of the region and identifying opportunities for commercial development; searching for a navigable water route across the continent; and establishing friendly relations with the Native American nations they encountered.

To prepare for the journey, Lewis received instruction from renowned experts in natural history, botany, zoology, astronomy, and other subjects. He also read books written by explorers who had visited the West and studied their sketchy maps of the region. While he completed his training, Lewis decided to add a co-leader to the expedition whose skills would complement his own. He chose William Clark, his former commanding officer.

Co-Captain of the Corps of Discovery

After gathering all the necessary supplies, Lewis traveled down the Ohio River in the fall of 1803 to meet Clark and a crew of experienced soldiers and outdoorsmen in Kentucky. The group then made their way to St. Louis, Missouri, which would be the starting point for their legendary adventure into the unknown western wilderness. On May 14, 1804, the Lewis and Clark Expedition launched their small boats on the Missouri River. Their plan involved following the river upstream to its source, then proceeding on foot or on horseback over the Rocky Mountains. When they reached the other side, they hoped to find a westward-flowing river that would take them all the way to the Pacific Ocean.

Throughout their twenty-eight month, 7,689-mile journey, Lewis and Clark proved to be a highly effective leadership team. Although the two men had very different temperaments, their strengths complemented each other and they got along well. As the more scientific-minded of the two, Lewis often walked along the shore collecting samples of rocks, soil, plants, and seeds. Clark, meanwhile, usually took charge of the boats and spent his time recording distances and landmarks to create maps. "Their relationship ranks high in the realm of notable human associations," a commemorative site noted. "It was a rare example of two men of noble heart and conscience sharing responsibilities for the conduct of a dangerous enterprise without ever losing each other's respect or loyalty. Despite frequent stress, hardships, and other conditions that could easily have bred jealousy, mistrust or contempt, they proved to be self-effacing brothers in command and leadership."[2]

Lewis had a number of close calls and dramatic, near-death experiences during the expedition. One time he fell down the face of a cliff and barely stopped his descent by wedging his knife into a rock crevice. Another time Lewis accidentally poisoned himself by tasting a mineral he discovered on the trail. Luckily, he realized his mistake quickly and saved himself by taking medicine to induce vomiting. On the return journey in 1806, Lewis was involved in a dangerous confrontation with a group of Blackfeet Indians who tried to steal the Americans' horses and guns. He ended up killing one of the Indians by shooting him in the chest. A short time later, one of Lewis's men mistook him for an elk while hunting and shot the captain in the upper thigh. None of these life-threatening events deterred him from the task at hand, however, and he was still able to carry out his mission.

The Lewis and Clark Expedition succeeded in reaching the Pacific Ocean in late 1805. After spending the winter on the coast, they returned safely to St.

Louis on September 23, 1806. Over the course of their travels, they mapped large sections of the unexplored West and described 200 previously unknown species of plants and animals. Lewis also accomplished his diplomatic mission, meeting with representatives of dozens of Native American nations and establishing trade relations between them and the United States. "In obedience to your orders we have penetrated the continent of North America to the Pacific Ocean," Lewis wrote to Jefferson, "and sufficiently explored the interior of the country to affirm with confidence that we have discovered the most practicable route which does exist across the continent by means of the navigable branches of the Missouri and Columbia Rivers."[3]

Struggles to Resume Ordinary Life

The return of the Corps of Discovery was widely celebrated, and Lewis was greeted as a hero for leading the successful expedition. He received double pay for his services, as well as a generous reward of 1,600 acres of land. Jefferson also appointed Lewis as governor of the Louisiana Territory. Despite all the acclaim, however, Lewis struggled to adjust to the demands of civilization upon his return from the wilderness. Jefferson encouraged him to publish a complete report of the expedition as quickly as possible, but Lewis seemed unable to organize the information and prepare his journals for publication. He also proved to be an ineffective governor, failing to communicate with federal authorities and refusing to cooperate with local leaders. His poor performance put a strain on his relationship with Jefferson.

Although Lewis had always been moody, he sunk into depression after the expedition ended. He hoped to get married, but two different women rejected his proposals. Clark and Jefferson both reached out to him, but Lewis increasingly turned to alcohol to try to cope with his problems. In the fall of 1809, Lewis decided to travel to Washington to meet with government officials and caught a riverboat through Tennessee. On October 11 he stopped at a roadhouse along the Natchez Trace, south of Nashville. It was there that Lewis died of gunshot wounds to the forehead and chest, at the age of thirty-five. His friends, aware that he had made attempts on his own life in the previous months, believed that he had committed suicide. But the mysterious circumstances surrounding his violent death have led some historians to think that he may have been murdered.

Lewis was buried in Tennessee. Jefferson chose a Latin inscription for his tombstone that translates to "I died young: but thou, O Good Republic, live out my years for me with better fortune."[4] Despite the tragic end to his heroic life, Lewis is remembered as "undoubtedly the greatest pathfinder this country has ever known."[5] Historian Stephen E. Ambrose paid respects to the legendary explorer by declaring that "If I were ever in a life-threatening situation, whether in armed combat, or in a ship sinking at sea, or an airplane in difficulty, Meriwether Lewis is the man I would want as my leader."[6]

Sources

Ambrose, Stephen E. *Undaunted Courage: Meriwether Lewis, William Clark, and the Opening of the American West.* New York: Simon and Schuster, 1996.

Dillon, Richard. *Meriwether Lewis: A Biography.* 3rd ed. Lafayette, CA: Great West Books, 2003.

"Inside the Corps: Captain Meriwether Lewis." *Lewis and Clark: The Journey of the Corps of Discovery.* PBS, 1997. Retrieved from http://www.pbs.org/lewisandclark/inside/mlewi.html.

"Meriwether Lewis." Virginia Center for Digital History, n.d. Retrieved from http://www2.vcdh.virginia.edu/lewisandclark/biddle/biographies_html/lewis.html.

"Meriwether Lewis (1774-1809)." *New Perspectives on the West.* PBS, 2001. Retrieved from http://www.pbs.org/weta/thewest/people/i_r/lewis.htm.

Notes

[1] Quoted in "Inside the Corps: Captain Meriwether Lewis." *Lewis and Clark: The Journey of the Corps of Discovery.* PBS, 1997. Retrieved from http://www.pbs.org/lewisandclark/inside/mlewi.html.

[2] Quoted in "Meriwether Lewis & William Clark." Lewis and Clark's Historic Trail. *Yankton Daily Press and Dakotan,* 2015. Retrieved from http://lewisclark.net/biography.

[3] Quoted in "Inside the Corps: Captain Meriwether Lewis."

[4] Quoted in "Meriwether Lewis & William Clark."

[5] Quoted in "Inside the Corps: Captain Meriwether Lewis."

[6] Dillon, Richard. *Meriwether Lewis: A Biography.* 3rd ed. Lafayette, CA: Great West Books, 2003, p. x.

Sacagawea (c. 1788-1812)
Interpreter and Guide for the Lewis and Clark Expedition

Sacagawea, whose name means "bird woman," was born in the Shoshone Indian nation in the area of the Bitterroot Mountains that is now Idaho. Although the exact date of her birth is unknown, historians estimate that it occurred around 1788. When Sacagawea was around twelve years old, she was kidnapped by an enemy tribe. The Hidatsa Indians had acquired rifles by bartering with white traders, so it was very difficult for the Shoshones to defend against Hidatsa attacks. As a result, the Hidatsas raided and pillaged Shoshone villages regularly, stealing their goods and killing or kidnapping their people.

The Hidatsa raiding party took Sacagawea and several other young women back to their villages on the Upper Missouri River in North Dakota. They sold Sacagawea and another Shoshone captive to Toussaint Charbonneau, a French-Canadian fur trader who had lived among them and the neighboring Mandan Indians for many years and adopted their way of life. Charbonneau considered the two women his wives.

Sacagawea did not receive a formal education, but she developed valuable outdoor knowledge and survival skills. She learned to recognize countless plants that grew in the region, for instance, and she knew which ones were edible and which could be used as medicine. She also became fluent in both the Shoshone and Hidatsa languages. Finally, Sacagawea grew familiar with the landscape features and Indian trails that surrounded both her Shoshone homeland and the Hidatsa-Mandan villages.

Hired as an Interpreter by Lewis and Clark

In the late fall of 1804, when Sacagawea was around sixteen years old, a group of American explorers arrived at the Mandan village near where she lived with her husband. The leaders, Captains Meriwether Lewis and William Clark, explained that they were on a scientific expedition sponsored by the U.S. government. They planned to continue up the Missouri River to its source, cross over the Rocky

Mountains, and then follow the Columbia River all the way to the Pacific Ocean. Since the arrival of winter was near, however, they asked to camp among the Indians for a few months before resuming their journey. The expedition members erected their winter quarters, Fort Mandan, just outside the village. They exchanged regular visits with the Indians and traded for food and other items they needed.

During that winter, Lewis and Clark met Toussaint Charbonneau, who offered to accompany the expedition and serve as a translator. Although the captains were not overly impressed with Charbonneau, they believed that his pregnant wife, Sacagawea, might be helpful to them. Lewis and Clark heard that her Shoshone people lived near the headwaters of the Missouri and had large herds of horses. They knew that they would need to acquire horses to carry their equipment and supplies over the mountains. The explorers believed that Sacagawea could help them locate and communicate with the Shoshone. They hired both Charbonneau and his young wife to serve as interpreters and guides for the expedition.

On February 11, 1805, Sacagawea gave birth to a son, Jean Baptiste Charbonneau. Lewis, who had undergone some medical training in preparation for the journey, assisted with the birth. He wrote in his journal that Sacagawea's labor was "tedious and violent with pain" until he gave her a potion of dried rattlesnake mixed with water. "Whether this medicine was truly the cause or not I shall not undertake to determine," Lewis noted, but "she had not taken it more than ten minutes before she brought forth."[1] Two months later, the Lewis and Clark Expedition set out from the Mandan villages with three new members: Charbonneau, Sacagawea, and baby Jean Baptiste, who made most of the journey strapped to his mother's back.

Finds Her Shoshone People

Sacagawea quickly became a respected and valued member of the crew. She assisted with many daily tasks, such as gathering and preparing food. In contrast to her husband, she also remained calm in dangerous situations. When a sudden storm nearly capsized their boat, for instance, Sacagawea bailed water and collected items that washed overboard, while Charbonneau panicked and cried for help. Without her clear-headedness and bravery, important equipment and documents would have been lost.

Sacagawea also aided Lewis and Clark by serving as an interpreter and helping them communicate with the Native Americans they encountered. At times the process of translation became very complicated. Communicating with the Salish Indians of the Bitterroot Valley, for instance, required Sacagawea to translate the complicated Salish language to Hidatsa, which Charbonneau understood. He then translated the Hidatsa to French, and another crew member translated the French to English for Lewis and Clark.

On August 17, 1805, Lewis and Clark met with the Shoshone. They asked Sacagawea to serve as an interpreter as they negotiated to obtain much-needed horses. To her amazement, Sacagawea recognized the Shoshone chief as her brother Cameahwait. She had not seen her family for many years, so the siblings had a joyous reunion. Sacagawea's participation in the negotiations increased the level of trust between the explorers and the Shoshone, and Cameahwait agreed to provide the group with thirty horses to transport their supplies over the Bitterroot Mountains.

Sacagawea's presence among the American explorers also helped keep them safe from Indian attacks. Native Americans who encountered the expedition believed that a war party would never include a woman and a baby, so they approached Lewis and Clark with curiosity rather than hostility. "The wife of [Charbonneau] ... reconciles all the Indians, as to our friendly intentions," Clark wrote. "A woman with a party of men is a token of peace."[2]

In the late fall of 1805 the crew succeeded in reaching the Pacific Coast. When the captains took a vote among the expedition members to decide where to make camp, they allowed Sacagawea to participate. This event was noteworthy because women did not receive voting rights in the United States until a century later. During that winter, the group heard that a whale had been beached on the shore. Lewis and Clark organized a group of men to hike several miles to the whale carcass and collect meat and blubber to feed the crew. Sacagawea firmly insisted that she be included. "The Indian woman was very importunate to be permitted to go, and was therefore indulged," Lewis wrote. "She observed that she had traveled a long way with us to see the great waters, and that now that monstrous fish was also to be seen, she thought it was very hard she could not be permitted to see either."[3]

Visits St. Louis

In the spring of 1806 the Lewis and Clark Expedition launched their return journey eastward across the continent. On August 14, 1806, they arrived back at the Hidatsa-Mandan villages. This marked the end of the journey for Sacagawea.

The captains paid Charbonneau $500 for his services and bid farewell to Sacagawea and little Jean Baptiste, whom Clark fondly called Pomp or Pompey. Sacagawea did not receive any direct payment or reward for her loyal service to the expedition. Clark later wrote to Charbonneau telling him that Sacagawea deserved far more than she got for her valuable assistance to the Corps of Discovery.

Along with other expedition members, the U.S. government granted Charbonneau title to 320 acres of land. In 1810 Sacagawea and her husband moved to St. Louis to claim the property. Sacagawea reportedly adopted a western style of dress at this time. Charbonneau did not enjoy the farming lifestyle, however, so the family did not remain in St. Louis for long. In 1811 Charbonneau sold the land to Clark for 100 dollars, and he and Sacagawea moved back west to Fort Manuel Lisa in South Dakota. They left Jean Baptiste with Clark, who offered to oversee his education.

Sacagawea gave birth to a daughter, Lisette, shortly after their arrival at Fort Manuel Lisa. Records indicate that Sacagawea died there of typhus on December 22, 1812, at the age of twenty-five. Eight months later, Clark legally adopted both of her children. Sacagawea's short yet remarkable life has fascinated people for two centuries. Lewis and Clark both commended her highly in their journals, and some experts argue that the expedition would not have succeeded without her. Sacagawea has been honored with statues, memorials, and historic sites across the country, and in 2000 her image was featured on a U.S. dollar coin.

Sources

"Early Life" and "Later Years and Death." Sacagawea Historical Society, n.d. Retrieved from http://www.sacagawea-biography.org/.

Howard, Harold P. *Sacajawea.* Norman: University of Oklahoma Press, 1979.

Hunsaker, Joyce Badgley. *Sacagawea Speaks: Beyond the Shining Mountains with Lewis and Clark.* Guilford, CT: TwoDot, 2001.

"Inside the Corps: Sacagawea." *Lewis and Clark: The Journey of the Corps of Discovery.* PBS, 1997. Retrieved from http://www.pbs.org/lewisandclark/inside/saca.html.

"Sacagawea." Lewis and Clark National Historic Trail. U.S. National Park Service, n.d. Retrieved from http://www.nps.gov/lecl/learn/historyculture/sacagawea.htm.

"Sacagawea (1786-1812)." National Women's History Museum. Retrieved from .

Notes

[1] Quoted in "Early Life." Sacagawea Historical Society, n.d. Retrieved from http://www.sacagawea-biography.org/biography-early-life/.

[2] Quoted in "Sacagawea." Lewis and Clark National Historic Trail. U.S. National Park Service, n.d. Retrieved from http://www.nps.gov/lecl/learn/historyculture/sacagawea.htm.

[3] Quoted in "Inside the Corps: Sacagawea." *Lewis and Clark: The Journey of the Corps of Discovery.* PBS, 1997. Retrieved from http://www.pbs.org/lewisandclark/inside/saca.html.

York (c. 1770-c. 1822)
Enslaved African-American Member of the Corps of Discovery

York was born in Caroline County, Virginia, around 1770. Some historians believe that his first name may have been Ben. York was descended from Africans who were forcibly brought to the American colonies to serve as slaves for white settlers. Like his parents, Old York and Rose, he was considered the property of John Clark and lived on his plantation. Since York was around the same age as Clark's youngest son, William, the two boys grew up together. York became William Clark's servant and companion.

In 1784 the Clark family moved to Kentucky, which was considered to be the western frontier of the newly established United States. Over the years, William Clark developed wilderness skills and served in the military. When John Clark died in 1799, he left York and several other enslaved African Americans to his son. York's life changed dramatically in 1803, when William Clark received an unexpected letter from his friend Meriwether Lewis inviting him to sign on as co-captain of the Corps of Discovery. This military unit had been specially commissioned by President Thomas Jefferson to explore, map, and study the Louisiana Territory—a vast wilderness on the west side of the Mississippi River that the United States had just purchased from France.

Member of the Corps of Discovery

On October 26, 1803, York accompanied Clark, Lewis, and a group of rugged outdoorsmen under their command as they set off on their historic journey across the continent. Unlike the other members of the group, who volunteered for the mission, York had no choice. As the property of William Clark, he had to do whatever his owner told him to do. But York quickly established himself as a valuable member of the crew. He performed his share of the duties required for the Corps of Discovery to reach the Pacific Ocean and return safely, and he was generally treated as an equal by the other men.

York is mentioned regularly in the journals kept by Lewis, Clark, and other expedition members. For instance, he performed work assignments to help build the winter quarters at Camp Wood in late 1803. The following spring, when the group began moving up the Missouri River, York helped gather and prepare food. On June 5 Clark wrote that "my servant York swam to the sand bar to gather greens for our dinner and returned with a sufficient quantity."[1] York also joined Clark and other expedition members in hunting for wild game. His participation in this task is noteworthy because laws in place at that time prohibited slaves from carrying guns. York also assisted in cooking, carrying supplies during portages, and scouting ahead on the trail.

Various journal entries also suggest that York played a role in attending to expedition members who got sick or injured. When Sergeant Charles Floyd became gravely ill in August 1804, Clark wrote, "every man attentive to him, York principally."[2] On another occasion, a sudden storm caused a dangerous flash flood that nearly washed Clark, Sacagawea, her husband Toussaint Charbonneau, and their son Jean Baptiste into the Missouri River. Without regard for his own safety, York searched for them at the height of the storm. Clark wrote that when his small group reached the rim of the canyon safely, "I found my servant in search of us greatly agitated, for our welfare."[3]

Since many of the Indian nations the expedition encountered had never seen an African American before, they tended to find York fascinating. York seemed to enjoy the attention he received, as he attracted even more by playing jokes on the Native American children. When the expedition camped among the Arikaras, for instance, Clark recorded that York "made himself more terrible in their view than I wished him to do, telling them that before I caught him he was wild and lived upon people, young children was very good eating."[4]

At times, York's presence among the white explorers aided the captains' efforts to establish peaceful relations with the Indians. When the group reached the headwaters of the Missouri River in August 1805 and needed to acquire horses to cross over the Rocky Mountains, Lewis scouted ahead of the main party and located the Shoshone Indians. They did not trust him, however, and prepared to leave the area. Lewis convinced them to wait for the main party to arrive by telling them that it included a man "who was black and had short curling hair."[5] Curious to meet this unusual person, the Shoshone stayed and eventually supplied the horses the expedition so desperately needed.

First African American Allowed to Vote

When the Lewis and Clark Expedition succeeded in reaching the Pacific Ocean in late 1805, York became the first African American to have crossed the North American continent. As winter closed in on the Corps of Discovery, the captains took a vote to decide where they should make camp. The results of the vote, which were recorded in their journals, show that both York and Sacagawea were allowed to participate. Historians have noted that their inclusion as equal members of the government-sponsored expedition may have marked the first time that a black man or a woman exercised voting rights in the United States.

When the captains divided the group on the return journey eastward in 1806, York accompanied Clark's crew that explored the Yellowstone River. In keeping with the practice of naming geographical features after members of the expedition, Clark named an empty streambed "York's Dry River." Earlier in the trip, the captains had called a braided section of the Missouri River "York's Eight Islands."

On September 23, 1806, the expedition made its triumphant return to St. Louis. Residents of the town flocked to greet the explorers, whom they had long given up hope of seeing again. Apparently York carried himself as a member of the crew, rather than as a slave, which surprised some of the people on shore. One observer noted that "Even the negro York, who was the body servant of Clark, despite his ebony complexion, was looked upon with decided partiality, and received his share of adulation."[6]

Sad Life Post-Expedition

After the expedition concluded, the other members of the Corps of Discovery received payment for their services and a gift of land as a reward for their accomplishments. But York received nothing and returned to a life of enslavement. He asked Clark to grant his freedom in exchange for the extraordinary services he had performed, but Clark refused. In fact, Clark grew increasingly frustrated with York for behaving as if he deserved better and should be treated equally. In a letter to his brother written in December 1808, Clark explained that "I did wish to do well by him. But as he has got such a notion about freedom…. I do not think with him, that his services have been so great or my situation would permit me to liberate him."[7] Clark even considered selling York to a cruel owner in an effort to change his attitude.

Clark took York with him to St. Louis when he became superintendent of Indian affairs for the Louisiana Territory. He eventually allowed York to return to Kentucky so he could be closer to his wife, who lived on a neighboring plantation. Finally, at least ten years after the expedition ended, Clark granted York his freedom and gave him a wagon and a team of horses. York then started a business hauling goods in Kentucky and Tennessee. Even as a free man, though, he still faced racial prejudice and discrimination. "Think about being an African-American free man in a world surrounded by race and slavery. And by racial attitudes that say freedom may only be what is written on a piece of paper," historian James Ronda noted. "York crossed the river, he crossed the mountains, he saw what freedom meant. And then re-entered a world of slavery."[8]

York reportedly died of cholera sometime in the 1820s. His participation in the Lewis and Clark Expedition is considered an important moment in African-American history, and he has served as the subject of books, Web sites, and monuments in recent years. "York's tale is perhaps one of the saddest of the biographies of expedition members," noted a National Park Service commemorative site. "Like so many other African Americans throughout history, he was held back not for lack of talents or ability, but merely because of the color of his skin."[9]

Sources

Betts, Robert B. *In Search of York: The Slave Who Went to the Pacific with Lewis and Clark.* Boulder, CO: Colorado Associated University Press, 1985.

"Inside the Corps: York." *Lewis and Clark: The Journey of the Corps of Discovery.* PBS, 1997. Retrieved from http://www.pbs.org/lewisandclark/inside/york.html.

Pringle, Laurence. *American Slave, American Hero: York of the Lewis and Clark Expedition.* Honesdale, PA: Calkins Creek, 2006.

"York." *Lewis and Clark National Historic Trail.* National Park Service, n.d. Retrieved from http://www.nps.gov/lecl/learn/historyculture/york.htm.

Notes

[1] Clark, William. June 5, 1804, entry in *The Journals of the Lewis and Clark Expedition,* ed. Gary Moulton. Lincoln: University of Nebraska Press / University of Nebraska-Lincoln Libraries-Electronic Text Center, 2005. Retrieved from http://lewisandclarkjournals.unl.edu/read/?_xmlsrc=1804-06-05.xml&_xslsrc=LCstyles.xsl.

[2] Clark, August 19, 1804, entry in *The Journals of the Lewis and Clark Expedition.* Retrieved from http://lewisandclarkjournals.unl.edu/read/?_xmlsrc=1804-08-19.xml&_xslsrc=LCstyles.xsl.

[3] Clark, June 29, 1805, entry in *The Journals of the Lewis and Clark Expedition.* Retrieved from http://lewisandclarkjournals.unl.edu/read/?_xmlsrc=1805-06-29&_xslsrc=LCstyles.xsl.

[4] Clark, October 10, 1804, entry in in *The Journals of the Lewis and Clark Expedition.* Retrieved from http://lewisandclarkjournals.unl.edu/read/?_xmlsrc=1804-10-10.xml&_xslsrc=LCstyles.xsl.

[5] Lewis, Meriwether. August 16, 1805, entry in *The Journals of the Lewis and Clark Expedition.* Retrieved from http://lewisandclarkjournals.unl.edu/read/?_xmlsrc=1805-08-16.xml&_xslsrc=LCstyles.xsl.

[6] Quoted in "Inside the Corps: York." *Lewis and Clark: The Journey of the Corps of Discovery.* PBS, 1997. Retrieved from http://www.pbs.org/lewisandclark/inside/york.html.

[7] Quoted in "Inside the Corps: York."

[8] Ronda, James. "Living History: York's Experience." *Lewis and Clark: The Journey of the Corps of Discovery.* PBS, 1997. Retrieved from http://www.pbs.org/lewisandclark/living/idx_5.html.

[9] Quoted in "Civilians of the Expedition: York." *Jefferson Expansion National Memorial.* National Park Service, n.d. Retrieved from http://www.nps.gov/jeff/learn/historyculture/york.htm.

PRIMARY SOURCES

Alexander Mackenzie Inspires American Exploration

Twelve years before the Lewis and Clark Expedition succeeded in reached the Pacific Ocean, a Scottish explorer named Alexander Mackenzie became the first European to cross North America by land. Searching for new trade routes on behalf of the British-owned North West Company, Mackenzie traveled westward through present-day Canada to the coast of British Columbia. On July 22, 1793—while being harassed by Heiltsuk Indians who had had negative experiences with seafaring Europeans—Mackenzie left an inscription on a large rock to mark the westernmost point of his journey. In 1801 he published an account of his expedition, which is excerpted below. One interested reader of this book was U.S. president Thomas Jefferson, who had a lifelong fascination with exploring the West. Worried that Mackenzie's accomplishment would bolster British claims to the land, Jefferson vowed to respond by organizing an American expedition.

As I could not ascertain the distance from the open sea, and being uncertain whether we were in a bay or among inlets and channels of islands, I confined my search to a proper place for taking an observation.... Under the land we met with three canoes, with fifteen men in them, and laden with their moveables, as if proceeding to a new situation, or returning for a former one. They manifested no kind of mistrust or fear of us, but entered into conversation with our young man [a coastal Indian who was traveling with Mackenzie's group], as I supposed, to obtain some information concerning us. It did not appear that they were the same people as those we had lately seen, as they spoke the language of our young chief, with a different accent. They then examined everything we had in our canoe, with an air of indifference and disdain. One of them in particular made me understand, with an air of insolence, that a large canoe had lately been in this bay, with people in her like me, and that one of them, whom he called *Macubah*, had fired on him and his friends, and that *Bensins* had struck him on the back, with the flat part of his sword. He also mentioned another name, the articulation of which I could not determine. At the same time he illustrated these circumstances by the assistance of my gun and sword; and I do not doubt but he well deserved the treatment which he described. He also produced several European articles, which could not have been long in his possession. From his conduct and appearance, I wished very much to be rid of him, and flattered myself that he would prosecute his voyage, which appeared to be in an opposite direction to our course. However, when I prepared to part from them, they turned their canoes about, and persuaded my young man to leave me, which I could not prevent.

We coasted along the land at about west-southwest for six miles, and met a canoe with two boys in it, who were dispatched to summon the people on that

157

part of the coast to join them. The troublesome fellow now forced himself into my canoe, and pointed out a narrow channel on the opposite shore, that led to his village, and requested us to steer towards it, which I accordingly ordered. His importunities now became very irksome, and he wanted to see everything we had, particularly my instruments, concerning which he must have received information from my young man. He asked for my hat, my handkerchief, and in short, everything that he saw about me. At the same time he frequently repeated the unpleasant intelligence that he had been shot at by people of my colour. At some distance from the land a channel opened to us, at south-west by west, and pointing that way, he made me understand that *Macubah* came there with his large canoe. When we were in mid-channel, I perceived some sheds, or the remains of old buildings on the shore; and as, from that circumstance I thought it probable that some Europeans might have been there, I directed my steersman to make for that spot. The traverse is upwards of three miles north-west.

We landed, and found the ruins of a village, in a situation calculated for defence. The place itself was overgrown with weeds.... We were soon followed by ten canoes, each of which contained from three to six men. They informed us that we were expected at the village, where we should see many of them. From their general deportment I was very apprehensive that some hostile design was meditated against us, and for the first time I acknowledged my apprehensions to my people. I accordingly desired them to be very much upon their guard, and to be prepared if any violence was offered to defend themselves to the last.

We had no sooner landed, than we took possession of a rock, where there was not space for more than twice our number, and which admitted of our defending ourselves with advantage, in case we should be attacked. The people in the three first canoes, were the most troublesome, but, after doing their utmost to irritate us, they went away.

They were, however, no sooner gone, than a hat, a handkerchief, and several other articles, were missing. The rest of our visitors continued their pressing invitations to accompany them to their village, but finding our resolution to decline them was not to be shaken, they about sun-set relieved us from all further importunities by their departure....

[Mackenzie and his crew spend an uneventful night on the rock. With clear skies the next morning, Mackenzie decides to take celestial readings to determine their position. While his navigational instruments are spread around the camp, more Indians arrive and warn him that a hostile group is approaching his location.]

The young man was now very anxious to persuade our people to depart, as the natives, he said, were as numerous as musquitoes, and of very malignant character. This information produced some very earnest remonstrances to me to hasten our departure, but as I was determined not to leave this place, except I was absolutely compelled to it, till I had ascertained its situation [geographic location], these solicitations were not repeated....

[After calculating his position, which confirms that he has succeeded in crossing North America by land, Mackenzie makes note of his achievement.] I now mixed up some vermillion in melted grease, and inscribed, in large characters, on the south-east face of the rock on which we had slept last night, this brief memorial—"Alexander Mackenzie, from Canada, by land, the twenty-second of July, one thousand seven hundred and ninety-three."

Source

Mackenzie, Alexander. *Voyages from Montreal, on the River St. Lawrence through the Continent of North America, to the Frozen and Pacific Oceans; in the years 1789 and 1793*. London: T. Cadell, 1801, pp. 433-438.

President Thomas Jefferson Asks Congress to Fund an Expedition

On January 18, 1803, President Thomas Jefferson sent the following confidential message to members of the U.S. Congress. He expresses concerns about ongoing land conflicts with Native Americans, who are growing increasingly reluctant to make way for white settlers. As one approach toward solving this problem, Jefferson suggests that the United States try to expand its territorial holdings west of the Mississippi River. He believes that the West holds great potential value for farming, trade, and settlement. The president asks Congress to fund a U.S. military expedition to explore the region, search for a navigable water route to the Pacific Ocean, and stake an American claim to western lands. Since U.S. interests in the region conflict with those of European powers, Jefferson made his request privately.

Gentlemen of the Senate, and of the House of Representatives:

As the continuance of the act for establishing trading houses with the Indian tribes will be under the consideration of the Legislature at its present session, I think it my duty to communicate the views which have guided me in the execution of that act, in order that you may decide on the policy of continuing it, in the present or any other form, or discontinue it altogether, if that shall, on the whole, seem most for the public good.

The Indian tribes residing within the limits of the United States, have, for a considerable time, been growing more and more uneasy at the constant diminution of the territory they occupy, although effected by their own voluntary sales: and the policy has long been gaining strength with them, of refusing absolutely all further sale, on any conditions; insomuch that, at this time, it hazards their friendship, and excites dangerous jealousies and perturbations in their minds to make any overture for the purchase of the smallest portions of their land. A very few tribes only are not yet obstinately in these dispositions. In order peaceably to counteract this policy of theirs, and to provide an extension of territory which the rapid increase of our numbers will call for, two measures are deemed expedient. First: to encourage them to abandon hunting, to apply to the raising stock, to agriculture and domestic manufacture, and thereby prove to themselves that less land and labor will maintain them in this, better than in their former mode of living. The extensive forests necessary in the hunting life, will then become useless, and they will see advantage in exchanging them for the means of improving their farms, and of increasing their domestic comforts. Secondly: to multiply trading houses among them, and place within their reach those things which will contribute more to their domestic comfort, than the possession of extensive, but uncultivated wilds. Experience and reflection will develop to them the wisdom of exchanging what they can spare and we want, for what we can spare and they want. In leading them to agriculture, to manufactures, and civilization; in bringing together their and our settlements, and in preparing them ultimately to participate in the benefits of our governments, I trust and believe we are acting for their greatest good. At these trading houses we have pursued the principles of the act of Congress, which directs that the commerce shall be carried on liberally, and requires only that the capital stock shall not be diminished. We consequently undersell private traders, foreign and domestic, drive them from the competition; and thus, with the good will of the Indians, rid ourselves of a description of men who are constantly endeavoring to excite in the Indian mind suspicions, fears, and irritations towards us. A letter now enclosed, shows the effect of our competition on the operations of the traders, while the Indians, perceiving the advantage of purchasing from us, are soliciting generally, our establishment of trading houses among them. In one quarter this is particularly interesting. The Legislature, reflecting on the late occurrences on the Mississippi, must be sensible how desirable it is to possess a respectable breadth of country on that river, from our Southern limit to the Illinois at least; so that we may present as firm a front on that as on our Eastern border. We possess what is below the Yazoo, and can probably acquire a certain breadth from the Illinois and Wabash to the Ohio; but between the Ohio and Yazoo, the country all belongs to the Chickasaws, friendly tribe within our limits, but the most decided against the alienation of lands. The portion of their country most important for us is exactly that which they do not inhabit. Their settlements are not on the Mississippi, but in the interior country. They have lately shown a desire to become agricultural; and this leads to the desire of buying implements and comforts. In the strengthening and gratifying of these wants, I see the only prospect of planting on the Mississippi itself, the means of its own safety. Duty has required me to submit these views to the judgment of the Legislature; but as their disclosure might embarrass and defeat their effect, they are committed to the special confidence of the two Houses.

While the extension of the public commerce among the Indian tribes, may deprive of that source of profit such of our citizens as are engaged in it, it might be worthy the attention of Congress, in their care of individual as well as of the general interest, to point, in another direction, the enterprise of these citizens, as profitably for themselves, and more usefully for the public. The river Missouri, and the Indians inhabiting it, are not as well known as is rendered desirable by their connexion with the Mississippi, and consequently with us. It is, however, understood, that the country on that river is inhabited by numerous tribes, who furnish great supplies of furs and peltry to the trade of another nation, carried on in a high latitude, through an infinite number of portages and lakes, shut up by ice through a long season. The commerce on that line could bear no competition with that of the Missouri, traversing a moderate climate, offering according to the best accounts, a continued navigation from its source, and possibly with a single portage, from the Western Ocean, and finding to the Atlantic a choice of channels through the Illinois or Wabash, the lakes and Hudson, through the Ohio and Susquehanna, or Potomac or James rivers, and through the Tennessee and Savannah, rivers. An intelligent officer, with ten or twelve chosen men, fit for the enterprise, and willing to undertake it, taken from our posts, where they may be spared without inconvenience, might explore the whole line, even to the Western Ocean, have conferences with the natives on the subject of commercial intercourse, get admission among them for our traders, as others are admitted, agree on convenient deposits for an interchange of articles, and return with the information acquired, in the course of two summers. Their arms and accoutrements, some instruments of observation, and light and cheap presents for the Indians, would be all the apparatus they could carry, and with an expectation of a soldier's portion of land on their return, would constitute the whole expense. Their pay would be going on, whether here or there. While other civilized nations have encountered great expense to enlarge the boundaries of knowledge by undertaking voyages of discovery, and for other literary purposes, in various parts and directions, our nation seems to owe to the same object, as well as to its own interests, to explore this, the only line of easy communication across the continent, and so directly traversing our own part of it. The interests of commerce place the principal object within the constitutional powers and care of Congress, and that it should incidentally advance the geographical knowledge of our own continent, cannot be but an additional gratification. The nation claiming the territory, regarding this as a literary pursuit, which is in the habit of permitting within its dominions, would not be disposed to view it with jealousy, even if the expiring state of its interests there did not render it a matter of indifference. The appropriation of two thousand five hundred dollars, "for the purpose of extending the external commerce of the United States," while understood and considered by the

Executive as giving the legislative sanction, would cover the undertaking from notice, and prevent the obstructions which interested individuals might otherwise previously prepare in its way.

TH. JEFFERSON
January 18, 1803

Source

Jefferson, Thomas. "Jefferson's Confidential Letter to Congress," January 18, 1803. Retrieved from http://www.monticello.org/site/jefferson/jeffersons-confidential-letter-to-congress.

The Louisiana Purchase Treaty

In April 1803, President Thomas Jefferson got an unexpected opportunity to expand the western frontier of the United States to include the vast Louisiana Territory west of the Mississippi River. Although French leader Napoleon Bonaparte had only acquired the area from Spain three years earlier, he quickly abandoned plans to reestablish French colonies in North America. Instead, he decided to sell 827,000 square miles of land to the United States for $15 million, or about 3 cents per acre. The historic Louisiana Purchase Treaty, which is excerpted below, doubled the size of the United States and extended its western border all the way to the Rocky Mountains.

The President of the United States of America and the First Consul of the French Republic [through their designated representatives or ministers plenipotentiary, Robert R. Livingston and James Monroe for the United States, and François de Barbé-Marbois for France] have agreed to the following Articles.

Article I

Whereas by the article the third of the Treaty concluded at St. Ildefonso the 9th Vendémiaire an 9 (1st October) 1800 between the First Consul of the French Republic and his Catholic Majesty [King Charles IV of Spain] it was agreed as follows.

"His Catholic Majesty promises and engages on his part to cede to the French Republic six months after the full and entire execution of the conditions and Stipulations herein relative to his Royal Highness the Duke of Parma, the Colony or Province of Louisiana with the Same extent that it now has in the hand of Spain, & that it had when France possessed it; and Such as it Should be after the Treaties subsequently entered into between Spain and other States."

And whereas in pursuance of the Treaty and particularly of the third article the French Republic has an incontestible title to the domain and to the possession of the said Territory—The First Consul of the French Republic desiring to give to the United States a strong proof of his friendship doth hereby cede to the United States in the name of the French Republic for ever and in full Sovereignty the said territory with all its rights and appurtenances as fully and in the Same manner as they have been acquired by the French Republic in virtue of the above mentioned Treaty concluded with his Catholic Majesty.

Article II

In the cession made by the preceding article are included the adjacent Islands belonging to Louisiana all public lots and Squares, vacant lands and all public buildings, fortifications, barracks and other edifices which are not private property. The Archives, papers & documents relative to the domain and Sovereignty of Louisiana and its dependances will be left in the possession of the Commissaries of the United States, and copies will be afterwards given in due form to the Magistrates and Municipal officers of such of the said papers and documents as may be necessary to them.

Article III

The inhabitants of the ceded territory shall be incorporated in the Union of the United States and admitted as soon as possible according to the principles of the federal Constitution to the enjoyment of all these rights, advantages and immunities of citizens of the United States, and in the mean time they shall be maintained and protected in the free enjoyment of their liberty, property and the Religion which they profess.

Article IV

There Shall be Sent by the Government of France a Commissary to Louisiana to the end that he do every act necessary as well to receive from the Officers of his Catholic Majesty the Said country and its dependances in the name of the French Republic if it has not been already done as to transmit it in the name of the French Republic to the Commissary or agent of the United States.

Article V

Immediately after the ratification of the present Treaty by the President of the United States and in case that of the first Consul's shall have been previously obtained, the commissary of the

French Republic shall remit all military posts of New Orleans and other parts of the ceded territory to the Commissary or Commissaries named by the President to take possession—the troops whether of France or Spain who may be there shall cease to occupy any military post from the time of taking possession and shall be embarked as soon as possible in the course of three months after the ratification of this treaty.

Article VI

The United States promise to execute Such treaties and articles as may have been agreed between Spain and the tribes and nations of Indians until by mutual consent of the United States and the said tribes or nations other Suitable articles Shall have been agreed upon.

Article VII

As it is reciprocally advantageous to the commerce of France and the United States to encourage the communication of both nations for a limited time in the country ceded by the present treaty until general arrangements relative to commerce of both nations may be agreed on; it has been agreed between the contracting parties that the French Ships coming directly from France or any of her colonies loaded only with the produce and manufactures of France or her Said Colonies; and the Ships of Spain coming directly from Spain or any of her colonies loaded only with the produce or manufactures of Spain or her Colonies shall be admitted during the Space of twelve years in the Port of New-Orleans and in all other legal ports-of-entry within the ceded territory in the Same manner as the Ships of the United States coming directly from France or Spain or any of their Colonies without being Subject to any other or greater duty on merchandize or other or greater tonnage than that paid by the citizens of the United States.

During that Space of time above mentioned no other nation Shall have a right to the Same privileges in the Ports of the ceded territory—the twelve years Shall commence three months after the exchange of ratifications if it Shall take place in France or three months after it Shall have been notified at Paris to the French Government if it Shall take place in the United States; It is however well understood that the object of the above article is to favour the manufactures, Commerce, freight and navigation of France and of Spain So far as relates to the importations that the French and Spanish Shall make into the Said Ports of the United States without in any Sort affecting the regulations that the United States may make concerning the exportation of the produce and merchandize of the United States, or any right they may have to make Such regulations.

Article VIII

In future and for ever after the expiration of the twelve years, the Ships of France shall be treated upon the footing of the most favoured nations in the ports above mentioned.

Article IX

The particular Convention Signed this day by the respective Ministers, having for its object to provide for the payment of debts due to the Citizens of the United States by the French Republic prior to the 30th Sept. 1800 (8th Vendémiaire an 9) is approved and to have its execution in the Same manner as if it had been inserted in this present treaty, and it Shall be ratified in the same form and in the Same time So that the one Shall not be ratified distinct from the other. Another particular Convention Signed at the Same date as the present treaty relative to a definitive rule between the contracting parties is in the like manner approved and will be ratified in the Same form, and in the Same time and jointly.

Article X

The present treaty Shall be ratified in good and due form and the ratifications Shall be exchanged in the Space of Six months after the date of the Signature by the Ministers Plenipotentiary or Sooner if possible.

In faith whereof the respective Plenipotentiaries have Signed these articles in the French and English languages; declaring nevertheless that the present Treaty was originally agreed to in the French language; and have thereunto affixed their Seals.

Done at Paris the tenth day of Floreal in the eleventh year of the French Republic; and the 30th of April 1803.

[The full treaty also included two separate conventions specifying the methods of payment.]

Robt. R. Livingston [seal]

Jas. Monroe [seal]

Barbé Marbois [seal]

Source

Louisiana Purchase Treaty, April 30, 1803. General Records of the U.S. Government, Record Group 11, National Archives. Retrieved from http://www.ourdocuments.gov/doc.php?flash=true&doc=18&page=transcript.

Jefferson Provides Meriwether Lewis with Detailed Instructions

Even before the Louisiana Purchase had been finalized, President Thomas Jefferson began organizing a U.S. military expedition to explore and map the newly acquired territory. He selected Captain Meriwether Lewis as its leader and gave him detailed instructions for achieving its many scientific, political, and military goals. In the letter excerpted below, dated June 20, 1803, Jefferson asks Lewis to record scientific data about the plants, animals, weather, and landscape of the West; create detailed maps of the region and identify opportunities for commercial development; search for a navigable water route across the continent; and establish friendly relations with the Native American nations he encounters. The president also acknowledges the danger inherent in the mission by offering contingency plans in the event Lewis is lost or killed.

To Meriwether Lewis, esquire, Captain of the 1st regiment of infantry of the United States of America.

Your situation as Secretary of the President of the United States has made you acquainted with the objects of my confidential message of Jan. 18, 1803, to the legislature. You have seen the act they passed, which, tho' expressed in general terms, was meant to sanction those objects, and you are appointed to carry them into execution.

Instruments for ascertaining by celestial observations the geography of the country thro' which you will pass, have been already provided. Light articles for barter, & presents among the Indians, arms for your attendants, say for from 10 to 12 men, boats, tents, & other travelling apparatus, with ammunition, medicine, surgical instruments & provision you will have prepared with such aids as the Secretary at War can yield in his department; & from him also you will receive authority to engage among our troops, by voluntary agreement, the number of attendants above mentioned, over whom you, as their commanding officer are invested with all the powers the laws give in such a case.

As your movements while within the limits of the U.S. will be better directed by occasional communications, adapted to circumstances as they arise, they will not be noticed here. What follows will respect your proceedings after your departure from the U.S.

Your mission has been communicated to the Ministers here from France, Spain, & Great Britain, and through them to their governments: and such assurances given them as to its objects as we trust will satisfy them. The country of Louisiana having been ceded by Spain to France, the passport you have from the Minister of France, the representative of the present sovereign of the country, will be a protection with all its subjects: and that from the Minister of England will entitle you to the friendly aid of any traders of that allegiance with whom you may happen to meet.

The object of your mission is to explore the Missouri river, & such principal stream of it, as, by its course & communication with the water of the Pacific ocean may offer the most direct & practicable water communication across this continent, for the purposes of commerce.

Beginning at the mouth of the Missouri, you will take observations of latitude and longitude at all remarkable points on the river, & especially at the mouths of rivers, at rapids, at islands & other places & objects distinguished by such natural marks & characters of a durable kind, as that they may with certainty be recognized hereafter. The courses of the river between these points of observation may be supplied by the compass, the log-line & by time, corrected by the observations themselves. The variations of the compass too, in different places should be noticed.

The interesting points of the portage between the heads of the Missouri & the water offering the best communication with the Pacific ocean should be fixed by observation, & the course of that water to the ocean, in the same manner as that of the Missouri.

Your observations are to be taken with great pains & accuracy to be entered distinctly, & intelligibly for others as well as yourself, to comprehend all the elements necessary, with the aid of the usual tables to fix the latitude & longitude of the places at which they were taken, & are to be rendered to the war office, for the purpose of having the calculations made concurrently by proper persons within the U.S. Several copies of these as well as of your other notes, should be made at leisure times, & put into the care of the most trustworthy of your attendants, to guard by multiplying them against the accidental losses to which they will be exposed. A further guard would be that one of these copies be written on the paper of the birch, as less liable to injury from damp than common paper.

The commerce which may be carried on with the people inhabiting the line you will pursue, renders a knowledge of these people important. You will therefore endeavor to make yourself acquainted, as far as a diligent pursuit of your journey shall admit, with

- the names of the nations & their numbers;
- the extent & limits of their possessions;

- their relations with other tribes or nations;

- their language, traditions, monuments;

- their ordinary occupations in agriculture, fishing, hunting, war, arts, & the implements for these;

- their food, clothing, & domestic accommodations;

- the diseases prevalent among them, & the remedies they use;

- moral and physical circumstance which distinguish them from the tribes they know;

- peculiarities in their laws, customs & dispositions;

- and articles of commerce they may need or furnish, & to what extent.

And considering the interest which every nation has in extending & strengthening the authority of reason & justice among the people around them, it will be useful to acquire what knowledge you can of the state of morality, religion & information among them, as it may better enable those who endeavor to civilize & instruct them, to adapt their measures to the existing notions & practices of those on whom they are to operate.

Other objects worthy of notice will be

- the soil & face of the country, its growth & vegetable productions, especially those not of the U.S.

- the animals of the country generally, & especially those not known in the U.S.

- the remains & accounts of any which may be deemed rare or extinct;

- the mineral productions of every kind; but more particularly metals, limestone, pit coal & saltpetre;

- salines & mineral waters, noting the temperature of the last & such circumstances as may indicate their character;

- volcanic appearances;

- climate as characterized by the thermometer, by the proportion of rainy, cloudy & clear days, by lightning, hail, snow, ice, by the access & recess of frost, by the winds, prevailing at different seasons, the dates at which particular plants put forth or lose their flowers, or leaf, times of appearance of particular birds, reptiles or insects.

Altho' your route will be along the channel of the Missouri, yet you will endeavor to inform yourself, by inquiry, of the character and extent of the country watered by its branches, & especially on its Southern side. The North river or Rio Bravo which runs into the gulf of Mexico, and the North river, or Rio Colorado which runs into the gulf of California, are understood to be the principal streams heading opposite to the waters of the Missouri, and running Southwardly. Whether the dividing grounds between the Missouri & them are mountains or flatlands, what are their distance from the Missouri, the character of the intermediate country, & the people inhabiting it, are worthy of particular enquiry. The Northern waters of the Missouri are less to be enquired after, because they have been ascertained to a considerable degree, and are still in a course of ascertainment by English traders & travelers. But if you can learn anything certain of the most Northern source of the Mississippi, & of its position relative to the lake of the woods, it will be interesting to us. Some account too of the path of the Canadian traders from the Mississippi, at the mouth of the Ouisconsin river, to where it strikes the Missouri, and of the soil and rivers in its course, is desirable.

In all your intercourse with the natives treat them in the most friendly & conciliatory manner which their own conduct will admit; allay all jealousies as to the object of your journey, satisfy them of its innocence, make them acquainted with the position, extent, character, peaceable & commercial dispositions of the U.S., of our wish to be neighborly, friendly & useful to them, & of our dispositions to a commercial intercourse with them; confer with them on the points most convenient as mutual emporiums, & the articles of most desirable interchange for them & us. If a few of their influential chiefs, within practicable distance, wish to visit us, arrange such a visit with them, and furnish them with authority to call on our officers, on their entering the U.S. to have them conveyed to this place at the public expense. If any of them should wish to have some of their young people brought up with us, & taught such arts as may be useful to them, we will receive, instruct & take care of them. Such a mission, whether of influential chiefs, or of young people, would give some security to your own party. Carry with you some matter of the kine pox [vaccine], inform those of them with whom you may be, of its efficacy as a preservative from the small pox; and instruct & encourage them in the use of it. This may be especially done wherever you may winter.

As it is impossible for us to foresee in what manner you will be received by those people, whether with hospitality or hostility, so is it impossible to prescribe the exact degree of perseverance with which you are to pursue your journey. We value too much the lives of citizens to offer them to probable destruction. Your numbers will be sufficient to secure you against the unauthorized opposition of individuals, or of small parties: but if a superior force, authorized or not authorized, by a nation, should be arrayed against your further passage, & inflexibly determined to arrest it, you must decline its further pursuit, and return. In the loss of yourselves, we should lose also the information you will have acquired. By returning safely with that, you may enable us to renew the essay with better calculated means. To your own discretion therefore must be left the degree of danger you may risk, & the point at which you should decline, only saying we wish you to err on the side of your safety, & to bring back your party safe, even if it be with less information.

As far up the Missouri as the white settlements extend, an intercourse will probably be found to exist between them and the Spanish posts at St. Louis, opposite Cahokia, or Ste. Genevieve opposite Kaskaskia. From still farther up the river, the traders may furnish a conveyance for letters. Beyond that you may perhaps be able to engage Indians to bring letters for the government to Cahokia or Kaskaskia, on promising that they shall there receive such special compensation as you shall have stipulated with them. Avail yourself of these means to communicate to us, at seasonable intervals, a copy of your journal, notes & observations of every kind, putting into cypher [code] whatever might do injury if betrayed.

Should you reach the Pacific ocean, inform yourself of the circumstances which may decide whether the furs of those parts may not be collected as advantageously at the head of the Missouri (convenient as is supposed to the waters of the Colorado & Oregon or Columbia) as at Nootka sound or any other point of that coast; & that trade be consequently conducted through the Missouri & U.S. more beneficially than by the circumnavigation now practiced.

On your arrival on that coast, endeavor to learn if there be any port within your reach frequented by the sea-vessels of any nation, and to send two of your trusty people back by sea, in such way as shall appear practicable, with a copy of your notes. And should you be of opinion that the return of your party by the way they went will be eminently dangerous, then ship the whole, & return by sea by way of Cape Horn or the Cape of Good Hope, as you shall be able. As you will be without money, clothes or provisions, you must endeavor to use the credit of the U.S. to obtain them; for which purpose open letters of credit shall be furnished you authorizing you to draw on the Executive of the U.S. or any of its officers in any part of the world, in which draughts can be disposed of, and to apply with our recommendations to the consuls, agents, merchants or citizens of any nation with which we have intercourse, assuring them in our name that any aids they may furnish you shall be honorably repaid, and on demand. Our consuls Thomas Howes at Batavia in Java, William Buchanan of the Isles of France and Bourbon, & John Elmslie at the Cape of Good Hope will be able to supply your necessities by draughts on us.

Should you find it safe to return by the way you go, after sending two of your party round by sea, or with your whole party, if no conveyance by sea can be found, do so; making such observations on your return as may serve to supply, correct or confirm those made on your outward journey.

In re-entering the U.S. and reaching a place of safety, discharge any of your attendants who may desire & deserve it: procuring for them immediate payment of all arrears of pay & clothing which may have incurred since their departure and assure them that they shall be recommended to the liberality of the legislature for the grant of a soldier's portion of land each, as proposed in my message to Congress: & repair yourself with your papers to the seat of government.

To provide, on the accident of your death, against anarchy, dispersion & the consequent danger to your party, and total failure of the enterprise, you are hereby authorized, by any instrument signed & written in your own hand, to name the person among them who shall succeed to the command on your decease, & by like instruments to change the nomination from time to time, as further experience of the characters accompanying you shall point out superior fitness: and all the powers & authorities given to yourself are, in the event of your death, transferred to & vested in the successor so named, with further power to him, & his successors in like manner to name each his successor, who, on the death of his predecessor shall be invested with all the powers & authorities given to yourself.

Given under my hand at the city of Washington, this 20th day of June 1803.

Th. Jefferson, Pr. U.S. of America.

Source

"Thomas Jefferson's Instructions to Meriwether Lewis," June 20, 1803. Monticello.org. Retrieved from http://www.monticello.org/site/jefferson/jeffersons-instructions-to-meriwether-lewis.

Lewis Buys Equipment and Supplies for the Expedition

After receiving his orders from President Jefferson, Captain Meriwether Lewis began purchasing equipment and supplies for his expedition into the western wilderness. The initial list of items he felt he would need, which appears below, includes food, clothing, medicine, camping gear, hunting rifles, and scientific instruments for navigation and mapmaking. Knowing that exchanging gifts was a traditional part of the interaction between white Americans and Native Americans on the frontier, Lewis also budgeted $696 for "Indian presents," such as beads, cloth, tobacco, and silver peace medals. He shipped all of the supplies to Pittsburgh, Pennsylvania, where they would be loaded onto a keelboat to begin the westward journey in the summer of 1803.

Mathematical Instruments

1 Hadley's quadrant

1 Mariner's compass & 2 pole chain

1 Set of plotting instruments

3 Thermometers

1 Cheap portable microscope

1 Pocket compass

1 Brass scale one foot in length

6 Magnetic needles in small straight silver or brass cases opening on the side with hinges

1 Instrument for measuring made of tape with feet & inches marked on it

2 Hydrometers

1 Theodolite

1 Set of planespheres

2 Artificial horizons

1 Patent log

6 Papers of ink powder

4 Metal pens, brass or silver

1 Set of small slates & pencils

2 Crayons Sealing wax, one bundle

1 Miller's edition of Linnaeus in 2 vol. [a book outlining the biological naming system of plants and animals]

Books

Maps

Charts

Blank vocabularies

Writing paper

1 Pair large brass money scales with two sets of weights

Arms & Accoutrements

15 Rifle

15 Powder horns & pouches complete

15 Pairs of bullet moulds

15 Pairs of wipers or gun worms

15 Ball screws

24 Pipe tomahawks

24 Large knives Extra parts of locks & tools for repairing arms

15 Gun slings

500 Best flints

Ammunition

200 Lbs. Best rifle powder

400 Lbs. Lead

Clothing

15 3 pt. blankets

15 Watch coats with hoods & belts

15 Woolen overalls

15 Rifle frocks of waterproof cloth if possible

30 Pairs of socks or half stockings

20 Fatigue frocks or hunting shirts

30 Shirts of strong linen

30 Yds. Common flannel

Camp Equipage

6 Copper kettles (1 of 5 gallons, 1 of 3, 2 of 2, & 2 of 1)

35 Falling axes

4 Drawing knives, short & strong

 2 Augers of the patent kind

 1 Small permanent vice

 1 Hand vice

36 Gimblets assorted

24 Files assorted

12 Chisels assorted

10 Nails assorted

 2 Steel plate hand saws

 2 Vials of phosphorus

 1 Vials of phosphorus made of alum & sugar

 4 Gross fishing hooks assorted

12 Bunches of drum line

 2 Foot adzes

12 Bunches of small cord

 2 Pick axes

 3 Coils of rope

 2 Spades

12 Bunches small fishing line assorted

 1 Lb. turkey or oil stone

 1 Iron mill for grinding corn

20 Yds. Oil linen for wrapping & securing articles

10 Yds. Oil linen of thicker quality for covering and lining boxes &c.

40 Yds. Oil linen to form two half faced tents or shelters

 4 Tin blowing trumpets

 2 Hand or spiral spring steelyards

20 Yds. Strong Oznaburgs [strong cloth]

24 Iron spoons

24 Pint tin cups (without handles)

30 Steels for striking or making fire

100 Flints for striking or making fire

2 Frows [cleaving tools with wedge-shaped blades]

6 Saddlers large needles

6 Saddlers large awls Mosquito curtains

2 Patent chamber lamps & wicks

15 Oil cloth bags for securing provisions

1 Sea grass hammock

Provisions and Means of Subsistence

150 Lbs. Portable Soup

3 Bushels of alum or rock salt Spices assorted

6 Kegs of 5 gallons each making 30 gallons of rectified spirits such as is used for the Indian trade

6 Kegs bound with iron hoops

Indian Presents

5 Lbs. White wampum [shell beads]

5 Lbs. White glass beads mostly small

20 Lbs. Red glass beads assorted

5 Lbs. Yellow or orange glass beads assorted

30 Calico shirts

12 Pieces of East India muslin handkerchiefs striped or checked with brilliant colors

12 Red silk handkerchiefs

144 Small cheap looking glasses

100 Burning glasses

4 Vials of phosphorus

288 Steels for striking fire

144 Small cheap scissors

20 Pair large scissors

12   Gross needles assorted no. 1 to 8 common points

12   Gross needles assorted with points for sewing leather

288   Common brass thimbles—part at War Office

10   Lbs. Sewing thread assorted

24   Hanks sewing silk

8   Lbs. Red lead

2   Lbs. Vermillion [red pigment]—at War Office

288   Knives small such as are generally used for the Indian trade, with fixed blades & handles inlaid with brass

36   Large knives

36   Pipe tomahawks—at Harpers Ferry

12   Lbs. Brass wire assorted

12   Lbs. Iron wire assorted generally large

6   Belts of narrow ribbons colors assorted

50   Lbs. Spun tobacco

20   Small falling axes to be obtained in Tennessee

40   Fish Griggs such as the Indians use with a single barbed point—at Harpers Ferry

3   Gross fishing hooks assorted

3   Gross moccasin awls assorted

50   Lbs. Powder secured in a keg covered with oil cloth

24   Belts of worsted feiret [woven wool tape used for embellishment] or gartering, colors brilliant and assorted

15   Sheets of copper cut into strips of an inch in width & a foot long

20   Sheets of tin

12   Lbs. Strips of sheet iron 1 in. wide 1 foot long

1   Piece red cloth second quality

1   Nest of 8 or 9 small copper kettles

100   Block-tin rings cheap kind ornamented with colored glass or mock-stone

2   Gross of brass curtain rings & sufficiently large for the finger

  1 Gross cast iron combs

18 Cheap brass combs

24 Blankets

12 Arm bands silver—at War Office

12 Wrist bands silver

36 Ear trinkets silver—part at War Office

  6 Gross drops of silver—part at War Office

  4 Dozen rings for fingers of silver

  4 Gross brooches of silver

12 Small medals silver

Means of Transportation

  1 Keeled boat light strong at least 60 feet in length her burthen [carrying capacity] equal to 8 tons

  1 Iron frame of canoe 40 feet long

  1 Large wooden canoe

12 Spikes for setting-poles

  4 Boat hooks & points complete

  2 Chains & pad-locks for confining the boat & canoes &c.

Medicine

15 Lbs. Best powder's bark

10 Lbs. Epsom or Glauber salts

  4 Oz. Calomel

12 Oz. Opium

 _ Oz. Tarter emetic

  8 Oz. Borax

  4 Oz. Powdered ipecacuanha

  8 Oz. Powdered jalap

  8 Oz. Powdered rhubarb

6 Best lancets

2 Oz. White vitriol

4 Oz. Lacteaum Saturni

4 Pewter penis syringes

1 Flour of Sulphur

3 Clyster pipes

4 Oz. Turlingtons balsam

2 Lbs. Yellow basilicum

2 Sticks of simple diachylon

1 Lb. Blistering ointments

2 Lbs. Nitre

2 Lbs. Copperas

Materials for Making Up the Various Articles into Portable Packs

30 Sheep skins taken off the animal as perfectly whole as possible, without being split on the belly as usual and dressed only with lime to free them from the wool; or otherwise about the same quantity of oil cloth bags well painted

Raw hide for pack strings

Dressed leather for hoppus [knapsack] straps

Other packing

Source

Jackson, Donald, ed., *Letters of the Lewis and Clark Expedition: With Related Documents 1783-1854.* Urbana and Chicago: University of Illinois Press, 1978, pp. 69-74. Retrieved from http://www.monti cello.org/site/jefferson/lewiss-packing-list.

Lewis Scouts the Great Falls of the Missouri River

As the leader of a U.S.-sponsored military expedition into the West, Captain Meriwether Lewis kept an extensive journal relating his experiences, cataloguing the plants and animals he found, describing the geographic features he saw, and recording the Native American cultures he observed. He wrote the entries excerpted below on June 14, 1805, as he walked overland—ahead of the boats carrying his crew and equipment—to scout the portage around the Great Falls of the Missouri River. In awe of the beauty of his surroundings, Lewis offers lyrical descriptions of the waterfalls and the abundant wildlife on the plains. He also provides a heart-pounding account of a "curious adventure" in which he is chased by a grizzly bear and threatened by an unfamiliar animal that he calls a "tiger cat."

About ten o'clock this morning while the men were engaged with the meat I took my gun and espontoon [spear] and thought I would walk a few miles and see where the rapids terminated above, and return to dinner. Accordingly I set out and proceeded up the river about southwest. After passing one continued rapid and three small cascades of about four or five feet each, at the distance of about five miles I arrived at a fall of about nineteen feet; the river is here about 400 yards wide. This pitch which I called the Crooked Falls occupies about three-fourths of the width of the river.... The water glides down the side of a sloping rock with a velocity almost equal to that of its perpendicular decent.

Just above this rapid the river makes a sudden bend to the right or northwardly. I should have returned from hence but hearing a tremendous roaring above me I continued my route across the point of a hill a few hundred yards further and was again presented by one of the most beautiful objects in nature, a cascade of about fifty feet perpendicular stretching at right angles across the river from side to side to the distance of at least a quarter of a mile. Here the river pitches over a shelving rock, with an edge as regular and as straight as if formed by art, without a niche or break in it; the water descends in one even and uninterrupted sheet to the bottom where dashing against the rocky bottom rises into foaming billows of great height and rapidly glides away, flashing and sparkling as it departs the spray rises from one extremity to the other to fifty feet. I now thought that if a skillful painter had been asked to make a beautiful cascade that he would most probably have presented the precise image of this one; nor could I for some time determine on which of those two great cataracts to bestow the [prize], on this or that which I had discovered yesterday; at length I determined between these two great rivals for glory that this was *pleasingly beautiful*, while the other was *sublimely grand....*

[He continues upstream several more miles, passing continuous rapids and a twenty-six-foot waterfall.] Below this fall at a little distance a beautiful little island well timbered is situated about the middle of the river. In this island on a cottonwood tree an eagle has placed her nest; a more inaccessible spot I believe she could not have found; for neither man nor beast dare pass those gulfs which separate her little domain from the shores. The water is also broken in such manner as it descends over this pitch that the mist or spray rises to a considerable height. This fall is certainly much the greatest I ever beheld except those two which I have mentioned below. It is incomparably a greater cataract and a more noble, interesting object than the celebrated falls of Potomac or Schuylkill [rivers back east].

Just above this is another cascade of about five feet, above which the water as far as I could see began to abate of its velocity, and I therefore determined to ascend the hill behind me which promised a fine prospect of the adjacent country, nor was I disappointed on my arrival at its summit. From hence I overlooked a most beautiful and extensive plain reaching from the river to the base of the snowclad mountains to the south and southwest; I also observed the Missouri stretching its meandering course to the south through this plain to a great distance filled to its even and grassy brim; another large river flowed in on its western side about four miles above me and extended itself though a level and fertile valley of three miles in width a great distance to the northwest, rendered more conspicuous by the timber which garnished its borders. In these plains and more particularly in the valley just below me immense herds of buffalo are feeding....

After feasting my eyes on this ravishing prospect and resting myself a few minutes I determined to proceed as far as the river which I saw discharge itself on the west side of the Missouri, convinced that it was the river which the Indians call Medicine River and which they informed us fell into the Missouri just above the falls. I descended the hills and directed my course to the bend of the Missouri near which there was a herd of at least a thousand buffalo; here I thought it would be well to kill a buffalo and leave him until my return from the river, and if I then found that I had not time to get back to camp this evening, to remain all night here, there being a few sticks of driftwood lying along shore which would answer for my fire, and a few scattering cottonwood trees a few hundred yards below which would afford me at least a semblance of a shelter.

Under this impression I selected a fat buffalo and shot him very well, through the lungs; while I was gazing attentively on the poor animal discharging blood in streams from his mouth and nostrils, expecting him to fall every instant, and having entirely forgotten to reload my rifle, a large white, or rather brown [grizzly] bear, had perceived and crept on me within twenty steps before I discovered him; in the first moment I drew up my gun to shoot, but at the same instant recollected that she was not loaded and that he was too near for me to hope to perform this operation before he reached me, as he was then briskly advancing on me; it was an open level plain, not a bush within miles nor a tree within less than 300 yards of me; the river bank was sloping and not more than three feet above the level of the water; in short there was no place by means of which I could conceal myself from this monster until I could charge my rifle; in this situation I thought of retreating in a brisk walk as fast as he was advancing until I could reach a tree about 300 yards below me, but I had no sooner turned myself about but he pitched at me, open mouthed and full speed. I ran about eighty yards and found he gained on me fast, I then ran into the water.

The idea struck me to get into the water to such depth that I could stand and he would be obliged to swim, and that I could in that situation defend myself with my espontoon; accordingly I ran hastily into the water about waist deep, and faced about and presented the point of my espontoon, at this instant he arrived at the edge of the water within about twenty feet of me; the moment I put myself in this attitude of defense he suddenly wheeled about as if frightened, declined the combat on such unequal grounds, and retreated with quite as great precipitation as he had just before pursued me. As soon as I saw him run off in that manner I returned to the shore and charged my gun, which I had still retained in my hand throughout this curious adventure. I saw him run through the level open plain about three miles, till he disappeared in the woods on Medicine River; during the whole of this distance he ran at full speed, sometimes appearing to look behind him as if he expected pursuit.... So it was and I felt myself not a little gratified that he had declined the combat. My gun reloaded I felt confidence once more in my strength; and determined not to be thwarted in my design of visiting Medicine River, but determined never again to suffer my piece to be longer empty than the time she necessarily required to charge her....

Having examined Medicine River I now determined to return, having by my estimate about twelve miles to walk. I looked at my watch and found it was half after six p.m. In returning through the level bottom of Medicine River and about 200 yards distant from the Missouri, my direction led me directly to an animal that I at first supposed was a wolf; but on nearer approach or about sixty paces distant I discovered that it was not, its color was a brownish yellow; it was standing near its burrow, and when I approached it thus nearly, it crouched itself down like a cat looking immediately at me as if it designed to spring on me. I took aim at it and fired, it instantly disappeared in its burrow; I loaded my gun and examined the place which was dusty and saw the track from which I am still further convinced that it was of the tiger kind [historians believe this animal was a wolverine]. Whether I struck it or not I could not determine, but I am almost confident that I did; my gun is true and I had a steady rest by means of my espontoon, which I have found very serviceable to me in this way in the open plains.

It now seemed to me that all the beasts of the neighborhood had made a league to destroy me, or that some fortune was disposed to amuse herself at my expense, for I had not proceeded more than 300 yards from the burrow of this tiger cat, before three bull buffalo, which were feeding with a large herd about half a mile from me on my left, separated from the herd and ran full speed towards me, I thought at least to give them some amusement and altered my direction to meet them; when they arrived within a hundred yards they made a halt, took a good view of me and retreated with precipitation.

I then continued my route homewards past the buffalo which I had killed, but did not think it prudent to remain all night at this place which really from the succession of curious adventures wore the impression on my mind of enchantment; at some times for a moment I thought it might be a dream, but the prickly pears [a form of cactus] which pierced my feet very severely once in a while, particularly after it grew dark, convinced me that I was really awake, and that it was necessary to make the best of my way to camp. It was sometime after dark before I returned to the party; I found them extremely uneasy for my safety; they had formed a thousand conjectures, all of which equally foreboding my death, which they had so far settled among them, that they had already agreed on the route which each should take in the morning to search for me. I felt myself much fatigued, but ate a hearty supper and took a good night's rest.

Source

Lewis, Meriwether. June 14, 1805, entry in *The Journals of the Lewis and Clark Expedition*, ed. Gary Moulton. Lincoln: University of Nebraska Press/Electronic Text Center, 2005. Retrieved from http://lewis andclarkjournals.unl.edu/journals.php?id=1805-06-14.

Sergeant Patrick Gass Crosses Treacherous Mountain Passes

Seven members of the Corps of Discovery kept journals of their experiences, including Sergeant Patrick Gass. Upon his return to civilization, Gass hired an editor and became the first expedition member to publish his account of the historic journey across the continent. The following excerpts from his book span September 2-19, 1805, after the group had exchanged their boats for horses and set off overland to cross the rugged, snowcapped Rocky Mountains. Gass describes the men's struggles with cold, hunger, and fatigue as they traverse the treacherous Lolo Pass through the Bitterroot Range. With wild game scarce, the expedition members eventually resort to killing their horses for food.

Monday, September 2

The morning was cloudy. We set out early; proceeded up the creek, and passed some part closely timbered with spruce and pine. We went on with difficulty on account of the bushes, the narrowness of the way and stones that injured our horses' feet, they being without shoes. In the forenoon we killed some pheasants and ducks, and a small squirrel. In the afternoon we had a good deal of rain, and the worst road (if road it can be called) that was ever travelled. The creek is become small and the hills come close in upon the banks of it, covered thick with standing timber and fallen trees; so that in some places we were obliged to go up the sides of the hills, which are very steep, and then down again in order to get along at all. In going up these ascents the horses would sometimes fall backwards, which injured them very much; and one was so badly hurt that the driver was obliged to leave his load on the side of one of the hills. In the low ground there are most beautiful tall straight pine trees of different kinds, except of white pine. Game is scarce; and a small quantity of dried salmon, which we got from the natives, is almost our whole stock of provisions. A son of our guide joined us today and is going on. We went thirteen miles and encamped; but some of the men did not come up till late at night.

Tuesday, September 3

…We pursued our journey up the creek, which still continued fatiguing almost beyond description. The country is very mountainous and thickly timbered; mostly with spruce pine. Having gone nine miles we halted for dinner, which was composed of a small portion of flour we had along and the last of our pork, which was but a trifle: Our hunters had not killed anything. We stayed here about two hours, during which time some rain fell, and the weather was extremely cold for the season. We then went on about three miles over a large mountain, to the head of another creek and encamped there for the night. This was not the creek our guide wished to have come upon; and to add to our misfortunes we had a cold evening with rain.

Wednesday, September 4

A considerable quantity of snow fell last night, and the morning was cloudy. After eating a few grains of parched corn, we set out at 8 o'clock; crossed a large mountain and hit on the creek and small valley, which were wished for by our guide. We killed some pheasants on our way, and were about to make use of the last of our flour, when, to our great joy, one of our hunters killed a fine deer. So we dined upon that and proceeded down a small valley about a mile wide, with a rich black soil; in which there are a great quantity of sweet roots and herbs, such as sweet myrrh, angelica, and several other, that the natives make use of, and of the names of which I am unacquainted. There is also timothy grass growing in it; and neither the valley nor the hills are so thickly timbered, as the mountains we had lately passed. What timber there is, is mostly pitch pine. We kept down the valley about five miles, and came to the [Salish] Flathead nation of Indians, or a part of them. We found them encamped on the creek and we encamped with them.

Thursday, September 5

This was a fine morning with a great white frost. The Indian dogs are so hungry and ravenous, that they ate four or five pair of our moccasins last night. We remained here all day, and recruited our horses to forty and three colts; and made four or five of this nation of Indians chiefs. They are a very friendly people; have plenty of robes and skins for covering, and a large stock of horses, some of which are very good; but they have nothing to eat, but berries, roots and such articles of food. This band is on its way over to the Missouri or Yellowstone rivers to hunt buffalo. They are the whitest Indians I ever saw....

[They spend several days passing through the Bitterroot Valley to Travelers Rest.]

Tuesday, September 10

We remained here all this day, which was clear and pleasant, to let our horses rest, and to take an observation. At night our hunters came in, and had killed five deer. With one of the hunters, three of the Flathead Indians came to our camp. They informed us that the rest of their band was over on the Columbia River, about five or six days' journey distant, with pack-horses....

Thursday, September 12

We started early on our journey and had a fine morning. Having travelled two miles we reached the mountains which are very steep; but the road over them pretty good, as it is much travelled by the natives, who come across to the Flathead River to gather cherries and berries. Our hunters in a short time killed four deer. At noon we halted at a branch of the creek, on the banks of which are a number of strawberry vines, haws, and service berry bushes. At 2 we proceeded on over a large mountain, where there is no water, and we could find no place to encamp until late at night, when we arrived at a small branch, and encamped by it, in a very inconvenient place, having come twenty-three miles.

Friday, September 13

A cloudy morning. Captain Lewis's horse could not be found; but some of the men were left to hunt for him and we proceeded on. When we had gone two miles, we came to a most beautiful warm spring, the water of which is considerably above blood-heat; and I could not bear my hand in it without uneasiness. There are so many paths leading to and from this spring, that our guide took a wrong one for a mile or two, and we had bad travelling across till we got into the road again. At noon we halted. Game is scarce; and our hunters killed nothing since yesterday morning; though four of the best were constantly out, and every one of them furnished with a good horse.... At 2 o'clock we proceeded on again over a mountain, and in our way found a deer, which our hunters had killed and hung up. In a short time we met with them, and Captain Lewis sent two back to look for the horse. We passed over a dividing ridge to the waters of another creek, and after travelling twelve miles we encamped on the creek, up which there are some prairies or plains.

Saturday, September 14

We set out early in a cloudy morning; passed over a large mountain, crossed Stony Creek, about thirty yards wide, and then went over another large mountain, on which I saw service-berry bushes hanging full of fruit; but not yet ripe, owing to the coldness of the climate on these mountains.... Being here unable to find a place to halt at, where our horses could feed, we went on to the junction of Stony Creek, with another large creek, which a short distance down becomes a considerable river, and encamped for the night, as it rained and was disagreeable travelling. The two hunters, that had gone back here joined us with Captain Lewis's horse, but none of the hunters killed anything except two or three pheasants; on which, without a miracle it was impossible to feed thirty hungry men and upwards, besides some Indians. So Captain Lewis gave out some portable soup, which he had along, to be used in cases of necessity. Some of the men did not relish this soup, and agreed to kill a colt; which they immediately did, and set about roasting it; and which appeared to me to be good eating. This day we travelled seventeen miles.

Sunday, September 15

Having breakfasted on colt, we moved on down the river three miles, and again took the mountains. In going up, one of the horses fell, and required eight or ten men to assist him in getting up again. We continued our march to 2 o'clock when we halted at a spring and dined on portable soup, and a handful of parched corn. We then proceeded on our journey over the mountain to a high point, where, it being dark, we were obliged to encamp. There was here no water; but a bank of snow answered as a substitute; and we supped upon soup.

Monday, September 16

Last night about 12 o'clock it began to snow. We renewed our march early, though the morning was very disagreeable, and proceeded over the most terrible mountains I ever beheld. It continued snowing until 3 o'clock p.m. when we halted, took some more soup, and went on till we came to a small stream where we encamped for the night. Here we killed another colt and supped on it. The snow fell so thick, and the day was so dark, that a person could not see to a distance of 200 yards. In the night and during the day the snow fell about ten inches deep.

Tuesday, September 17

Our horses scattered so much last night, that they were not collected until noon, at which time we began our march again. It was a fine day with warm sunshine, which melted the snow very fast on the south sides of the hills, and made the travelling very fatiguing and uncomfortable. We continued over high desert mountains, where our hunters could find no game, nor signs of any except a bear's track which they observed today. At dark we halted at a spring on the top of a mountain; killed another colt, and encamped there all night.

Wednesday, September 18

This was a clear cold frosty morning. All our horses except one were collected early: Six hunters went on ahead; one man to look for the horse; and all the rest of us proceeded on our journey over the mountains, which are very high and rough. About 12 we passed a part where the snow was off, and no appearance that much had lately fallen. At 3 we came to snow again, and halted to take some soup, which we made with snow water, as no other could be found. Here the man who had been sent for the horse came up, but had not found him. Except on the sides of hills where it has fallen, the country is closely timbered with pitch and spruce pine, and what some call balsam-fir. We can see no prospect of getting off these desert mountains yet, except the appearance of a deep cove on each side of the ridge we are passing along. We remained here an hour and an half, and then proceeded on down a steep mountain, and encamped after travelling eighteen miles. We had great difficulty in getting water, being obliged to go half a mile for it down a very steep precipice.

Thursday, September 19

Our hunters did not join us last night, which was disagreeably cold. About 8 this morning we set out, and proceeded on in our way over the mountains; the sun shining warm and pleasant. We travelled a west course, and about 12 o'clock halted at a spring to take a little more soup. The snow is chiefly gone except on the north points of the high mountains. At 2 p.m. we again went on, and descended a steep mountain into a cove on our left hand, where there is a large creek, which here runs towards the east. The hills on each side, along which the trail or path passes, are very steep. One of our horses fell down the precipice about 100 feet, and was not killed, nor much hurt: the reason was, that there is no bottom below, and the precipice the only bank which the creek has; therefore the horse pitched into the water, without meeting with any intervening object which could materially injure him. We made seventeen miles this day and encamped on a small branch of the creek. Having heard nothing from our hunters, we again supped upon some of our portable soup. The men are becoming lean and debilitated, on account of the scarcity and poor quality of the provisions on which we subsist: our horses' feet are also becoming very sore. We have, however, some hopes of getting soon out of this horrible mountainous desert, as we have discovered the appearance of a valley or level part of the country about forty miles ahead. When this discovery was made there was as much joy and rejoicing among the corps, as happens among passengers at sea, who have experienced a dangerous and protracted voyage, when they first discover land on the long-looked-for coast.

Source

Gass, Patrick. September 2-September 19, 1805, entries in *The Journals of the Lewis and Clark Expedition*, ed. Gary Moulton. Lincoln: University of Nebraska Press/Electronic Text Center, 2005. Retrieved from http://lewisandclarkjournals.unl.edu/journals.php?id=1805-09-02.

William Clark Searches for Winter Quarters on the Pacific Coast

In November 1805 the Lewis and Clark Expedition finally succeeded in reaching the Pacific Ocean after traveling more than 4,000 miles across the continent. Their joy quickly turned to gloom, however, as they were confronted with terrible weather, troublesome Indians, and poor options for establishing winter quarters on the coast. In the following excerpts from his journal, dated November 24-December 5, 1805, Captain William Clark describes taking a historic vote of all crew members—including an African-American man and a Native-American woman—to decide where to camp for the winter. He also recalls his frustration and discomfort at being socked in for two weeks by relentless rain, wind, and waves before the group finally finds a suitable camping spot, at which point he inscribes his name on a tree.

Sunday, November 24

...Being now determined to go into winter quarters as soon as possible, as a convenient situation to procure the wild animals of the forest which must be our dependence for subsisting this winter, we have every reason to believe that the natives have not provisions sufficient for our consumption, and if they had, their prices are so high that it would take ten times as much to purchase their roots & dried fish as we have in our possession, including our small remains of merchandise and clothes &c. This certainly induces every individual of the party to make diligent inquiries of the natives the part of the country in which the wild animals are most plenty. They generally agree that the most elk is on the opposite shore, and that the greatest numbers of deer is up the river at some distance above.

The elk being an animal much larger than deer, easier to kill, better meat (in the winter when poor and skins better for the clothes of our party): added to, a convenient situation to the sea coast where we could make salt, and a probability of vessels coming into the mouth of the Columbia (which the Indians inform us would return to trade with them in three months) from whom we might procure a fresh supply of Indian trinkets to purchase provisions on our return home: together with the solicitations [votes] of every individual, except one of our party, induced us conclude to cross the river and examine the opposite side.... Added to the above advantages in being near the sea coast one most striking occurs to me, i.e., the climate which must be from every appearance much milder than that above the first range of mountains. The Indians are slightly clothed and give an account of but little snow, and the weather which we have experienced since we arrived in the neighborhood of the sea coast has been very warm, and many of the few days past disagreeably so. If this should be the case it will most certainly be the best situation of our naked party dressed as they are altogether in leather....

[After deciding to build a winter camp on the opposite side of the Columbia River, the expedition is socked in by bad weather.]

Thursday, November 28

Wind shifted about to the southwest and blew hard accompanied with hard rain all last night, we are all wet, bedding and stores, having nothing to keep ourselves or stores dry, our lodge nearly worn out, and the pieces of sails & tents so full of holes & rotten that they will not keep anything dry, we sent out the most of the men to drive the point for deer, they scattered through the point; some stood on the peninsula, we could find no deer, several hunters' attempts to penetrate the thick woods to the main south side without success, the swan & geese wild and cannot be approached, and wind too high to go either back or forward, and we have nothing to eat but a little pounded fish which we purchased at the Great Falls. This is our present situation, truly disagreeable! Added to this the robes of ourselves and men are all rotten from being continually wet, and we cannot procure others, or blankets in their places. About 12 o'clock the wind shifted about to the northwest and blew with great violence for the remainder of the day. At many times it blew for fifteen or twenty minutes with such violence that I expected every moment to see trees taken up by the roots, some were blown down. Those squalls were succeeded by rain, O! how tremendous is the day. This dreadful wind and rain continued with intervals of fair weather, the greater part of the evening and night.

Sunday, December 1

...The immense seas and waves which break on the rocks & coasts to the southwest and northwest roars like an immense fall at a distance, and this roaring has continued ever since our arrival in the neighborhood of the sea coast, which has been twenty-four days since we arrived in sight of the Great Western (for I cannot say Pacific) Ocean, as I have not seen one pacific day since my arrival in its vicinity, and its waters are foaming and perpetually break with immense waves on the sands and rocky coasts, tempestuous and horrible.

Tuesday, December 3

A fair windy morning wind from the east. The men returned with the elk which revived the spirits of my party very much. I am still unwell and can't eat even the flesh of the elk. An Indian canoe of eight Indians came too, those Indians are on their way down to the Clatsops with wapato to barter with that nation, I purchased a few of those roots for which I gave small fish hooks, those roots I ate with a little elk soup which I found gave me great relief. I found the roots both nourishing and as a check to my disorder. The Indians proceeded on down through immense high waves, many times their canoe was entirely out of sight before they were half a mile distant....

I marked my name on a large pine tree immediately on the isthmus [a narrow spit of land], William Clark, December 3rd, 1805. By land from the U. States in 1804 & 1805.

Thursday, December 5

Some hard showers of rain last night, this morning cloudy and drizzly at some little distance above the isthmus the rain is much harder. High water today at 12, this tide is two inches higher than that of yesterday. All our stores and bedding are again wet by the hard rain of last night. Captain Lewis's long delay below, has been the source of no little uneasiness on my part of his probable situation and safety, the repeated rains and hard wind which blows from the southwest renders it impossible for me to move with loaded canoes along an unknown coast. We are all wet & disagreeable; the party much better of indispositions.

Captain Lewis returned with three men in the canoe and informs me that he thinks that a sufficient number of elk may be procured convenient to a situation on a small river which falls into a small bay a short distance below, that his party had killed six elk & five deer in his route, two men of his party left behind to secure the elk. This was very satisfactory information to all the party. We accordingly determined to proceed on to the situation which Captain Lewis had viewed as soon as the wind and weather should permit and commence building huts &c.

Source

Clark, William. November 24-December 5, 1805, entries in *The Journals of the Lewis and Clark Expedition*, ed. Gary Moulton. Lincoln: University of Nebraska Press/Electronic Text Center, 2005. Retrieved from http://lewisandclarkjournals.unl.edu/journals.php?id=1805-11-24.

Sergeant John Ordway Returns to Civilization

The following excerpts from the journals of Sergeant John Ordway, dated September 21-23, 1806, describe the final few days of the Lewis and Clark Expedition. As the Corps of Discovery floats down the Missouri River toward St. Louis and reaches American outposts—including some that have been built since they set out more than two years earlier—none of the settlers on shore can believe that the explorers made it back safely. Historians have noted that "we proceeded on," which Ordway repeats several times, was the most commonly used phrase in all of the records of the expedition. Ordway and the other crew members maintained this determined, matter-of-fact attitude even during their triumphant return to civilization.

Sunday, September 21

We set out at the usual time and proceeded on. Passed the scattering houses along the shores. Met a great number of Indians in canoes moving up the river. The people of the settlements were making inquiries of us & were surprised to see us as they said we had been given out for dead above a year ago. Towards evening we arrived at St. Charles, fired three rounds, and camped at the lower end of the town. The people of the town gathered on the bank and could hardly believe that it was us, for they had heard and had believed that we were all dead and were forgotten. The most of the party got quarters in town and refreshments. Late in the evening hard rain commenced and continued hard during the night.

Monday, September 22

The hard rain continued this morning until about 11 o'clock a.m. at which time the party was collected and we set out & proceeded on. Towards evening we arrived at Bell Fountain, a fort or cantonment on the south side which was built since we ascended the Missouri & a handsome place. We moved a short distance below and camped, the Company of Artillery who lay at this fort fired seventeen rounds with the field pieces. The most of our party was quartered in the cantonment. Several flat boats are built at this place. Some rain this evening. A number of these soldiers are acquaintances of ours &c.

Tuesday, September 23

A wet, disagreeable morning. We set out after breakfast and proceeded on. Soon arrived at the mouth of the Missouri, entered the Mississippi River, and landed at River Dubois [Camp Wood] where we wintered in 1804. Here we found a widow woman who we left here & has a plantation under tolerable good way since we have been on the expedition. We delayed a short time and about 12 o'clock we arrived in site of St. Louis, fired three rounds as we approached the town, and landed opposite the center of the town, the people gathered on the shore and huzzaed three cheers. We unloaded the canoes and carried the baggage all up to a store house in town. Drew out the canoes then the party all considerable much rejoiced that we have the expedition completed, and now we look for boarding in town and wait for our settlement and then we intend to return to our native homes to see our parents once more, as we have been so long from them. —*Finis.*

Source

Ordway, John. September 21–23, 1806, entries in *The Journals of the Lewis and Clark Expedition*, ed. Gary Moulton. Lincoln: University of Nebraska Press/Electronic Text Center, 2005. Retrieved from lewisandclarkjournals.unl.edu/read/?_xmlsrc=1806-09-21.xml&_xslsrc=LCstyles.xsl.

Lewis Informs Jefferson That He Completed His Mission

As soon as the Corps of Discovery reached St. Louis, Captain Meriwether Lewis sent the letter excerpted below to President Thomas Jefferson. Lewis notifies the president that he and his men have completed their mission and returned safely. He describes the route the expedition followed across the continent and emphasizes its potential for future trade and commerce. The captain says that he plans to travel to Washington as soon as possible, along with the Mandan chief Sheheke and a variety of plant and animal specimens he collected during the journey. Finally, Lewis mentions the valuable services rendered by his partner, Captain William Clark, and expresses eagerness to see his friends and family again.

St. Louis
September 23, 1806
Sir,

It is with pleasure that I announce to you the safe arrival of myself and party at 12 o'clock today at this place with our papers and baggage. In obedience to your orders we have penetrated the Continent of North America to the Pacific Ocean, and sufficiently explored the interior of the country to affirm with confidence that we have discovered the most practicable route which does exist across the continent by means of the navigable branches of the Missouri and Columbia Rivers. Such is that by way of the Missouri to the foot of the rapids five miles below the great falls of that river a distance of 2,575 miles, thence by land passing the Rocky Mountains to a navigable part of the Kooskooske 340 miles; with the Kooskooske 73 miles, a southeasterly branch of the Columbia 154 miles, and the latter river 413 miles to the Pacific Ocean; making the total distance from the confluence of the Missouri and Mississippi to the discharge of the Columbia into the Pacific Ocean 3,555 miles.

The navigation of the Missouri may be deemed safe and good; its difficulties arise from its falling banks, timber imbedded in the mud of its channel, its sand bars and steady rapidity of its current, all which may be overcome with a great degree of certainty by taking the necessary precautions. The passage by land of 340 miles from the Missouri to the Kooskooske is the most formidable part of the tract proposed across the continent; of this distance 200 miles is along a good road, and 140 over tremendous mountains which for 60 miles are covered with eternal snows; however a passage over these mountains is practicable from the latter part of June to the last of September, and the cheap rate at which horses are to be obtained from the Indians of the Rocky Mountains and west of them, reduces the expenses of transportation over this portage to a mere trifle. The navigation of the Kooskooske, the southeast branch of the Columbia itself is safe and good from the first of April to the middle of August, by making three portages on the latter.... [Lewis specifies the size of boats that can navigate various rivers.]

We view this passage across the continent as affording immense advantages to the fur trade, but fear that the advantages which it offers as a communication for the productions of the East Indies to the United States and thence to Europe will never be found equal on an extensive scale to that by way of the Cape of Good Hope; still we believe that many articles not bulky, brittle, nor of a very perishable nature may be conveyed to the United States by this route with more facility and at less expense than by that at present practiced.

The Missouri and all its branches from the Cheyenne upwards abound more in beaver and common otter than any other streams on earth, particularly that proportion of them lying within the Rocky Mountains. The furs of all this immense tract of country including such as may be collected on the upper portion of the River St. Peters, Red River, and the Assiniboine with the immense country watered by the Columbia, may be conveyed to the mouth of the Columbia by the first of August in each year and from thence be shipped to, and arrive in London....

In the infancy of the trade across the continent, or during the period that the trading establishments shall be confined to the Missouri and its branches, the men employed in this trade will be compelled to convey the furs collected in that quarter as low on the Columbia as tide water, in which case they could not return to the falls of the Missouri until about the first of October, which would be so late in the season that there would be considerable danger of the river being obstructed by ice before they could reach this place and consequently that the commodities brought from the East Indies would be detained until the following spring; but this difficulty will at once vanish when establishments are also made on the Columbia, and a sufficient number of men employed at them to convey annually the productions of the East Indies to the upper establishment on the Kooskooske, and there exchange them with the men of the Missouri for their furs, in the beginning of July. By this means the furs not only of the Missouri but those also of the Columbia may be shipped to the East Indies by the season before mentioned, and the commodities of the East Indies arrive at St. Louis or the mouth of the Ohio by the last of September in each year.

Although the Columbia does not as much as the Missouri abound in beaver and otter, yet it is by no means despicable in this respect, and would furnish a valuable fur trade distinct from any other consideration in addition to the otter and beaver which it could furnish. There might be collected considerable quantities of the skins of three species of bear affording a great variety of colors and of superior delicacy, those also of the tiger cat [wolverine], several species of fox, marten, and several others of an inferior class of furs, besides the valuable sea otter of the coast.

If the government will only aid, even in a very limited manner, the enterprise of her citizens I am fully convinced that we shall shortly derive the benefits of a most lucrative trade from this source, and that in the course of ten or twelve years a tour across the Continent by the route mentioned will be undertaken by individuals with as little concern as a voyage across the Atlantic is at present.

The British North West Company of Canada has for several years, carried on a partial trade with the Minitari, Amahami, and Mandans on the Missouri from their establishments on the Assiniboine at the entrance of Mouse River; at present I have good reason for believing that they intend shortly to form an establishment near those nations with a view to engross the fur trade of the Missouri. The known enterprise and resources of this company, latterly strengthened by an union with their powerful rival the X. Y. Company, renders them formidable in that distant part of the continent to all other traders; and in my opinion if we are to regard the trade of the Missouri as an object of importance to the United States; the strides of this company towards the Missouri cannot be too vigilantly watched nor too firmly and speedily opposed by our government. The embarrassments from which the navigation of the Missouri at present labors from the unfriendly dispositions of the Kansas, the several bands of Tetons, Assiniboines and those tribes that resort to the British establishments on the Saskatchewan is also a subject which requires the earliest attention of our government. As I shall shortly be with you I have deemed it unnecessary here to detail the several ideas which have presented themselves to my mind on those subjects, more especially when I consider that a thorough knowledge of the geography of the country is absolutely necessary to their being understood, and leisure has not yet permitted us to make but one general map of the country which I am unwilling to risk by the mail.

As a sketch of the most prominent features of our peregrination since we left the Mandans may not be uninteresting, I shall endeavor to give it to you by way of letter from this place, where I shall necessarily be detained several days in order to settle with and discharge the men who accompanied me on the voyage as well as to prepare for my route to the City of Washington.

We left Fort Clatsop where we wintered near the entrance of the Columbia on the 27th of March last, and arrived at the foot of the Rocky Mountains on the 10th of May, where we were detained until the 24th of June in consequence of the snow which rendered a passage over the those mountains impracticable until that moment; had it not been for this detention I should ere this have joined you at Monticello. In my last communication to you from the Mandans I mentioned my intention of sending back a canoe with a small party from the Rocky Mountains; but on our arrival at the great falls of the Missouri on the 14th of June 1805, in view of that formidable snowy barrier, the discouraging difficulties which we had to encounter in making a portage of eighteen miles of our canoes and baggage around those falls were such that my friend Captain Clark and myself conceived it inexpedient to reduce the party, lest by doing so we should lessen the ardor of those who remained and thus hazard the fate of the expedition, and therefore declined that measure, thinking it better that the government as well as our friends should for a moment feel some anxiety for our fate than to risk so much; experience has since proved the justice of our decision, for we have more than once owed our lives and the fate of the expedition to our number, which consisted of thirty-one men.

I have brought with me several skins of the sea otter, two skins of the native sheep of America, five skins and skeletons complete of the bighorn or mountain ram, and a skin of the mule deer besides the skins of several other quadrupeds and birds, natives of the countries through which we have passed. I have also preserved a pretty extensive collection of plants, and collected nine other vocabularies.

I have prevailed on the great chief of the Mandan nation to accompany me to Washington; he is now with my friend and colleague Captain Clark at this place, in good health and spirits, and very anxious to proceed.

With respect to the exertions and services rendered by that esteemable man Captain William Clark in the course of late voyage I cannot say too much; if sir any credit be due for the success of that arduous enterprise in which we have been mutually engaged, he is equally with myself entitled to your consideration and that of our common country.

The anxiety which I feel in returning once more to the bosom of my friends is a sufficient guarantee that no time will be unnecessarily expended in this quarter. I have detained the post several hours for the purpose of making you this hasty communication. I hope that while I am pardoned for this detention of the mail, the situation in which I have been compelled to write will sufficiently apologize for having been this laconic....

I am very anxious to learn the state of my friends in Albemarle, particularly whether my mother is yet living. I am with every sentiment of esteem your obedient and very humble servant.

Meriwether Lewis
Captain 1st U.S. Regiment Infantry

N.B. [*nota bene,* or take note] The whole of the party who accompanied me from the Mandans have returned in good health, which is not, I assure you, to me one of the least pleasing considerations of the voyage.

Source

Lewis, Meriwether. Letter to Thomas Jefferson, September 23, 1806. Thomas Jefferson Papers, Library of Congress. Retrieved from http://www.loc.gov/resource/mtj1.036_0912_0917/?sp=1&st=text.

Jefferson Meets with an American Indian Delegation

One of President Thomas Jefferson's goals for the Lewis and Clark Expedition was to establish friendly relations with the Native Americans who lived west of the Mississippi River. The captains convinced several Indian nations of the Upper Missouri to send representatives to Washington, D.C., to meet with the "great chief" of the United States. Jefferson delivered the following address to this delegation on January 4, 1806. The president explains that the United States is very powerful and now controls lands across North America. He emphasizes his good intentions, however, and offers to supply goods they want in exchange for furs and other valuable resources from the frontier.

My friends & children. I take you by the hand of friendship and give you a hearty welcome to the seat of the government of the U.S. The journey which you have taken to visit your fathers on this side of our island is a long one, and your having undertaken it is a proof that you desired to become acquainted with us. I thank the great spirit that he has protected you though the journey and brought you safely to the residence of your friends, and I hope he will have you constantly in his safekeeping and restore you in good health to your nations and families.

My friends & children. We are descended from the old nations which live beyond the great water: but we & our forefathers have been so long here that we seem like you to have grown out of this land: we consider ourselves no longer as of the old nations beyond the great water, but as united in one family with our red brethren here. The French, the English, the Spaniards, have now agreed with us to retire from all the country which you & we hold between Canada & Mexico, and never more to return to it. And remember the words I now speak to you my children, they are never to return again. We are become as numerous as the leaves of the trees, and, tho' we do not boast, we do not fear any nation. We are now your fathers; and you shall not lose by the change. As soon as Spain had agreed to withdraw from all the waters of the Missouri & Mississippi, I felt the desire of becoming acquainted with all my red children beyond the Mississippi, and of uniting them with us, as we have done those on this side of that river, in the bonds of peace & friendship. I wished to learn what we could do to benefit them by furnishing them the necessaries they want in exchange for their furs & peltries. I therefore sent our beloved man Captain Lewis, one of my own family, to go up the Missouri River, to get acquainted with all the Indian nations in its neighborhood, to take them by the hand, deliver my talks to them, and to inform us in what way we could be useful to them. Some of you who are here have seen him & heard his words. You have taken him by the hand, and been friendly to him. My children I thank you for the services you rendered him, and for your attention to his words. When he returns he will tell us where we should establish factories to be convenient to you all, and what we must send to them. In establishing a trade with you we desire to make no profit. We shall ask from you only what everything costs us, and give you for your furs & pelts whatever we can get for them again. Be assured you shall find your advantage in this change of your friends. It will take us some time to be in readiness to supply your wants, but in the meanwhile & till Captain Lewis returns, the traders who have heretofore furnished you will continue to do so.

My friends & children. I have now an important advice to give you. I have already told you that you are all my children, and I wish you to live in peace & friendship with one another as brethren of the same family ought to do. How much better is it for neighbors to help than to hurt one another, how much happier must it make them. If you will cease to make war on one another, if you will live in friendship with all mankind, you can employ all of your time in providing food & clothing for yourselves and you families. Your men will not be destroyed in war and your women & children will lie down to sleep in their cabins without fear of being surprised by their enemies & killed or carried away. Your numbers will be increased, instead of diminishing, and you will live in plenty & in quiet. My children, I have given this advice to all your red brethren on this side of the Mississippi, they are following it, they are increasing in their numbers, are learning to clothe & provide for their families as we do, and you see the proofs of it in such of them as you happened to find here. My children, we are strong, we are numerous as the stars in the heavens, & we are all gun-men. Yet we live in peace with all nations; and all nations esteem & honor us because we are peaceable & just. Then let my red children be peaceable & just also; take each other by the hand, and hold it fast. If ever bad men among your neighbors should do you wrong, and their nation refuse you justice, apply to the beloved man whom we shall place nearest to you; he will go to the offending nation, & endeavor to obtain right, & preserve peace. If ever bad men among yourselves injure you neighbors, be always ready to do justice. It is always honorable in those who have done wrong to acknowledge & make amends for it; and it is the only way in which peace can be maintained among men. Remember then my advice, my children, carry it home to your people, and tell them that from the day that they have become all the same family, from the day that we become father to them all, we wish as a true father should do, that we may all live together as one household, and that before they strike one another, they should come to their father & let him endeavor to make up the quarrel.

My children. You are come from the other side of our great island, from where the sun sets to see your new friends at the sun rising. You have now arrived where the waters are constantly rising & falling every day, but you are still distant from the sea. I very much desire that you should not stop here, but go on and see your brethren as far as the edge of the great water. I am persuaded you have so far seen that every man by the way has received you as his brothers, and has been ready to do you all the kindnesses in his power. You will see the same thing quite to the sea shore; and I wish you therefore to go and visit our great cities in that quarter, & to see how many friends & brothers you have here. You will then have travelled a long line from West to East, and if you had time to go from North to South, from Canada to Florida, you would find it as long in that direction, & all the people as sincerely your friends. I wish you, my children, to see all you can and to tell your people all you see; because I am sure the more they know of us, the more they will be our hearty friends. I invite you therefore to pay a visit to Baltimore, Philadelphia, New York, & the cities still beyond that if you should be willing to go further. We will provide carriages to convey you, & a person to go with you to see that you want for nothing. By the time you come back, the snows will be melted on the mountains, ice in the rivers broken up and you will be wishing to set out on your return home.

My children. I have long desired to see you. I have now opened my heart to you; let my words sink into your hearts & never be forgotten. If ever lying people or bad spirits should raise up clouds between us: let us come together as friends & explain to each other what is misrepresented or misunderstood. The clouds will fly away like the morning fog and the sun of friendship appear, & shine forever bright & clear between us.

My children. It may happen that while you are here, occasion may arise to talk about many things which I do not now particularly mention. The Secretary at War will always be ready to talk with you: and you are to consider whatever he says as said by myself. He will also take care of you & see that you are furnished with all comforts here.

Th. Jefferson
January 4, 1806

Source

Jefferson, Thomas. Speech delivered January 4, 1806. In Jackson, Donald, ed. *Letters of the Lewis and Clark Expedition with Related Documents 1783-1854.* Volume 1. Urbana and Chicago: University of Illinois Press, 1978. Retrieved from http://www.loc.gov/exhibits/lewisandclark/transcript45.html.

Native Americans Offer Their Perspective on Westward Expansion

Lewis and Clark sent a delegation of American Indians from seven nations along the Upper Missouri River back east to meet with President Thomas Jefferson. After hearing a speech by the president on January 4, 1806, they issued the following response. The Native American leaders express affection for the captains and a willingness to accept Jefferson's offers of peace, friendship, and trade. But they also express concerns about whether American traders and settlers on the western frontier will follow through on the president's promises to treat them fairly. As it turned out, their concerns were well founded. In the decades following the Lewis and Clark Expedition, the U.S. government betrayed its promises to the Native Americans countless times by breaking treaties and stealing their land to make room for white settlement.

My Grandfather & My Father

It is with an open heart that we receive your hands, friendship stretches ours in yours & unites them together.

Fathers

We feel entirely our happiness at this day, since you tell us that we are welcome in the grand lodge of prosperity. We perceive that we are numbered among your most cherished children.

Fathers

You observe that we have undertaken a very long journey in order to see our fathers & brethren; it is most true: but fathers, we will tell you that we did not look back for to measure the road, & our sight stretching to the rising sun, discovered every new day the pleasure rising with him, as we were reflecting our daily approach, our hearts were overjoyed, for we were soon to see our new good fathers who wish to pity us.

Fathers

There is a long while that we wish to be acquainted with our fathers & brothers of the rising sun & we hope that, when we will return back, where the sun sets, we will dispel all the thick clouds whose darkness obscures the light of the day.

Fathers

That Great Spirit who disposes of everything, & fixes into our bosom the ardent desire of seeing you, we thank him & we will thank him more when we will be at home amongst our wives & children, for, then, our eyes will be satisfied, our ears full with your words, & our hearts with joy.

But fathers

We have to thank our interpreters who advised us to strengthen our hearts, & listen not to the sense of those men who wanted to prevent us from coming to see you, alleging that we would be unwelcome & all of us should die. Our interpreters told us that our fathers were good & would pity us, that they wanted to be acquainted with their new red children; & that we ought not to listen to the crowing of bad birds.

Fathers

You do not know yet your new red children, & we see that you are as much worthy of pity as we are; flatterers came before you, made vast promises, but when far away, they constitute themselves masters, deceive you & your children suffer....

Fathers

We believe that you wish to pity us & to prevent our wants by sending us supplies of goods, but look sharp & tell to your men to take not too much fur for a little of goods, should they act in that way we would not be better off than we are now with our actual traders.

Fathers

We have seen the beloved man [Captain Meriwether Lewis], we shook hands with him & we heard the words you put in his mouth. We wish him well, where he is, we have him in our hearts, & when he will return we believe that he will take care of us, prevent our wants & make us happy: he told us you wished us to come to see you & our brethren of the rising sun: here we are happy to see you & glad to hear the words of good fathers.

Fathers

You tell us to be in peace & amity with our brethren: we wish to be so: misunderstanding sometimes breaks peace & amity, because we listen too much to those men who live yet amongst us & who do not belong to your family, but when we will have but your own children with us, then it will be easy for you to maintain the peace of your red children & we will all acknowledge that we have good fathers.

Fathers

Meditate what you say, you tell us that your children of this side of the Mississippi hear your word, you are mistaken, since every day they raise their tomahawks over our heads, but we believe it be contrary to your orders & inclination, & that, before long, should they be deaf to your voice, you will chastise them.

Fathers

Though your forefathers were inhabiting the other side of the big lake, we consider you as ourselves, since, like us, you spring out of our land, for the same reason, we believe you consider us to be your children, that you pity us & wish to make us happy should we follow your advices.

Fathers

You say that the French, English & Spanish nations have left the waters of the Missouri & Mississippi, we are all glad of it, & we believe that the day they will leave us the weather will be clear, the paths clean, & our ears will be no more affected with the disagreeable sounds of the bad birds who wish us to relinquish the words of our good fathers whose words we keep in our hearts.

Although fathers

Do not believe that the number of our new brethren would be able to frighten us, were we not inclined to acknowledge you for our fathers; but we wish to live like you & to be men like you; we hope you will protect us from the wicked, you will punish them who won't hear your word, open their ears, & lead them in the good path....

Fathers

You say that you are as numerous as the stars in the skies, & as strong as numerous. So much the better, fathers, tho', if you are so, we will see you ere long punishing all the wicked red skins that you'll find amongst us, & you may tell to your white children on our lands, to follow your orders, & do not as they please, for they do not keep your word. Our brothers who came here before told us you had ordered good things to be done & sent to our villages, but we have seen nothing, & your waged men think that truth will not reach your ears, but we are conscious that we must speak the truth, truth must be spoken to the ears of our fathers, & our fathers must open their ears to truth to get in.

Fathers

You tell us to complain to the beloved man, should anyone commit injury & decline compensation, but you know fathers that the beloved man is gone far away, that he cannot do the justice which you want him to do; while he is absent we do better to complain to his fathers, & when he will arrive we will complain to him, then he will have justice done to the injured man & if he loves his fathers he will chastise the one who broke the peace which our good fathers told us to make together & to maintain.

Fathers

We hear your word, we will carry it into our villages, & spread it all over our fields, we will tell to our warriors, wives & children that, ever since you became the fathers of all the red skins, like good fathers, you wish us to live like children of but one family who have but one father, & that before we should go at war we have to take the advice of our good fathers & then we shall know what these latter will tell us.

Fathers

Our hearts are good, though we are powerful & strong, & we know how to fight, we do not wish to fight but shut the mouth of your children who speak war, stop the arm of those who raise the tomahawk over our heads & crush those who strike first, then we will confess that we have good fathers who wish to make their red children happy & peace maintained among them. For when we are at peace we hunt freely, our wives & children do not stand in want, we smoke & sleep easy....

Fathers

As you spoke that we had brethren inhabiting the shores of the big Lake & that you offered us to visit them, we do wish to be acquainted with them, to shake hands with them & to tell them that we are their brothers & if they are good children we will tell them that we are so, for you know fathers we acknowledge you for our fathers.

Fathers

After shaking hands with all our new brothers, being acquainted with them all, then we will tell to our warriors, our wives, our children how many things we have seen, they all will listen to our sayings, they will gather around us, hear the words of their new fathers & brethren, love them all & wonder at all things;

yes fathers, we will speak the truth, you know the truth must come out of the mouth of a father.

Fathers

We hope the more we will see our new brethren the more we will love them for we hope they will welcome us & receive us as their brethren....

Fathers

You say, that, when we will come back the ice will be broken, the snow melted, & then we will return into our villages: yes, fathers, when we will see our warriors, when we will see our wives, when we will see our children, our hearts will be overjoyed, their hearts will be overjoyed, they will hear the word you put in our mouth, we will carry it to them deeply engraved in our hearts. Our warriors will bury the tomahawk, the wicked will be good, whenever they will hear the word of their fathers & know them to be good to all the red skins.

Fathers

We will keep your word in our bosom; the stinking cloud may rise, it will melt away when we will remember the word of our fathers, the bad birds may fly over our heads, & crow mischief, their flesh will be poor, their voice weak, they will hush & fly away when hearing the word of our fathers; we will be happy with your word, fathers, & never part with it....

Fathers

We give you again the hand of friendship.

Source

"Speech of the Osages, Missouri, Otos, Panis, Cansas, Ayowais & Sioux Nations to the President of the U.S. & to the Secretary at War," January 4, 1806. In Jackson, Donald, ed. *Letters of the Lewis and Clark Expedition with Related Documents 1783-1854*. Volume 1. Urbana and Chicago: University of Illinois Press, 1978. Retrieved from http://www.loc.gov/exhibits/lewisandclark/transcript46.html.

Historian James Ronda Explores the Legacy of Lewis and Clark

The bicentennial of the Lewis and Clark Expedition in 2004-2006 generated a surge in public inter-
est in the courageous explorers and their epic journey across the continent. It also prompted James
P. Ronda, a prominent historian and author of several books about the Corps of Discovery, to con-
sider the importance of the expedition in American history and in the lives of Americans today. His
article "Why Lewis and Clark Matter" appeared in Smithsonian *magazine and is reprinted below.*

As the Lewis and Clark bicentennial approaches—the Corps of Discovery
set out from Camp Dubois at the confluence of the Mississippi and Missouri
rivers on May 14, 1804—all the signs of a great cultural-historical wallow are
in place. Hundreds of Lewis and Clark books are flooding the market—everything from *The Journals of the Lewis and Clark Expedition* to Gary Moulton's magnificent 13-volume edition of the expedition's journals, to cookbooks, coloring
books and trail guides. A gift catalog from Thomas Jefferson's Monticello offers
stuffed versions of a prairie dog, a bison and a Newfoundland dog made to look
like Seaman, the animal that accompanied Lewis on the trip. You can even order
dolls of Meriwether Lewis and William Clark, Sacagawea and York "with
detailed removable clothing."

There are Corps of Discovery television documentaries, an IMAX movie
and dozens upon dozens of Internet Web sites. There are Lewis and Clark conferences, museum exhibitions and trail rides. Last summer Harley-Davidson
motorcycle riders drove parts of the trail. When Harley hogs discover Lewis and
Clark, you know something big is going on!

Now I would be the last person to dump mashed potatoes on all of this; after
all, I've written four books about the expedition. Much of this bicentennial celebration is good, clean family fun that's both informative and entertaining. But
in all this hoopla I fear that we may miss the underlying significance of the Lewis
and Clark story and the chance to connect these early explorers to the larger and
richer stories of our past. On the road with Thomas Jefferson's Corps of Discovery, or even standing alongside the trail as they pass by, we meet ourselves,
and more important, we meet people who are not ourselves.

Lewis and Clark were not the first white men to cross the continent from
the Atlantic to the Pacific north of Mexico. (Scottish fur trader Alexander Mac-

Ronda, James P. "Why Lewis and Clark Matter." *Smithsonian*, August 2003. Used by permission of the author.

kenzie crossed Canada a decade earlier.) Nor did they visit places not already seen and mapped by generations of native people. You could even say that Lewis and Clark began the American invasion of the West, which aimed at making it safe for cows, corn and capital at the expense of bison, prairie grasses and cultures not fitting the expansionist agenda. If we want to be hard edged, we could even make a case that the Lewis and Clark story is a mainstay of the same shelf-worn narrative that glorifies and justifies the American conquest and dispossession of the North America natives. (Textbook history often portrays Lewis and Clark as the vanguard of America's triumphant westward expansion, a movement that brought civilization and progress to a savage wilderness.) But it does seem to me that there are several reasons why Lewis and Clark *do* matter—and why we are so drawn to them.

First, what happened to the Corps is a great story, brimming with energy and full of forward motion. In extraordinary settings, a remarkable cast of characters encountered adversity of epic proportions and struggled through one adventure after another.

American novelist Willa Cather once noted that there are only two or three great human stories—and that we are destined to keep repeating them over and over again. One of these is the journey. Some of the oldest Indian stories are about journeys. There are the journeys of Africans and Europeans coming to North America, settlers pushing west by way of the Oregon Trail and the transcontinental railroad, and Chinese women and men traveling from places such as Shanghai and Guangdong Province to California, Idaho and Wyoming. Journeys took—and continue to take—Spanish-speaking men and women to El Norte. In the 20th century, the journeys of African-Americans from the rural South to the urban, industrial North re-made the racial, cultural and political map of the United States.

We are a people in motion, whether on the Trail of Tears, Route 66 or the Interstate System. From Jack Kerouac to Willie Nelson, the lure of the road and the promise of the journey still hold us. And it was Lewis and Clark who gave us our first great national road story.

Second, the Lewis and Clark expedition resonates because it's not just a white man's army, but rather a group of people from many different racial, ethnic, cultural and social backgrounds—a human community as diverse as any in America today. Consider York, William Clark's slave and fellow adventurer, or Pierre Cruzatte, the one-eyed fiddle player, who was part French and part

211

Omaha Indian. There was German-born Pvt. John Potts, a miller by trade and a soldier most likely by necessity. Here is Sacagawea, a Shoshone woman who spent formative years with the Hidatsa Indians, and Jean Baptiste Charbonneau, a child of mixed Shoshone-French ancestry. Imagine the sounds around the campfire: William Clark's Virginia-Kentucky drawl, Sgt. John Ordway's New Hampshire inflections, George Drouillard's Shawnee-flavored French, and the cries and first words of Jean Baptiste, the baby born to Sacagawea on the trip. This is the crazy quilt that was and is America.

But Sacagawea aside, isn't the expedition a man's story? Not entirely. A close reading of the expedition records reveals that women were a part of the journey every step of the way. Philadelphia seamstress Matilda Chapman sewed 93 shirts for the expedition; women did laundry and sold provisions to the expedition as it overwintered outside St. Louis; Arikara, Mandan and Hidatsa women were a constant part of expedition life up the Missouri, providing food and friendship; Lemhi Shoshone women carried expedition baggage over the Continental Divide; a Nez Perce woman named Watkuweis brokered friendly relations between the Americans and her tribe; Chinook women, camped outside Fort Clatsop, offered themselves in return for valued trade goods, including metal tools, cloth and even uniform buttons.

Indeed, native people of both sexes lie at the heart of the Lewis and Clark journey; it is they who make it such a compelling story. On the day before the expedition's official start, William Clark wrote that the expedition's "road across the continent" would take the Corps through "a multitude of Indians." We can name the names: the Otoe chief Big Horse (Shingto-tongo), the Brulé Teton Sioux chief Black Buffalo Bull (Un-tongar-Sar-bar), the Mandan chief Black Cat (Posecopsahe), the Lemhi Shoshone chief Cameahwait (Too-et-te-conl), the Nez Perce chief Five Big Hearts (Yoom-park-kar-tim), the Walula chief Yelleppit and the Clatsop village headman Coboway.

Finally, this is a story of the kind novelist Henry James once called "the visitable past." We can still float the Upper Missouri and look on what Lewis described as "seens of visionary inchantment." We can stand at Lemhi Pass and see the distant Bitterroots. We can hike parts of the Lolo Trail and visit Fort Clatsop.

Historian Donald Jackson once observed that Lewis and Clark were the "writingest" explorers in American history. The expedition diarists—all seven if we count the still-missing Robert Frazer journal—wrote about everything from bison, thunderstorms and tribal politics to river currents, mountain ranges and prairie plants. Some of it is dull, recording miles traveled and campsites set up. But there are also passages of the most marvelous, flashing prose, which brings the West alive, leaps the abyss of time and dances for us across the page. And all of it, whether dull or delightful, is written in a way we can understand.

Lewis and Clark matter today because they act as a benchmark by which we can measure change and continuity in everything from the environment to relations between peoples. But more than that, their adventure reminds us that we are not the first Americans (native and newcomers alike) to face difficult choices in troubled times. William Clark, Sacagawea and Coboway lived in a complex, often violent age. The winds of change blew as hard then as now.

When honestly told, the Lewis and Clark story inspires without leading us into simpleminded platitudes. History humanizes us by giving names, faces and texture to our physical and mental landscapes. Not only do the Lewis and Clark stories entertain us, they serve as a map and guide for life on the American road.

Source

Ronda, James P. "Why Lewis and Clark Matter." *Smithsonian,* August 2003. Retrieved from http://www.smithsonianmag.com/history/why-lewis-and-clark-matter-87847931/?all.

IMPORTANT PEOPLE, PLACES, AND TERMS

Bonaparte, Napoleon (1769-1821)
Emperor of France who sold the Louisiana Territory to the United States in 1803.

Cameahwait
Shoshone Indian chief and brother of Sacagawea who provided horses to the Lewis and Clark Expedition in August 1805, allowing the explorers to cross the Rocky Mountains.

Charbonneau, Jean Baptiste (1805-1866)
Son of Sacagawea and Toussaint Charbonneau who accompanied his parents on the Lewis and Clark Expedition as a baby and went on to become an explorer and fur trader.

Charbonneau, Toussaint (c. 1760-1843)
French Canadian fur trader and husband of Sacagawea who served as a translator for the Lewis and Clark Expedition.

Clark, William (1770-1838)
Co-captain and primary mapmaker for the Corps of Discovery.

Clatsop
Indian nation with territory near the mouth of the Columbia River in present-day Washington, where the Lewis and Clark Expedition spent the winter of 1805-1806.

Colter, John (c. 1774-1813)
Member of the Corps of Discovery who went on to become a fur trapper, explorer, and legendary mountain man.

Corps of Discovery
   The unofficial name of the U.S. military and scientific expedition led by Lewis and Clark.

Drouillard, George (c. 1774-1810)
   French Canadian-Shawnee Indian civilian member of the Corps of Discovery who was the expedition's best hunter.

Enlightenment
   A historical era, also known as the Age of Reason, in which leading thinkers emphasized questioning traditional authority, pursuing knowledge and individual improvement, and reforming government, society, and culture.

Floyd, Charles (1782-1804)
   Sergeant in the Corps of Discovery who died of a ruptured appendix during his journey with Lewis and Clark.

Gass, Patrick (1771-1870)
   Sergeant and carpenter in the Corps of Discovery who published an unauthorized account of the Lewis and Clark Expedition.

Indian Removal Act
   A controversial 1830 law that authorized the U.S. government to forcibly deport Native Americans from their ancestral territory to reservation lands west of the Mississippi River.

Jefferson, Thomas (1743-1826)
   Author of the Declaration of Independence, third president of the United States, and organizer of the Lewis and Clark Expedition.

Lewis, Meriwether (1774-1809)
   Explorer, naturalist, soldier, personal secretary of President Thomas Jefferson, and co-captain of the Corps of Discovery.

Livingston, Robert (1746-1813)
   Lawyer, politician, and Founding Father who represented the United States in the successful negotiations to purchase the Louisiana Territory from France in 1803.

Louisiana Purchase
   A treaty in which the United States acquired 827,000 square miles of territory from France for $15 million. The deal doubled the size of the Unit-

ed States and shifted the nation's western border all the way from the Mississippi River to the Rocky Mountains.

Mackenzie, Alexander (1764-1820)

Scottish explorer who became the first European to cross North America by land and reach the Pacific Ocean in 1793.

Mandan

A Native American nation of the Upper Missouri River that assisted the Lewis and Clark Expedition during the winter of 1804-1805.

Manifest destiny

The idea, popular in the mid-1800s, that the United States had a national mission to spread freedom and democracy and would be serving God's purpose by extending its borders all the way to the Pacific Ocean.

Monroe, James (1758-1831)

Founding Father who helped negotiate the Louisiana Purchase in 1803 and also promoted Indian removal as the fifth president of the United States (1817-1825).

Nez Perce

A Native American nation with territory on the west side of the Bitterroot Range that provided food and guidance to Lewis and Clark when they crossed the mountains in 1805 and 1806.

Ordway, John (1775-1817)

Sergeant in the Corps of Discovery who kept records, issued provisions, made duty assignments, and led teams in the absence of Lewis and Clark.

Sacagawea (c. 1788-1812)

Shoshone Indian woman who served as an interpreter and guide for the Lewis and Clark Expedition.

Shoshone

A Native American nation with territory near modern-day Salmon, Idaho, that provided horses and guidance to the Lewis and Clark Expedition in 1805.

York (c. 1770-c. 1822)

Enslaved African-American man who was considered the property of Captain William Clark and participated in the journey of the Corps of Discovery.

CHRONOLOGY

1762

At the end of the French and Indian War, France is forced to turn over control of Louisiana to Spain. *See p. 10.*

1776

The American colonies declare independence from Great Britain. *See p. 7.*

1783

The United States is established following the end of the Revolutionary War. *See p. 7.*

1787

The Northwest Ordinance, which opens the Great Lakes region to white settlement, also includes protections for Native American inhabitants. *See p. 92.*

1792

American sea captain Robert Gray sails into the mouth of the Columbia River on the Pacific Coast of North America. *See p. 16.*

1793

Scottish explorer Alexander Mackenzie, traveling through Canada, becomes the first European to cross North America by land and reach the Pacific Ocean. *See p. 16.*

1795

Meriwether Lewis and William Clark meet when they serve in the same frontier military unit. *See p. 21.*

1799

Napoleon Bonaparte seizes power in France and begins working to reclaim former French colonies in North America. *See p. 10.*

1801

Thomas Jefferson takes office as the third president of the United States. *See p. 7.*

Jefferson invites Lewis to Washington, D.C., to serve as his personal secretary. *See p. 20.*

Mackenzie publishes a book about his North American exploration, which encourages Jefferson to organize a U.S. expedition. *See p. 17.*

1802

King Charles IV of Spain signs a decree transferring ownership of the Louisiana Territory back to France. *See p. 10.*

1803

January 18 – Jefferson delivers a confidential message to Congress requesting funds to mount a U.S. military expedition to explore the Louisiana Territory. *See p. 17.*

April 11 – French foreign minister Charles Maurice de Talleyrand informs U.S. ambassador Robert Livingston that France is willing to sell Louisiana to the United States for $15 million. *See p. 13.*

April 30 – Livingston and U.S. envoy James Monroe sign the Louisiana Purchase Treaty. *See p. 13.*

Jefferson officially organizes a U.S. military expedition into the West and names Lewis as its leader. *See p. 20.*

Lewis visits with leading experts from the American Philosophical Society in Philadelphia to brush up on scientific skills. *See p. 21.*

June 19 – Lewis sends a letter to Clark asking him to be a partner in the expedition. *See p. 21.*

June 20 – Jefferson sends a long, detailed letter to Lewis outlining his many scientific, political, and military goals for the expedition. *See p. 22.*

Lewis purchases equipment and supplies for the expedition and ships them to Pittsburgh. *See p. 24.*

July 5 – Lewis travels to Pittsburgh, only to find that the construction of his keelboat has been delayed. *See p. 25.*

August 31 – With the keelboat finally finished, Lewis departs down the Ohio River from Pittsburgh. *See p. 25.*

October 14 – Lewis meets up with Clark and the "nine young men from Kentucky" in Clarksville, Indiana Territory. *See p. 26.*

November 13 – The Corps of Discovery reaches the junction of the Ohio and Mississippi Rivers and stops to fix the latitude and longitude of the spot. *See p. 27.*

December 10 – The expedition arrives at St. Louis and builds Camp Dubois just upstream from the city at Wood River, Illinois. *See p. 28.*

1804

March 9 – Lewis attends a ceremony marking the official transfer of the Louisiana Territory from Spain to the United States. *See p. 28.*

April 1 – Lewis and Clark file a military detachment order indicating the final composition of the permanent party that will accompany them to the Pacific and the return party that will take the keelboat back to St. Louis. *See p. 32.*

Lewis receives official military paperwork from Washington denying his request that Clark be granted the rank of captain; he ignores the order and refers to Clark as captain throughout the expedition. *See p. 32.*

May 14 – After spending five months camped at Wood River, the expedition launches its journey up the Missouri River. *See p. 32.*

May 21 – The expedition passes St. Charles, the last American settlement on the Missouri River. *See p. 33.*

June 26 – The Corps of Discovery reaches the site of present-day Kansas City, Missouri, nearly 400 miles upstream from St. Louis. *See p. 38.*

July 21 – Lewis and Clark pass the confluence of the Platte River in present-day Nebraska, nearly 650 miles upstream from Camp Wood, and enter the Great Plains. *See p. 38.*

August 2 – The captains meet with a group of Otoe and Missouri Indians near present-day Council Bluffs, Iowa. *See p. 41.*

August 20 – Sergeant Charles Floyd dies from a ruptured appendix and is buried with military honors near Sioux City, Iowa; he is the only member of the Corps of Discovery to die during the expedition. *See p. 39.*

August 27 – The Corps makes contact with the Yankton Sioux at the mouth of the James River in present-day South Dakota. *See p. 41.*

September 11 – Expedition member George Shannon relocates the group after being lost for two weeks. *See p. 40.*

September 25 – Lewis and Clark have a tense confrontation with the Teton Sioux (Lakota) near present-day Pierre, South Dakota. *See p. 42.*

October 15 – The group reaches the Hidatsa villages on the Upper Missouri; having never seen a black person before, the Hidatsa are fascinated with York, Clark's enslaved African-American servant. *See p. 47.*

November 2 – The Corps of Discovery begins building a winter camp on the east side of the Missouri River near present-day Bismarck, North Dakota; they name it Fort Mandan after the neighboring Mandan Indians. *See p. 46.*

November 4 – The captains add two more people to the expedition as interpreters and guides, the French Canadian fur trader Toussaint Charbonneau and his Shoshone Indian wife, Sacagawea. *See p. 47.*

December 17 – Clark notes a temperature of 45 degrees below zero. *See p. 47.*

1805

February 11 – Sacagawea gives birth to a son, Jean Baptiste Charbonneau, who accompanies the expedition across the continent by riding on his mother's back. *See p. 49.*

April 7 – After five months at Fort Mandan, Lewis and Clark embark with the permanent party toward the Pacific Ocean, while Corporal Richard Warfington leaves for

St. Louis in the keelboat with the return party and a shipment of scientific samples and geographic information for Jefferson. *See p. 49.*

April 29 – The expedition has its first encounter with grizzly bears. *See p. 52.*

May 14 – Lewis and Clark watch helplessly from shore as a sudden squall tips over one of the pirogues; fortunately, Sacagawea calmly collects the important documents and equipment that have washed overboard while another crew member rights the boat. *See p. 53.*

May 26 – Lewis climbs a tall bluff and sees snowcapped mountains in the distance. *See p. 55.*

May 31 – The expedition enters the scenic White Cliffs of the Missouri River. *See p. 55.*

July 15 – Following a month-long struggle, the crew finally completes the portage around the Great Falls of the Missouri River. *See p. 57.*

July 25 – The expedition reaches Three Forks, where three smaller rivers converge to form the Missouri; Sacagawea recognizes it as the spot where she was captured by the Hidatsa. *See p. 58.*

August 12 – Lewis climbs Lemhi Pass and finds the source of the Missouri River; he also sees mountain ranges stretching into the distance on the other side, meaning that the fabled Northwest Passage does not exist. *See p. 60.*

August 12 – Jefferson receives the first shipment of scientific specimens and Indian artifacts sent back by Lewis and Clark. *See p. 60.*

August 17 – The expedition locates the Shoshone Indians; Sacagawea recognizes the chief as her long-lost brother, Cameahwait, and negotiates the purchase of horses to cross the Rocky Mountains. *See p. 61.*

August 23 – Clark scouts the Salmon River and finds that its rapids are not navigable. *See p. 61.*

September 1 – The Corps of Discovery leaves its canoes at Camp Fortunate and travels overland into the mountains. *See p. 62.*

September 9 – The expedition makes camp near present-day Missoula, Montana, at a spot they called Travelers Rest. *See p. 62.*

September 11 – The expedition begins climbing into the Bitterroot Range on the treacherous Lolo Trail. *See p. 62.*

September 23 – The group descends into the open country known as Weippe Prairie near present-day Orofino, Idaho, and camps among the Nez Perce Indians. *See p. 64.*

October 7 – The men leave their horses with the Nez Perce for safekeeping and load their gear into dugout canoes to travel down the Clearwater and Snake Rivers. *See p. 64.*

October 16 – The expedition finally reaches the Columbia River. *See p. 65.*

November 7 – When the Columbia widens into a large bay, Clark believes it is the Pacific Ocean; in reality, the coast is still twenty miles away. *See p. 65.*

November 24 – Lewis and Clark take a vote of all expedition members, including Sacagawea and York, to decide where to camp for the winter. *See p. 66.*

1806

March 23 – The Corps of Discovery loads its gear into canoes and launches its return journey eastward across the continent. *See p. 71.*

April 27 – After a month of traveling upstream on the Columbia, Lewis and Clark make arrangements with the Wallawalla Indians to exchange their canoes for horses in order to continue their journey overland. *See p. 74.*

May 14 – The expedition begins a month-long wait at Camp Chopunnish, on the east side of the Clearwater River at the site of present-day Kamiah, Idaho, for snow to clear from Lolo Pass. *See p. 74.*

June 10 – The men attempt to cross the Bitterroot Range, but deep snow forces them to turn back and return to the Nez Perce village. *See p. 75.*

June 24 – The expedition launches a second, successful attempt to cross the Bitterroots. *See p. 75.*

July 3 – After reaching Travelers Rest, Lewis and Clark divide the Corps into two groups to explore separate sections of the Louisiana Territory. *See p. 75.*

July 8 – Clark's group reaches Camp Fortunate and retrieves the expedition's boats and supplies. *See p. 76.*

July 11 – Lewis's group reaches the Missouri River. *See p. 78.*

July 15 – Clark reaches the Yellowstone River. *See p. 77.*

July 25 – Clark engraves his signature on Pompeys Pillar, a large, distinctive sandstone outcropping near Billings, Montana. *See p. 78.*

July 27 – Lewis has a deadly confrontation with Blackfeet Indians on the Marias River. *See p. 78.*

July 28 – Lewis reaches the Missouri River and rejoins Sergeant John Ordway's group that has carried the expedition gear around the Great Falls. *See p. 80.*

August 11 – The expedition nearly loses one of its leaders when Lewis is accidentally shot by one of his own hunters. *See p. 80.*

August 12 – Lewis and Clark's parties are reunited. *See p. 80.*

August 14 – The expedition reaches the Mandan villages, where they part ways with Sacagawea, her son Jean Baptiste, Toussaint Charbonneau, and John Colter. *See p. 80.*

August 30 – The captains refuse to meet with Lakota leaders, with whom they had a tense encounter two years earlier. *See p. 81.*

September 23 – The Lewis and Clark Expedition returns safely to St. Louis after two and a half years and 7,689 miles. *See p. 83.*

Lewis writes a letter to Jefferson announcing the successful conclusion of the expedition. *See p. 83.*

1807

Sergeant Patrick Gass publishes his journals from the Lewis and Clark Expedition. *See p. 84.*

American explorer Zebulon Pike is taken into custody by Spanish authorities in Mexico. *See p. 106.*

1814

Clark finally publishes the official version of the journals of the Corps of Discovery, ten years after the expedition began. *See p. 85.*

1828

Upon taking office, President Andrew Jackson makes Indian removal a top priority. *See p. 94.*

1830

Congress passes the Indian Removal Act, a ruthless piece of legislation that formally authorizes Jackson to relocate all eastern tribes to reservations west of the Mississippi River. *See p. 94.*

1836

Texas declares its independence from Mexico and asks to become part of the United States. *See p. 96.*

The first migrant wagon train departs from Independence, Missouri, on the Oregon Trail. *See p. 98.*

1838

May 26 – Federal troops forcibly evict thousands of Cherokee Indians from their homes and march them to official reservation land in eastern Oklahoma; an estimated 4,000 tribal members die from disease, exhaustion, or starvation during the thousand-mile journey, which becomes known as the Trail of Tears. *See p. 94.*

1842

Explorer John C. Frémont leads the first in a series of U.S. government-sponsored expeditions into the West. *See p. 106.*

1845

Journalist John L. O'Sullivan coins the term "manifest destiny." *See p. 95.*

Texas is annexed to the United States and then admitted as a state, creating a conflict with Mexico over the disputed territory. *See p. 96.*

1846

The Mexican-American War begins. *See p. 96.*

President James K. Polk signs the Oregon Treaty, which provides for the acquisition of new territory in the Pacific Northwest and establishes the U.S. border along the 49th Parallel. *See p. 97.*

1848

February 2 – The Treaty of Guadalupe Hidalgo ends the Mexican-American War; under its terms, the United States takes possession of 750,000 square miles of Mexican territory—including California, Texas, and the Southwest—and expands its boundaries south to the Rio Grande and west to the Pacific Ocean. *See p. 97.*

The discovery of gold near Sacramento, California, launches the Gold Rush, which greatly increases the pace of westward migration. *See p. 98.*

1850

The U.S. population reaches 23 million, up from 5 million in 1800; an estimated 4 million of these people have left the crowded industrial cities of the East to seek new opportunities in the West. *See p. 102.*

More than 100,000 American Indians from twenty-eight tribes have been deported from their ancestral homelands to reservations west of the Mississippi River since 1817. *See p. 93.*

1861

The first coast-to-coast telegraph communication is completed. *See p. 98.*

Indian Wars flare up across the West as various nations resist U.S. encroachment on their territory. *See p. 100.*

1867

With the purchase of Alaska from Russia, U.S. territory comes close to assuming its final form. *See p. 102.*

1869

May 10 – The 1,900-mile transcontinental railroad connects the existing eastern U.S. rail network to the Pacific Coast in California, making cross-country travel easier and safer than ever before. *See p. 98.*

Explorer John Wesley Powell launches an expedition to explore one of the last remaining blank spaces on the map of the West: the Grand Canyon of the Colorado River. *See p. 106.*

1879

Congress creates the U.S. Geographical Survey (USGS) to coordinate efforts to map the West. *See p. 109.*

1880

The population of the city of San Francisco is nearly 250,000. *See p. 102.*

1890

> Government analysts announce that U.S. Census population figures no longer show a clear line of advancing settlement across the continent, which they interpret to mean that the nation has achieved its manifest destiny and tamed the West. *See p. 102.*

1893

> Historian Frederick Jackson Turner delivers his famous speech entitled "The Significance of the Frontier in American History." *See p. 103.*

1900

> The nation's population reaches 76 million, more than tripling in only fifty years. *See p. 102.*

1904

> Editor Reuben Gold Thwaites publishes an eight-volume edition of the Lewis and Clark journals. *See p. 85.*

1961

> May 25 – Following in the tradition of exploration established by Jefferson, President John F. Kennedy proposes that the United States attempt to land a man on the Moon. *See p. 109.*

1969

> July 20 – American astronauts fulfill Kennedy's dream by walking on the Moon; the historic event is broadcast live on television to a worldwide audience. *See p. 109.*

1978

> Congress establishes the Lewis and Clark National Historic Trail, with parks and monuments stretching from St. Louis to the mouth of the Columbia River. *See p. 112.*

1985

> The definitive, thirteen-volume version of the Lewis and Clark journals, edited by Gary Moulton, is published by the University of Nebraska Press. *See p. 85.*

2004

> The bicentennial of the Lewis and Clark Expedition is marked by books, films, commemorative Web sites, and special celebrations across the United States. *See p. 114.*

SOURCES FOR FURTHER STUDY

Ambrose, Stephen E. *Lewis and Clark: Voyage of Discovery*. Washington, DC: National Geographic Society, 1998. In this beautifully illustrated volume, a leading historian intersperses the history of the Lewis and Clark Expedition with his own modern-day travels in the explorers' footsteps.

Ambrose, Stephen E. *Undaunted Courage: Meriwether Lewis, Thomas Jefferson, and the Opening of the American West*. New York: Simon and Schuster, 1996. Although this book is primarily a biography of Lewis, it captures all the excitement and adventure of the journey of the Corps of Discovery.

Discovering Lewis and Clark. Lewis and Clark Fort Mandan Association, 1998-2005. Retrieved from http://www.lewis-clark.org/. This extensive, highly informative Web site, maintained by a nonprofit educational foundation, features dozens of essays on the expedition, its natural history discoveries, the members of the Corps of Discovery, the Native American nations of the West, and more.

Duncan, Dayton, and Ken Burns. *Lewis and Clark: The Journey of the Corps of Discovery*. New York: Knopf, 1997. This companion volume to the PBS documentary is heavily illustrated and provides valuable background on the expedition and its members.

The Lewis and Clark Expedition. Monticello, n.d. Retrieved from http://www.monticello.org/site/jefferson/lewis-and-clark-expedition. The official Internet site of Thomas Jefferson's historic home covers the president's interest in the West, acquisition of the Louisiana Territory, and decision to mount the expedition. It also provides access to many historic documents.

Lewis and Clark Expedition: A National Register of Historic Places Travel Itinerary. National Park Service, n.d. Retrieved from http://www.nps.gov/nr/travel/lewisandclark/index.htm. This Web site serves as a guide to modern-day travelers on the Lewis and Clark National Historic Trail, with introductory essays and links to trail sites, maps, and suggested travel itineraries.

Lewis and Clark: Great Journey West. National Geographic, 1996. Retrieved from http://www.nationalgeographic.com/lewisandclark/index.html. This informative and entertaining Web site features an interactive journey into the West, games, photos, articles, maps, and more.

Lewis and Clark Trail Heritage Foundation, 2014. Retrieved from http://www.lewisandclark .org/. This Web site provides state-by-state listings of historic sites, monuments, and museums dedicated to preserving the legacy of Lewis and Clark and educating the public about the expedition's important role in U.S. history.

Lewis and Clark: The Journey of the Corps of Discovery. PBS, 1997. Retrieved from http://www .pbs.org/lewisandclark/. A companion to the documentary film by Ken Burns, this Web site includes biographies, a timeline, an interactive trail map, classroom activities, and a searchable archive of the expedition journals.

Moulton, Gary, ed. *The Journals of the Lewis and Clark Expedition.* Lincoln: University of Nebraska Press/Electronic Text Center, 2005. Retrieved from http://lewisandclarkjournals .unl.edu/index.html. This site features the full text of the most definitive and complete version of the expedition journals, along with a gallery of images, supplemental articles and texts, and Native American perspectives.

Rivers, Edens, Empires: Lewis and Clark and the Revealing of America. Library of Congress Exhibitions, n.d. Retrieved from http://www.loc.gov/exhibits/lewisandclark/index.html. Divided into historical periods before, during, and after the expedition, this online exhibition offers interactive maps, links to documents and images, resources for teachers, and activities for students.

BIBLIOGRAPHY

Books

Ambrose, Stephen E. *Lewis & Clark: Voyage of Discovery*. Washington, DC: National Geographic Society, 1998.

Ambrose, Stephen E. *Undaunted Courage: Meriwether Lewis, Thomas Jefferson, and the Opening of the American West*. New York: Simon and Schuster, 1996.

Beckham, Stephen Dow. *Lewis and Clark: From the Rockies to the Pacific*. Portland, OR: Graphic Arts Center, 2011.

Bedini, Silvio A. *Thomas Jefferson, Statesman of Science*. New York: Macmillan, 1990.

Betts, Robert B. *In Search of York: The Slave Who Went to the Pacific with Lewis and Clark*. 2nd ed. Boulder: Colorado Associated University Press, 2000.

Biddle, Nicholas, ed. *History of the Expedition under the Command of Captains Lewis and Clark*. 2 vols. Philadelphia: 1814.

Buckley, Jay H. *William Clark: Indian Diplomat*. Norman: University of Oklahoma Press, 2008.

Clark, Charles G. *The Men of the Lewis and Clark Expedition*. Lincoln: University of Nebraska Press, 2002.

Coues, Elliott, ed. *History of the Expedition under the Command of Lewis and Clark*. 3 vols. New York: Frances P. Harper, 1893.

Cutright, Paul R. *Lewis and Clark: Pioneering Naturalists*. Lincoln: University of Nebraska Press, 1989.

DeVoto, Bernard. *The Journals of Lewis and Clark*. New York: Mariner Books, 1997.

Dillon, Richard. *Meriwether Lewis: A Biography*. 3rd ed. Lafayette, CA: Great West Books, 2003.

Duncan, Dayton, and Ken Burns. *Lewis and Clark: The Journey of the Corps of Discovery: An Illustrated History*. New York: Knopf, 1997.

Foley, William E. *Wilderness Journey: The Life of William Clark*. Columbia: University of Missouri Press, 2004.

Grossman, Elizabeth. *Adventuring along the Lewis and Clark Trail*. San Francisco: Sierra Club Books, 2003.

Hawke, David Freeman. *The Tremendous Mountains: The Story of the Lewis and Clark Expedition.* New York: Norton, 1980.

Holmberg, James J., ed. *Dear Brother: Letters of William Clark to Jonathan Clark.* New Haven, CT: Yale University Press, 2002.

Howard, Harold P. *Sacajawea.* Norman: University of Oklahoma Press, 1979.

Hoxie, Frederick E., and Jay T. Nelson, eds. *Lewis & Clark and the Indian Country: The Native American Perspective.* Urbana: University of Illinois Press, 2008.

Hunsaker, Joyce Badgley. *Sacagawea Speaks: Beyond the Shining Mountains with Lewis and Clark.* Guilford, CT: TwoDot, 2001.

Jackson, Donald, ed. *Letters of the Lewis and Clark Expedition, with Related Documents 1783-1854.* 2 vols. Urbana: University of Illinois Press, 1978.

Jones, Landon Y. *The Essential Lewis and Clark.* New York: Ecco Press, 2000.

Jones, Landon Y. *William Clark and the Shaping of the West.* New York: Hill and Wang, 2004.

Lavender, David Sievert. *The Way to the Western Sea: Lewis and Clark Across the Continent.* New York: Harper & Row, 1988.

Malone, Dumas. *Jefferson and His Time.* 6 vols. Charlottesville: University of Virginia Press, 2006.

Ronda, James P. *Jefferson's West: Journey with Lewis and Clark.* Charlottesville, VA: Thomas Jefferson Foundation, 2000.

Ronda, James P. *Lewis and Clark among the Indians.* Lincoln: University of Nebraska Press, 1984.

Ronda, James P., ed. *Voyages of Discovery: Essays on the Lewis and Clark Expeditions.* Helena, MT: Montana Historical Society Press, 1998.

Thwaites, Reuben Gold, ed. *Original Journals of the Lewis and Clark Expedition, 1804-1806.* 8 vols. New York: 1904.

Online Resources

Discovering Lewis and Clark. Lewis and Clark Fort Mandan Association, 1998-2005. Retrieved from http://www.lewis-clark.org/.

Gass, Patrick. *Gass's Journal of the Lewis and Clark Expedition.* Chicago: A. C. McClurg, 1904. Retrieved from https://archive.org/details/gasssjournallew01hosmgoog.

Hall, Jolene. "Lewis and Clark for the Modern-Day Adventurer." Recreation.gov, 2014. Retrieved from http://www.recreation.gov/outdoors/Explore_And_More/exploreArticles/Lewis-and-Clark-for-the-Modern-Day-Adventurer.htm?utm_source=JulyNewsletter-&utm_medium=Link&utm_campaign=LewisClark.

The Journals of Captain Meriwether Lewis and Sergeant John Ordway, Kept on the Expedition of Western Exploration, 1803-1806. Madison, WI: The Society, 1916. Retrieved from https://archive.org/details/journalsofcaptai00lewirich.

Lewis and Clark Expedition. American Treasures in the Library of Congress, 2010. Retrieved from http://www.lcweb.loc.gov/exhibits/treasures/trr001.html.

Lewis and Clark: The Journey of the Corps of Discovery. PBS, 1997. Retrieved from http://www.pbs.org/lewisandclark/.

Lewis and Clark: The National Bicentennial Exhibition. Missouri Historical Society, 1999-2003. Retrieved from http://www.lewisandclarkexhibit.org/2_0_0/index.html.

Murphy, Cullen. "Lewis and Clark and Us." *The Atlantic Monthly,* March 1998, p. 32. Retrieved from http://www.theatlantic.com/magazine/archive/1998/03/lewis-and-clark-and-us/377073/.

Perry, Douglas. "Teaching with Documents: The Lewis and Clark Expedition." U.S. National Archives, n.d. Retrieved from http://www.archives.gov/education/lessons/lewis-clark/#\documents.

Ronda, James P. "Why Lewis and Clark Matter." *Smithsonian,* August 2003. Retrieved from http://www.smithsonianmag.com/history/why-lewis-and-clark-matter-87847931/?all.

PHOTO AND ILLUSTRATION CREDITS

Cover and title page: "Lewis and Clark at Three Forks" by Edgar S. Paxson, Oil on Canvas, 1912. Detail of Mural in the Montana State Capitol, Courtesy of the Montana Historical Society, Don Beatty, photographer.

Chapter One: Library of Congress, LC-DIG-ppmsca-15715 (p. 8); Aquatint print by J. L. Bouqueto de Woiseri, 1803 via Wikimedia Commons (p. 11); U.S. Capitol fresco by Constantino Brumidi, 1875. Official Architect of the Capitol photograph (p. 12); National Atlas of the United States (p. 14); Granger, NYC (p. 16).

Chapter Two: Library of Congress, LC-USZ62-20214 (p. 20); Library of Congress, LC-USZ62-10609 (p. 22); National Museum of American History, Washington, DC. Photo by Daderot via Wikimedia Commons (p. 24); Michael Haynes/www.mhaynesart.com (p. 27); Calabria Design, ©2015 Omnigraphics, Inc. (p. 29).

Chapter Three: ©ullstein bild/The Image Works (p. 36); Watercolor by Karl Bodmer, 1833 via Wikimedia Commons (p. 39); Library of Congress, LC-USZ62-17372 (p. 42); John Reddy/KRT/Newscom (p. 46); Granger, NYC (p. 48).

Chapter Four: Library of Congress, LC-USZ62-17371 (p. 52); Everett Collection/Newscom (p. 54); ©Mary Evans Picture Library/The Image Works (p. 56); Brigham Young Harold B. Lee Library, L. Tom Perry Special Collections, MSS 1608. William Henry Jackson, artist (p. 60); Washington State Historical Society. Painting by Gustav Sohon, 1855 (p. 63); Library of Congress, LC-USZ62-50631 (p. 67).

Chapter Five: Granger, NYC (p. 72); Everett Collection/Newscom (p. 74); Bureau of Land Management (p. 77); Library of Congress, LC-USZ62-19231 (p. 79); Michael Haynes/www.mhaynesart.com (p. 82); CMSP Education/Newscom (p. 87).

Chapter Six: Picture History/Newscom (p. 93); Library of Congress, LC-DIG-ppmsca-03213 (p. 95); Library of Congress, LC-USZ62-116413 (p. 99); Library of Congress, LC-USZC4-7421 (p. 102).

Chapter Seven: Photo by Laurie Collier Hillstrom (p. 107); NASA, AS11-40-5874 (p. 108); Bureau of Land Management. Photo by Bob Wick (p. 111); Cape Disappointment with Lighthouse, Washington. Photo by Adbar, via Wikimedia Commons (p. 112).

Biographies: Michael Haynes/www.mhaynesart.com (p. 117); Library of Congress, LC-USZ6-633 (p. 121); Michael Haynes/www.mhaynesart.com (p. 125); Michael Haynes/www

INDEX